Charles Ray Palmer

The Bi-centennial celebration of the First Congregational Church and Society of Bridgeport, Connecticut : June 12th and 13th, 1895

Charles Ray Palmer

The Bi-centennial celebration of the First Congregational Church and Society of Bridgeport, Connecticut : June 12th and 13th, 1895

ISBN/EAN: 9783337261443

Printed in Europe, USA, Canada, Australia, Japan

Cover: Foto ©Lupo / pixelio.de

More available books at **www.hansebooks.com**

THE

BI-CENTENNIAL CELEBRATION

OF THE

First Congregational Church and Society

OF

BRIDGEPORT, CONNECTICUT

June 12th and 13th, 1895

NEW HAVEN:
THE TUTTLE, MOREHOUSE & TAYLOR PRESS
1895

PREFACE.

✠

The First Church and Society of Bridgeport — originally the Parish of Stratfield — looked forward to the two-hundredth anniversary of its organization for some years previous with increasing interest. The celebration was carefully planned and most successfully carried out. The decorations of the church were extremely effective; the weather was perfect; the attendance of interested and sympathetic audiences was from beginning to end as great as could be accommodated; the music — rendered by the combined choirs of the First, the Second, the Park Street Congregational Churches, and the Presbyterian Church — was admirable; in short, the occasion seemed to those most concerned to be a delightful one in every particular. It appeared desirable to preserve a permanent record of it. As far as practicable, to do this is the purpose of the present volume.

One feature of the celebration was of necessity an incident of the occasion only. By dint of much research and labor, and the contribution of many willing hands, a remarkable loan-collection of relics was gathered and exhibited in the Chapel. The Committee take this opportunity of tendering their hearty thanks to all who lent their aid toward this most valuable and interesting illustration of the history which the celebration commemorated.

The proceedings in the several services were stenographically reported by Mr. F. G. Fowler. The lists of members have been compiled by the sub-committee constituted for the purpose — among whom it is not invidious to name Mr. Richard B. Cogswell. While the result is avowedly and inevitably incomplete, his indefatigable industry has accomplished a task to which few could have proved equal, which many will count invaluable. This volume has been edited for the committee of arrangements, at their request, by its chairman. The frontispiece has been added by their direction. The editor hopes that the result of his endeavors will be accepted by the dear friends he has served for so many years with the gracious consideration which he has always experienced at their hands, and that one abiding fruitage of the Bi-Centennial may be an increased consciousness on the part of the citizens of Bridgeport of the inspiration to be derived from its honorable history.

CHARLES RAY PALMER.

New Haven, Sept. 10, 1895.

TABLE OF CONTENTS.

✣

		PAGE.
1.	List of Committees, .	7, 8
2.	The Letter of Invitation,	9
3.	The Programme, ...	10–14
4.	The services on Wednesday afternoon, the 12th, including the Historical Discourse, .	15
5.	The services on Wednesday evening,	47
6.	The services on Thursday forenoon, the 13th, .	65
7.	The services on Thursday afternoon, ...	109
8.	The services on Sunday, the 16th, including the second part of the Historical Discourse, . .	142
9.	List of Sites marked for their Historic interest, .	156
10.	Extracts from Letters, .	157
11.	Lists of Members,	163

1695   1895

BI-CENTENNIAL CELEBRATION COMMITTEE.

✠

Committee of First Church and Society.

CHARLES RAY PALMER, *Chairman.*

ROWLAND B. LACEY,	HENRY R. PARROTT,
WILLIAM B. HINCKS,	HENRY C. COGSWELL,
MORRIS B. BEARDSLEY,	SILAS BURTON,
HOWARD G. HUBBELL,	WILLARD P. ABERNETHY,
ROBERT E. WHEELER,	JOHN T. STERLING,
N. EUGENE WORDIN,	HORACE W. SMITH,
CHARLES SHERWOOD,	EBENEZER BURR.

Coöperative Committee of South Church.

SAMUEL W. BALDWIN,	EDWARD STERLING,
ALEXANDER HAWLEY,	LEWIS B. SILLIMAN,

CURTIS THOMPSON.

Sub-Committees.

On Exercises.

C. R. PALMER,	H. R. PARROTT,
H. C. COGSWELL,	R. B. LACEY,

E. BURR.

On Music.

H. R. PARROTT,	MRS. E. BEARDSLEY,
JOHN A. BARRI,	A. T. GOODSELL,

MISS E. DURAND.

On Invitations.

C. R. PALMER,	F. RUSSELL,
C. SHERWOOD,	O. H. BROTHWELL,

R. B. COGSWELL.

On Hospitality.

L. B. SILLIMAN,	M. B. BEARDSLEY,
W. G. LINEBURGH,	I. W. BIRDSEY,

E. F. MELKER.

On Reception and Information.

A. Hawley,
E. Sterling,
F. C. Lyon,

E. P. Hincks,
H. D. Simonds,
F. W. Parrott.

On Finance.

W. B. Hincks,
E. Burr,
E. C. Smith,
T. C. Wordin,

W. E. Seeley,
W. P. Abernethy,
G. Comstock,
J. C. Curtis.

On Decorations.

Silas Burton,
W. A. Smith,

W. N. Middlebrook.
J. G. Howland.

A. H. Gamsby.

On Printing and Publication.

H. C. Cogswell,
A. W. Stillman,

E. F. Strong,
C. Thompson,

N. E. Wordin.

On Historic Sites and Relics.

R. B. Lacey,
R. B. Cogswell,

S. W. Baldwin,
F. B. Hawley,

David S. Beach.

On Luncheon.

H. G. Hubbell,
F. Trubee,
H. Birdsey,

J. T. Sterling,
H. W. Smith,
R. E. Wheeler.

On List of Members.

A. H. Gamsby,
E. Sterling,

R. B. Cogswell,
O. H. Brothwell.

A. W. Stillman.

1695   1895

✣

JUNE THIRTEENTH.

The First Church and Society in Bridgeport—the South Church co-operating—cordially invite you to be present at the celebration of the

TWO HUNDREDTH ANNIVERSARY

of the organization of the Church of Christ in Stratfield, June 13th, 1695.

The exercises will commence on Wednesday afternoon and conclude on Thursday afternoon, June 12th and 13th, 1895. They will comprise a historical discourse by the Pastor, appropriate papers and addresses, music, and a collation.

Please inform Mr. Charles Sherwood of your acceptance of this invitation as early as June 1st, if you desire arrangements made for your entertainment.

Cordially yours,

CHARLES RAY PALMER,
CHARLES SHERWOOD,
FRANK RUSSELL,
ORLANDO H. BROTHWELL,
RICHARD B. COGSWELL,

Committee of Invitation.

Bridgeport, May 1st, 1895.

THE PROGRAMME.

✣

1695   JUNE THIRTEENTH.   1895

✣

ORDER OF SERVICES

ON

JUNE TWELFTH AND THIRTEENTH, 1895,

COMMEMORATIVE OF THE

TWO HUNDREDTH ANNIVERSARY

OF THE

ORGANIZATION OF THE CHURCH AT STRATFIELD, JUNE 12TH, 1695.

ORDER OF SERVICES.

✠

WEDNESDAY, TWELFTH JUNE.

AFTERNOON.

(Commencing at half past two.)

———

1. ORGAN PRELUDE.
2. DOXOLOGY.
3. READING OF SCRIPTURE.
4. PRAYER, ... By Rev. FRANK RUSSELL, D.D.
5. ANTHEM, "We Praise Thee, O God!" *J. Baptiste Calkin.*
6. HISTORICAL DISCOURSE, . . By Rev. CHARLES RAY PALMER, D.D.
7. HYMN 1312,
   "O God! beneath thy guiding hand
   Our exiled fathers crossed the sea."
8. BENEDICTION.

ORDER OF SERVICES.

✢

WEDNESDAY, TWELFTH JUNE.

EVENING.

(Commencing at quarter before eight.)

---

1. ORGAN PRELUDE.
2. ANTHEM, "Great is the Lord." *Dr. Calcott.*
3. PRAYER.
4. WELCOME TO INVITED GUESTS.
5. ANCIENT PSALMODY—Hymn 97. *Kethe,* 1561.
 "All people that on earth do dwell."
6. ADDRESSES FROM INVITED GUESTS.
 (1) The Rector of St. John's Parish, Rev. WILLIAM H. LEWIS.
 (2) The Pastor of the First Baptist Church,
  Rev. GEORGE W. NICHOLSON.
 (3) The Pastor of the First Methodist Church,
  Rev. JOSEPH PULLMAN, D.D.
 (4) The Pastor of the First Presbyterian Church,
  Rev. HENRY A. DAVENPORT.
7. ANCIENT PSALMODY, *W. Billings.*
 "The Lord descended from on high."
8. BENEDICTION.

ORDER OF SERVICES.

✣

THURSDAY, THIRTEENTH JUNE.

MORNING.

(Commencing at ten o'clock.)

———

1. DRUM PRELUDE.
2. ORGAN VOLUNTARY.
3. ANTHEM, "Send Out Thy Light." *Gounod.*
4. PRAYER OF COMMEMORATION.
5. PAPER ON THE LIMITS OF STRATFIELD PARISH AS ORIGINALLY CONSTITUTED, . . . By Dea. ROWLAND B. LACEY.
6. ROLL CALL OF ORIGINAL MEMBERS OF THE STRATFIELD CHURCH, TO BE RESPONDED TO BY THEIR DESCENDANTS.
7. HYMN 1046, "O God of Bethel, by whose hand!"
8. COMMEMORATIVE ADDRESSES.
    (1) The Saybrook Constitution and the Connecticut Churches, Prof. GEORGE P. FISHER, D.D., LL.D.,
    New Haven.
    (2) The Memory of the Fathers the Inspiration of their Children, Hon. ELIPHALET W. BLATCHFORD,
    Chicago, Ill.
    INTERLUDE, "The breaking waves dashed high."
    (3) The Service of Learning the Service of the Churches, Rev. TIMOTHY DWIGHT, D.D., LL.D.,
    New Haven.
    (4) The Debt of a Community to its Founders, Hon. JOSEPH HAWLEY, LL.D.,
    U. S. Senate.
9. LETTERS FROM ABSENT BUT NOT FORGOTTEN FRIENDS.
10. PAPER ON THE RELATION OF THE PARISH OF STRATFIELD TO THE CITY OF BRIDGEPORT, TO BE FOLLOWED BY A GREETING FROM HIS HONOR, THE MAYOR, HON. FRANK E. CLARK.
11. HYMN 1019, "O where are kings and empires now?"
12. RECESS FOR THE LUNCHEON.

ORDER OF SERVICES.

✦

THURSDAY, THIRTEENTH JUNE.

AFTERNOON.

(Commencing at half past two.)

"Should auld acquaintance be forgot?"

1. ORGAN PRELUDE.
2. ANTHEM, "Praise the Lord." *Randegger.*
3. WORDS FROM THE MOTHER CHURCHES.
    (1) First Church in Fairfield, Rev. FRANK S. CHILD.
    (2) First Church in Stratford, Rev. JOEL S. IVES.
4. HYMN 329, "Ye tribes of Adam join."
5. WORDS FROM THE DAUGHTER CHURCHES.
    (1) The South Church, Rev. FRANK RUSSELL, D.D.
    (2) The Park Street Church, Rev. EDWARD GRIER FULLERTON.
    (3) Olivet Church, Rev. EDWIN K. HOLDEN.
    (4) The West-End Church, Rev. CYRUS F. STIMSON.
    (5) The King's Highway Church, Rev. WILSON R. STEWART.
6. HYMN 854, "Happy the souls to Jesus joined."
7. BENEDICTION.

SERVICES OF
WEDNESDAY AFTERNOON.

✠

ORGAN PRELUDE, BY A. T. GOODSELL.

✠

DOXOLOGY.

✠

READING OF THE SCRIPTURE AND PRAYER,

BY REV. FRANK RUSSELL, D.D.

The Scripture Lesson.

"We have heard with our ears, O God, our fathers have told us,
What work thou didst in their days, in the days of old.
Thou didst drive out the nations with thy hand, and plantedst
    them in :
Thou didst afflict the peoples, and didst spread them abroad.
For they got not the land in possession by their own sword,
Neither did their own arm save them :
But thy right hand, and thine arm, and the light of thy coun-
    tenance,
Because thou hadst a favor unto them."

[Ps. xliv : 1–3.]

"We have thought on thy loving kindness, O God,
In the midst of thy temple.
As is thy name, O God,
So is thy praise unto the ends of the earth,
Thy right hand is full of righteousness.
Let Mount Zion be glad,
Let the daughters of Judah rejoice,
Because of thy judgments.
Walk about Zion, and go round about her :
Tell the towers thereof.
Mark ye well her bulwarks,
Consider her palaces ;
That ye may tell it to the generation following.
For this God is our God forever and ever.
He will be our guide even unto death."
                        [Ps. xlviii : 9-14.]

"Thou, O Lord, shalt abide forever
And thy memorial unto all generations."
"This shall be written for the generation to come :
And a people which shall be created shall praise the Lord."
Of old hast thou laid the foundation of the earth ;
And the heavens are the work of thy hands.
They shall perish, but thou shalt endure ;
Yea, all of them shall wax old like a garment ;
As a vesture shalt thou change them, and they shall be
    changed :
But thou art the same,
And thy years shall have no end,
The children of thy servants shall continue,
And their seed shall be established before thee."
                        [Ps. cii : 12, 18, 25-28.]

✝

Let us unite our hearts in prayer:—

Our Father, Thou hast been our dwelling place in all generations. Before the mountains were brought forth, or ever Thou hast formed the earth and the world, from everlasting to everlasting Thou art God. Thou dost sit above the heavens watching the stream of human history, which Thou didst Thyself form. This stream pours beyond our sight, for Thou art ever calling hence from our number those that are saved. Many have been the mightiest of men, filled with Thee; and they strove divinely for the truth. Thou gavest them the truth and made it clear to their eyes, and they handed it down to their children. They were also strong because of Thine own presence with them. Thou didst enlighten the generations by means of them. Thou didst exalt some in every generation to be leaders of men, to work Thy will on the earth. We bless Thee for those who sought to know Thy will and to do it in Thy fear—for these leaders, examples, benefactors on the earth. We thank Thee for the gifts and graces with which Thou didst endow them; for the experiences by which Thou didst edify them; for the characters Thou didst perfect in them; that they have been in the midst of Thine assemblies as golden candlesticks placed by Thine own hand at the altar.

We praise Thee and we bless Thee for the throngs of martyrs and apostles who have known Thee and lived to work Thy praise on the earth, who have gone hence, leaving the heritage of their good work and their influence on their children behind them. To-day we almost see them in gathering ranks about Thee, some gone so long we would question whether they would recognize us, in the ranks of the glorified before Thee; and yet we know there is nothing that would more heighten their joy than to see us carrying on the good work which they so nobly commenced. We see them now in the innumerable company of those that sing the song of Moses and the Lamb; and above them all we see the pierced hands of the Great Head of the Church.

We bless Thee for Thy Church in this world—the Church of the Living God, the pillar and ground of the truth. We praise Thee that Thou didst establish it, and hast preserved it, and given honor unto it. We bring Thee thanksgiving that it still stands; that the glory has not departed from the temples which Thou hast built. We praise Thee that the gospel of redemption is preached among men, with altogether wider extent and, as we would fain believe, with a deeper and more pervasive spirit than ever before. Thy servants are not retreating among men, they are sending Thy light with increasing brightness into the life of the world.

When we look back to see older times of great darkness, that there were nations living in wickedness, who knew not the name of Christ, we are grateful to Thee that now His name is known among all nations, and almost by all mankind. May the whole earth be filled with the knowledge of Him, and all flesh see Thy salvation!

Bless Thy people, as they have gathered to wait before Thee. We praise Thee that in successive generations this church has not failed. Thou hast kept it; Thou hast given wisdom and power and learning unto it. Thou hast declared that the law should go forth out of Zion, and Thy law has gone forth and men have received it, and have been drawn near to Thyself, and have lived for Thee, and have done with great courage and with great success that which Thou didst require at their hands. We bring Thee thanksgiving and praise for this church of Christ. We bless Thee that Thou hast given it for preaching and for prayer, and to spread the gospel among men, that the songs of Zion have been learned here, and messages of divine grace and love have come with power in the sanctuary, and thousands have been moved to serve Thee and so order their household that their children after them should be Thy children, and should rise up to praise Thee.

We thank Thee for the privilege of coming together at this time to rehearse the goodly things of the past, among which Thy hand has been clearly seen, and to commemorate Thy goodness to the children of men; and of looking unto Thee for the presence of Thy spirit in the work that is to come. We pray that at the beginning of this commemorative exercise Thy spirit may pervade every heart; that Thou wilt bless us in hearing, bless us in praying, bless us in singing, and bless us in speaking, that in all which shall be said, thought or done may, on the part of every one of us, be such as to reflect the influence of Thy presence among these Thy people.

We pray for Thy blessing upon Thy servant who shall address us. We thank Thee for his exalted labors in this place. We thank Thee that Thou hast been around about him, and hast kept him, and we pray Thou wilt still continue his years in whatever work Thou shalt appoint to him.

Bless us, we pray Thee, in the exercises of this afternoon, this evening, and on the morrow. Do Thou dwell with Thy people, and in all the future lead them.

We ask it in the great name of Jesus, the Head of the Church, who died that we may never die, to whom be all the glory. AMEN.

ANTHEM, "We Praise Thee, O God."—*J. Baptiste Calkin.*

✠

Dr. PALMER: My friends, it is desired, so far as possible, to register the names of all who are here to-day. A list will be increasingly interesting as time goes on. The register is in the vestibule; I will thank any of you who have not registered to do so before leaving the house.

I want to call your attention also to a collection of relics in the upper room of the chapel, which may be seen any time to-day or to-morrow.

I want to say further, before the close of these services, a photographer will take a view of the house and audience in it. I shall request you to wait a moment, at the close of the services, for this purpose; it will take but a moment, and will represent the house, just as it is, to the generations who will come after us.

HISTORICAL DISCOURSE

✣

The text which I will prefix to my discourse is in the thirty-second chapter of Deuteronomy, seventh verse: "Remember the days of old. Consider the years of many generations. Ask thy father and he will show thee; Thine elders and they will tell thee."

Two centuries of human history cannot be reviewed in a day. Two centuries of the history of a single community cannot be set forth in a single discourse. I am embarrassed at the very threshold of my task by its magnitude and complexity. Yet that something be said on this interesting anniversary of what has transpired since the fathers in the fear of God and in Christian solicitude for their families organized this venerable church, is a most reasonable expectation. Relying upon your considerate kindness, I address myself to my obvious duty.

It has always been an interesting fact to me that this church originated in the period commonly spoken of as "the dark days" of Colonial history. Many historical students have set forth with graphic delineations the special hardships, anxieties, discouragements, perils, and calamities of the ten years from 1685 to 1695. There was abundant cause for the gloom and depression which prevailed. The Indian wars, in which it has been estimated that one in six of the able-bodied men in New England lost their lives, and which laid upon the colonies heavy burdens of taxation, and wrought a very general demoralization; the political excitements which followed the death of Charles II. and convulsed the colonies with the fear of entirely losing the liberties, ecclesiastical and civil, that the fathers had crossed the sea to secure, and that the struggles of sixty years had made precious; the revolution in 1689, and the new movements that followed it; the suffering and the losses ensuing from the raids of pirates upon the coasts; floods and storms and frosts of unusual severity, with short crops and depressed trade; the panic about witchcraft and satanic agencies, due to an epidemic of superstition;—these and other incidents of that extremely critical period made it a time of despondency and of apprehension to a degree hardly to be appreciated by us in these more favored days. It is difficult for us, without entering deeply into the history of "the woful decade," as it has been called, even approximately to measure the gloom which prevailed. Does it not add dignity and sacredness to the beginnings we commemorate that they were made in this particular period? Does it not enhance our estimate of the labors and the sacrifices of which the organization of this church was the fruitage, to remember just when it was that an undaunted faith and a resolute public spirit prompted them? We shall not do justice to the memory of the fathers unless we recognize what discouragements they overcame.

Could we reproduce in imagination the site of our fair city as it was two hundred and fifty years ago, we should see it a wilderness, without inhabitants other than a tribe of Indians on Golden Hill. About twenty-five years later it became—so far west as Park Avenue—part of the township of Stratford, having been acquired by purchase. West of Park Avenue the territory pertained to Fairfield. The settlement of this site began in the pushing forth of Stratford and Fairfield families in this direction. Absolutely the first to locate here, it is said, were two Stratford families, who came as early as 1665, that of Henry Summers and that of Samuel Gregory.* Their homes were near the corner of Park and Washington Avenues. Next came John and Samuel Beardsley, and then the community was fairly begun. By 1678 it was large enough to have a school of its own with forty-seven scholars, and to sue for release from school rates to Fairfield. By 1690 it had grown so large as to seek for church privileges as well. Just when religious services began to be held, one cannot say. But the movement

* Brothers-in-law.

which issued in the formation of this church seems to have had its impulse in the presence of Mr. Charles Chauncey. This young man came here, I imagine, as a school master. He was made freeman of Fairfield on March 18, 1690, but he had then been here for some time and had already done duty as a minister, although not ordained. He was the son of Rev. Israel Chauncey of Stratford, and grandson of Charles Chauncey, the second President of Harvard College, one of the Puritan Divines silenced and driven from England in 1637.* Israel Chauncey was his youngest son, a graduate of Harvard in 1661, and one of the founders of Yale. His son Charles was born in Stratford September 3, 1668, and graduated at Harvard in 1686. There is evidence of his being here as early as 1687; there is a receipt signed by him dating from 1688; I incline to the belief that he came here not very long after his college graduation to teach; that while employed as teacher he began to hold informal religious meetings, and that very gradually this kind of labor developed into the relation of a minister which he afterwards sustained. The earliest approach to a formal organization seems to have been in the formation of the Fairfield Village Society in 1693, when we find a vote that "Mr. Chauncey for his encouragement in the ministry in this place shall have sixty pounds in good provisions for the year ensuing." This action of course implies that his ministry had become a recognized fact. The householders here had, some three years before the last named date, begun the movement which culminated in the organization of this church. A petition dated May 2, 1690, and signed by forty-six taxpayers—thirteen of Stratford and thirty-three of Fairfield—was sent to the General Court, asking that they be exempted from paying any minister's rates in Stratford and Fairfield, with a view to their providing for themselves. Although the Fairfield minister approved the project, his townsmen generally did not; the representatives of Fairfield opposed it and the petition was refused. In May 1691 the application was

---

* Reached Plymouth in 1638.

CONJECTURAL APPEARANCE OF FIRST EDIFICE.

renewed and the General Court granted liberty to the applicants to procure and settle a minister of their own, provided that such as belonged to Fairfield should still pay their rates in that town. In October of the same year they were released from this provision; in December 1692 the town of Stratford voted land for a meeting-house; in 1693, as we have seen, a Society was organized and the foundation of the first edifice was commenced; in May 1694 the General Court gave permission to organize a church; in June 1695 the humble edifice was completed, and on the thirteenth it was first occupied and the church was duly organized. Slow and tedious must this long process have seemed, and persistent must have been the sturdy promoters of it. As it was the first instance in which a parish had been erected independent of town lines, still further legislation proved to be necessary; but at length its liberties were satisfactorily settled and its name fixed as Stratfield.

The first edifice stood in what we call Park Avenue, on what became known as Meeting-house hill. The site was acquired half from Stratford, half from Fairfield, and the building stood on the division-line. It was probably a humble one—nobody knows how it looked. But doubtless it was dear to those who built it, and the day we celebrate was a joyful one—the crowning of a difficult and patient struggle and the beginning of an honorable history.

The community was composed mainly of farmers and laborers. They built their own houses; no doubt they built their meeting-house. In the older parts of New England shingles superseded thatching about 1691; whether they were available in the far western frontier, i. e., in this locality—is perhaps questionable. We shall naturally think of the earliest gatherings for worship as composed of plain people, living in plain homes, but they were resolute and vigorous men, who coveted for themselves and their families the best they could attain, and when the initial difficulties of clearing the lands and subduing the soil were overcome, doubtless improvements in the homes they had reared were effected as soon as they were practicable. Framed houses succeeded to log-cabins, and two-story structures furnished accommodations for the households with which the log-cabins had been crowded. What we call North Avenue was laid out in 1687, and Park Avenue somewhat later, and upon these for the most part lay the dwellings of Stratfield two hundred years ago.

I have said forty-six householders signed the petition in 1690 for the erection of the new parish. The list probably included all that were here. The first members of the church were nine—their wives, and some other women to the number of fifteen in all, joining shortly after its organization by letter. Mr. Chauncey had already become entirely identified with the enterprise and became pastor of course. Three years previously (June 29, 1692) he had married Sarah, daughter of Major John Burr of Fairfield, and granddaughter of Mr. Jehu Burr, who came from England and died in Fairfield in 1670. Sarah Burr was born July 25, 1675, and hence was less than seventeen on her wedding-day. On a corner of Major Burr's farm, in what was afterwards known as Cooke's Lane, a house was built for them, and here the young pair commenced their married life. It was to end too soon. She died in her twenty-second year, leaving two sons. But she was here two hundred years ago. It is my conviction that Mr. Chauncey's character and abilities commanded high respect, and that his personal influence was a large factor in the making of this church. He had the advantage of as good an education as New England afforded, and both his father and his grandfather were scholars of unusual attainments. His ministry here was for its time most successful. He received to full communion ninety-seven, and under the Half-way Covenant one hundred and thirty-three. He exercised an influence beyond his parish. He was a member of the Synod which framed the Saybrook Platform, and one of the founders of the Fairfield Consociation. His views of church polity had a decided bent toward Presbyterianism, and his general attitude was conservative. He died in his forty-seventh year (December 31, 1714), too young to have reached the full measure of his usefulness or his influence in the Colony, but having already wrought a work for which we honor his memory, and to which this community was deeply indebted. It should not be forgotten in this connection that Commodore Isaac Chauncey of the United States Navy was his great-grandson, whose distinguished services in the war of 1812-15 added lustre to his honored name. Mr. Chauncey married the second time, March 16, 1698, Sarah, daughter of Henry Wolcott, by whom he had three children. She died January 5, 1703. March 14, 1710, he married again, this time Elizabeth, daughter of John Sherwood, who survived him. He had property in Stratford and in England, and left an estate valued at £743.

The first deacon of the church was David Sherman, the son of Mr. Samuel Sherman, who came here about 1685 and died here in 1700. Deacon David was thirty years old at the time we celebrate, a farmer, and lived at the summit of Toilsome Hill. Well-authenticated tradition reports him a man of good abilities and very much esteemed. He was specially gifted in prayer, and in the minister's absence took his place acceptably. He served the church for fifty-eight years, dying January 1, 1753. Mr. Elijah Burritt, who died at an advanced age, within the memory of some who are here, remembered him distinctly. Although he had no son, he had through his daughters many descendants, among others the present senior deacon of this church. This is a felicitous circumstance of our celebration.

Of the other members of the church, one, Matthew Sherman, was a brother of the deacon; two—each named Richard Hubbell—were father and son. Richard, Senior, was an immigrant from Wales, was made freeman in New Haven March 7, 1647, and married there, in 1650, Elizabeth Meigs. After residing there for some years, and for some time at Guilford, he came here in 1670. He died October 23, 1699. His son Richard was born in New

Haven in 1654. The family homestead was on what we call Clinton Avenue. Samuel Gregory has been mentioned as one of the first settlers here; he came here from Stratford. James Bennet and Isaac Wheeler were sons of settlers in Fairfield, the latter a large landholder. Samuel Beardsley was the son of William and Mary Beardsley, who came from Stratford-on-Avon, in England, in 1635, and he was born in 1638, the year in which his father settled in Stratford. He acquired land here near the site of the present jail, about 1670, and he, too, became a large landholder. The other was John Odell, Jr., from Fairfield. The well-known names of Sherwood, Wells, and Wakeley appear among the female members, and not long after came Thomas Hawley, the second deacon, and the head of a numerous line; and probably in 1698 Jacob Sterling, another of the fathers of this town. Among the promoters of the organization who did not become communicants, we recognize the familiar names of Knapp, Bishop, Burr, Morehouse, Hall, Seeley, Jackson, and Somers.

Thus we have seen the infant community gather, supply itself with homes, school, minister, and church. Evidence is abundant that before twenty years from the day we commemorate had passed it had attained no inconsiderable proportions, and comprised within it substantial citizens and comfortable households. But, as has been mentioned, Mr. Chauncey was gone, and one of the pressing needs of the year 1715 was the procuring of a new minister. There was another—the need of a larger church edifice. Both these needs were faced with a good courage.

The choice of a pastor fell upon Mr. Samuel Cooke. He was born in Guilford, Nov. 22, 1687—the son of Thomas and Sarah (Mason) Cooke. He graduated at Yale in 1705. He probably commenced the study of Divinity at once, but in January, 1707, became Rector of the Hopkins Grammar School, and held that position for nine years. He found it practicable to combine with his duties in it, however, occasional preaching, and three years service as Deputy from New Haven to the General

THE SECOND EDIFICE.

Court. In his second session he became clerk of the House. This dignity he still enjoyed at the May session of 1715. In the following month—June 16th—he was called hither. The First Church in New Haven was vacant at the same time, and Mr. Cooke became a candidate for that pastorate. Another was preferred, however, and then he accepted this call to Stratfield, July 11. He began his ministry here at once, but also fulfilled the duties of his rectorship at New Haven until the end of the year. He was ordained here Feb. 14, 1716. His home was nearly opposite that of his predecessor in the lane long known by his name. He brought here his wife, and four children. Mrs. Cooke was Anne, the only daughter of John Trowbridge of New Haven, and granddaughter of Governor Leete. She was born July 22, 1688. The date of the marriage was November 30, 1708.

About two months before Mr. Cooke's ordination, Richard Hubbell, Thomas Hawley and James Seeley were appointed a committee to consult with carpenters about the enlargement of the meeting-house. This was the beginning of a movement which ended in the building of a new edifice farther north, i. e., on the north-west corner of Park and North Avenues. This was erected in 1717, and here the church worshipped for upwards of ninety years. It was at a later date enlarged, and a steeple built, and a fair representation of it is preserved. It stood until 1835. In the erection of this church we find there were grants of permission to make pews; there was a seating committee appointed, to seat the worshippers "by dignity, age and estate." There was a "men's side," and a "women's side," and a gallery. These facts are suggestive, in their way, of the development of the social life of the community.

Mr. Cooke's personal influence undoubtedly operated in favor of the increase of ceremony and formality. He seems to have been the first to ask permission to build a family pew. He was a man whose personal dignity was long remembered in the parish. He was punctilious in his ministerial dress—comprising a heavy curled wig, black

coat and small clothes, shoes with silver buckles, and
over all a black gown or cloak. He was held in the highest
respect—somewhat in fear. He was a man of resolution,
often impetuous; had strong friends, and determined
opponents. His home was thrice desolated. He complains
of many sorrows and afflictions, in a note in the
church-record. He had difficulty in his later days in
getting his dues. His estate sued the parish for £3000
arrears. He alienated a number of the principal supporters
of the church to such a degree that they became the
promoters of the movement which resulted in the organization
of an Episcopal church. These facts do not make
a pleasant impression. He was a Fellow of the Corporation
of Yale College from 1732 to 1746, when he resigned
to avoid being excluded. This again does not sound well.
But to understand these things one must appreciate the
times in which he lived, and get below the surface of the
narrative. Mr. Cooke entered deeply into the controversies
and the conflicts of an exciting period. It would have
been strange indeed had he come out of them unscathed.
The Saybrook Synod of 1708, comprising the leading ministers,
and backed by the General Court, made an honest
endeavor to remedy evils in the condition of the Colony
which were recognized. The state of religion in the
churches was unsatisfactory. Morality was at a low ebb.
The signs of the time were ominous. These excellent
men aimed to establish an ecclesiastical constitution under
which the churches could be more effectually governed.
They sought to enforce discipline and to repress disorders.
But the churches did not take kindly to the system, and
viewed the attempts to put it in operation with jealousy.
Only as it was in practice construed more liberally than
its promoters had intended, did the churches finally
acquiesce in it. Dr. Bacon says of it that for a half-century
it made more difficulties than it healed. In the friction
between the party of order and the party of liberty,
I imagine the sympathies of Mr. Cooke were with the latter.
They certainly were in a celebrated case. Whether
the controversy on church-psalmody, which nearly rent

asunder some churches in this period, disturbed this one, I find no information. It may have done so. The issue was between singing by ear and singing by note. The latter innovation found it hard to make its way. Then, also, arose the excitements attending the Great Awakening—the Revivals of 1735 and 1740 and onward. It is difficult for us to get at the real merits of the conflicts of this time. When we hear of the blessed results of these works of grace, we are apt to wonder what arrayed against the promoters of them the great majority of the leading pastors. When we read how bitterly from the outset these pastors were assailed and reviled by itinerant ministers and lay exhorters, and what disorders and scandals often attended the Revival meetings, we wonder how there could have been any good in them. When we read the lamentations in President Edwards' letters written in 1750, and later, over the contentions, the confusions, the separations, the apostacies, the prevailing declensions and abounding iniquity of "the unhappy time" which followed the Revivals, we cannot but recognize that even their most zealous promoters had occasion for searchings of heart concerning them. I have no call to speak minutely of these difficulties here, beyond their relation to Mr. Cooke. He was heart and soul with the New Light men; lent all his influence to promote the Revival measures, and by his ability, activity and zeal provoked the antagonism from which he suffered. His own preaching was fervid and pungent. How far the church increased under his ministry cannot be told with accuracy from his carelessness in keeping the records, for which he himself apologizes. He died December 2, 1747. He was four times married. His first wife died August 11, 1721. His second wife was Esther, daughter of Nathaniel and Ann Burr, and widow of John Sloss of Fairfield. This wedding was May 3, 1722; and certain probate proceedings show she died previous to May 1, 1723. He married, third, Elizabeth, daughter of Joseph Platt of Norwalk, who died May 16, 1732, in her 31st year. His fourth wife was Abigail, eldest daughter of Rev. Samuel Russell of Branford, and widow of Rev. Joseph Moss of Derby. This marriage took place August 6, 1733, and she survived him. He left four sons and two daughters, and is honorably represented by their descendants to-day.

Nearly two years passed before the vacant pastorate was filled. Then came a man best known through his services in quite another field. Mr. Lyman Hall was born in Wallingford, April 12, 1724, and graduated at Yale in 1747. He studied theology with an uncle in Cheshire, and was ordained here September 27, 1749. His pastorate was short. It ended, not altogether happily, June 18, 1751. His views were not acceptable to the more ardent friends of Mr. Cooke, and the antagonism to him which was developed during his stay led to the forming, shortly after his dismission, of the Stratfield Baptist Society. So far as I know, this was the most abiding result of his ministry. He married the following spring, [May 20, 1752] Miss Abigail, daughter of Thaddeus and Abigail [Sturgis] Burr. She died July 8, 1753, in her 25th year. He turned his attention to the study of medicine, was in Fairfield as late as 1757, but eventually removed to Georgia. Early in 1775 he took a seat in the Continental Congress from that Colony. He was one of the signers of the Declaration of Independence, and afterwards the first Governor of the State of Georgia. He died October 19, 1790, leaving a widow but no children. He is buried in Wallingford, and a monument commemorates him there.

The date of his dismission, above mentioned, takes us just past the middle of the eighteenth century. The community had then, I judge, not far from a thousand inhabitants. It was a fair representative of the typical New England democracies—more self-complete than anything else the world knew—each with its elected magistrates, its school, its church, its minister of its own choosing, its annual town meeting; its cherished traditions of chartered rights and liberties. Connecticut had many such—had in all upward of a hundred and thirty thousand people. Here, as elsewhere, there were substantial men—

capable in business, in industry, in all manner of affairs. In spite of troubles with currency—with too much paper and too little coin—there was no little wealth and comfort. And there was a growing restlessness under the limitations imposed upon the development of these Colonies in the interest of the mother-country.* The age of Colonial dependence was drawing to its close. Men were already born who would see the war of independence, and the American Union.

After another interval of more than two years, a new pastor was elected. It indicates how generally the church had failed to sympathize with the views of Mr. Cooke that again they chose a man of the more conservative sort, but this time also a man of mark. Rev. Robert Ross was a native of Ireland, brought to this country in his infancy.† He was born in 1726. He graduated at Princeton College in 1751. It is said upon his monument that he was subsequently a tutor there, but this the Princeton Triennial does not confirm.‡ He was ordained here November 28, 1753, and spent here the rest of his days. About three weeks after his ordination [December 18, 1753] he married Mrs. Sarah, widow of Samuel Hawley. She was a granddaughter of Capt. John Edwards, an early settler here. Mr. Ross's home was on North Avenue, where Laurel Avenue now intersects it. The house was taken down within my memory.

He was definitely remembered far into the present century for his personal appearance, his personal qualities, and his force of character. In person he was fully six feet tall, and well proportioned. His presence was imposing, and his ruffled shirt, wig and cocked hat, his black suit, knee-breeches and white-topped boots, seemed to be peculiarly in keeping with it. But his ardent nature, his

---

* Ban. III., 464.

† A letter to me from a venerable lady, the great-granddaughter of Parson Ross, received after this discourse had been delivered, confirms what is said above, but adds the statement that the parents were originally Scotch, that the mother died previous to the father's immigration, and that the latter event was in the boy's third year.—C. R. P.

‡ He had an Honorary M. A. from Yale in 1754.

decisiveness, his strong and plain speaking, his impatience of contradiction, made him a man to be reckoned with, and he was among the foremost in all local affairs. He was a classical scholar, he was interested in education, and compiled text-books for schools. He was a stalwart Calvinist, and accounted a sound theologian; he was naturally a champion of the Standing Order, and a resolute antagonist to the various Separatists of his day. A work of his is extant in which he deals with these in a style far more noteworthy for its vigor than for its fulness of charity. In a word, we recognize in the man a good deal of the heat and combativeness of the Celtic race. To this in part he owed the impulse from which resulted his earnest devotion to the cause of the colonies. From the beginning to the end of the great struggle he was among the warmest on the patriotic side, and proportionally obnoxious to those who through interest or affection were loyal to the British crown. He was an early and a persistent advocate of the rights of the colonists as against the harassing restrictions upon their development imposed by the British government. He was impatient of these restrictions and keenly alive to the wrong of them. As time went on, sermons and prayers revealed how absorbed he was in the coming struggle. At the outbreak of the war he preached on the text "for the divisions of Reuben there were great searchings of heart" in a way long remembered. We can readily imagine that such a period as his ministry covered—including the war which expelled the French from this continent, and the war for independence, while it made heavy demands upon the heads and the hearts of men; while it tested the strength of their convictions, their fortitude and courage, their faith and persistence,—was not one favorable to the development of spiritual religion, or of religious institutions. Well was it that there were stout-hearted religious leaders; well was it that there was prayer in the homes, in the churches, in the colonial assemblies and in the camps; for if ever men needed the support and the inspirations of religion, they did in that tremendous time; but he knows little of human nature who would expect to hear that churches throve and piety abounded when the absorbing task of every town and colony was the war, the desperate, all-but-hopeless war for independence. Churches were scattered; churches were impoverished; churches were made into barracks, or burned; it was hardly a time to see them filled with happy worshippers, adorned with votive offerings, or multiplied through works of grace.

The history of this church in this period corresponded with the general trend of the time. Up to the outbreak of the Revolution, the community was prosperous, and its wealth increased. I have alluded to the renovation of the meeting-house, and the addition of its steeple. This was completed in 1771; and in 1774 the Society voted to have a bell. In the years succeeding this community was not wanting in the spirit of '76. In the autumn of 1775, we hear of the parading, at an early morning hour, of a company of soldiers in Mr. Ross' front yard, which, after his fervent prayer in their behalf, marched to join in the invasion of Canada. In 1776 the Stratfield company was engaged in the defense of New York. There is no doubt this was but the beginning of Stratfield's contributions to the long and heroic struggle; but as it went on, and the heavy burdens of it increased, the prosperity in which the community had rejoiced and felt strong, gave place to adversity which tasked its courage and endurance to the utmost. When we read deeply into the records of this time, and become acquainted with the long train of evils which accompanied and followed upon the war, we wonder that anything survived the stress and the misery of days so unfavorable to every interest of society. The last ten or twenty years of Mr. Ross' ministry were for many reasons times of hardship. The diseases, the vices, the sufferings, the losses, the universal insolvency, the impoverishment, the social disorders, which came with the war, or were entailed by it, gave reason for the saying of a recent historian that with the end of the war the worst troubles of the colonists commenced. The difficulties, the depressions, the straits of the church must have tasked even so ardent and zealous a man as Mr. Ross. He had his domestic sorrows also. His first-born son, when a child, was drowned in his father's well. Mrs. Ross died October 10, 1772. She left a daughter, also Sarah, who has descendants now living. Mr. Ross married, second, Eulilia, daughter of Ebenezer and Elizabeth (Williams) Bartram, of Fairfield. She was born June 24, 1737. She made herself greatly beloved, and died, much lamented, December 5, 1785, after several months' illness. Mr. Ross married again, Sarah, daughter of Rev. Jonathan Merrick, of North Branford. She survived him about twenty-four hours. He resigned his charge April 30, 1796, and died August 29, 1799. He is described on his monument as "a person who long sustained a high character for Christian literature, and general knowledge. In his principles orthodox; in his preaching, practical and judicious. He advocated the truths of the Gospel by doctrine and example, and was therefore a pious guide and instructor." I must confess to not a little tenderness toward the memory of "Parson Ross," who for more than forty-two years, against many discouragements, held up the standard here, and left behind him so honorable a reputation.

It is part of the ecclesiastical history of the latter part of his ministry that in it began what is now the First Methodist Church of our city. The first preacher of Methodism to come here was the Rev. William Black, in 1784. He preached several times in the Congregational Church, and was heard with favor, but at length offended Mr. Ross' Calvinistic convictions, and, as the story goes, was by him somewhat vehemently denounced. From this time, however, there seem to have been those who were favorable to his doctrine, and who were accustomed to gather in private houses. On September 26, 1789, the first Methodist society in New England was organized by Rev. Jesse Lee, in a house on the west side of the Toilsome Hill road. It was a class consisting of three good women, and this proved the nucleus of the church we have since known so well. I do not suppose Parson

Ross approved this new conventicle in his parish, but that has not prevented our living on the best of terms with our Methodist brethren, and rejoicing in their prosperity. The seedling he would have suppressed became a tree of great fruitfulness.

A single incident of the church life during Mr. Ross's ministry, although often described, was too remarkable and too tragic to be passed over here. On the 28th July, 1771, the congregation assembled for worship at the usual morning hour. A storm was gathering, but the service proceeded. The storm proved to be one of appalling severity. The church grew dark, until the form of the minister was hardly visible, as he stood in the exercise of prayer. Suddenly a dazzling flash of lightning filled the house, made more terrific by the crash of thunder which followed instantaneously. The voice of the minister broke the awful stillness which ensued, with the question, "*Are we all here?*" It was found that two of the best men of the community, David Sherman and Captain John Burr, who had come to church in the fulness of vigorous life, had been struck dead, and several others had been injured. The impression made by this painful occurrence was profound and lasting.

The mention of these excellent men reminds me that there were many noteworthy laymen in the first century of this church's existence, whom, did time permit, it would be interesting to commemorate. Richard Hubbell, the third of the name, was born in the year 1695. He lived until 1788, and at his death had been deacon for fifty years. His house is still standing, although it has been moved. John Cooke, the son of Rev. Samuel Cooke, born in 1715, lived until the end of 1813. Lieut. Benjamin Fayerweather, born in 1717, lived until 1791, and was a substantial citizen. Capt. Stephen Burroughs, born in 1730, lived to 1818, and was a man of distinguished attainments in mathematics and other sciences. He is said to have been the inventor of Federal money. He was an ardent patriot, and raised and commanded a company called the "Householders," of those exempt from military service. Capt. William Wordin, born in 1733, lived until 1808. He was another ardent patriot, and in his turn commanded the "Householders." He was a tall, spare, indefatigable man, and took a leading part in the parish affairs. Capt. Abijah Sterling, born 1745, lived until 1802, and left the impression of a strong personality. He was described as "one of Nature's noblemen." He was captain in the militia, and a justice of the peace; a man of great sagacity, acuteness, and strong moral sense. He was the umpire in all disputes, the general pacificator. Dea. Abel Seelye (1725-1810), and Dea. Seth Seelye (1738-1817) also deserve mention, and others as well. These were men who, in the times that tried men's souls, stood the fiery test and lived to tell the story. Nearly all of them lived to see the slow process of the recuperation of the community and of the church, and to see the great change which the former underwent. After the Revolution, the trade and commerce which the mother country had done her utmost to prevent, began to be of importance. The little collection of houses and stores which had acquired the name of Newfield, to the eastward, and in the vicinity of the intersection of Main and State streets, gradually increased and became in due time the nucleus of the future town of Bridgeport, in which the individuality of the rural parish of Stratfield was eventually lost. It is an indication of the progress of this change that the home of the next minister was not on North Avenue but where is now 644 Main street.

This was the Rev. Samuel Blatchford. He was the eldest son of Henry and Mary (Heath) Blatchford, and born in Devonport, Devonshire, England, in the year 1767, and grew up there. The fate of prisoners of war in British hands during the Revolution was as a rule very hard. They were often herded in prison ships and treated with great inhumanity. Vast numbers of them perished. Those who were taken to England fared little better at the hands of officials, but sometimes experienced kindness from English people. Not very far from the early home of Mr. Blatchford was one of the prisons where American prisoners were confined, and his parents were interested in their behalf. When a lad he was employed in conveying to sufferers the means of relief. The sympathies thus awakened occasioned in him an early resolution to come to this country. That resolution gave to the United States a useful citizen and the founder of a distinguished family. But it was not at once carried out. He was educated in England. He was sent to a school at Willington in Somersetshire, and thence to Homerton College near London. After completing his studies he was employed as an assistant minister, and subsequently ordained pastor at Kingsbridge near Dartmouth. His ordination was in November, 1789. He married, March 25, 1788, Alicia, daughter of Thomas Windeatt, Esq., of Bridgetown-Totwas, a woman admirably fitted to her station, and, happily, spared to him to the end of his life.* In 1791 he removed to Topsham, near Exeter, and thence, in 1795, executed his long-cherished purpose of emigration. He arrived in New York August 1. He preached first in Bedford, N. Y.; then for a year at Greenfield Hill, succeeding President Dwight. In February, 1797, he was invited to preach here for six months, with a view to settlement. He accepted and was installed November 22 of the same year. His salary being inadequate, he eked it out by teaching an academy for boys. I imagine he had rather a hard time here, but he commanded the respect of the community. Unfamiliar with American life, scantily supported, burdened with care and with work in his double duties, he could hardly do justice to himself. But his labors were of great service to the church, and only too soon terminated. He resigned March 20, 1804, to accept a call to the Presbyterian Church in Lansingburgh, where he continued until his death, March 17, 1828. He was honored with the degree of Doctor of Divinity in 1808 by Williams College. He was an able, an excellent and, in his later years, a prominent man. As a preacher he was instructive in

---

* She died December 2, 1846.

matter, unaffected and impressive in manner. He was well read in theology and decided in his convictions. He was social in his disposition, noted for his hospitality, and generous in his sympathies. He retained his interest in the education of young men, and was responsive to all benevolent enterprises. He was the father of seventeen children, of whom ten survived him. I need only mention in this connection his son John, who a generation later succeeded him; another son, the Hon. R. M. Blatchford, the friend and executor of Daniel Webster, whose splendid services to his country as a jurist, a financier, a commissioner of great trusts, and a representative abroad, are not forgotten; and the late Hon. Samuel Blatchford, Associate Justice of the United States Supreme Court, the son of the last-named—to remind you how rich was the gift this parish received in its fifth pastor.

In this seven years' pastorate a number were added to the church, and a movement was successfully inaugurated to build a new church edifice. It was time to do this—and time to remove the center of the church life from the old site at the Four Corners into the midst of the new and rapidly increasing village by the harbor. But it was not altogether an easy thing to do. Those long accustomed to worship in the old church clung to it, and very reluctantly yielded to a necessity which from our point of view seems obvious enough. The transition took place under the ministry of Rev. Elijah Waterman. He was the great restorer and second founder of this church, in the Providence of God, and he is commemorated here opposite to Mr. Chauncey. He was happy in his opportunity, and nobly used it. He was born in Bozrah, Conn., November 28, 1769.[*] He graduated at Yale in 1791, with creditable rank. He betook himself to teaching, intending ultimately to study law, but changed his purpose, and in 1792 became a student with Dr. Dwight at Greenfield Hill, and afterward with Dr. Jonathan Edwards of New

---

[*] He was the son of Nehemiah and Susannah (Isham) Waterman. The father was a magistrate, and an active patriot during the Revolutionary war.

THE THIRD EDIFICE.

Haven. In April, 1794, he went to Windham to preach as a candidate, and in October following was ordained there, and fulfilled a pastorate of ten years. He married November 18, 1795, Lucy, daughter of Shubael Abbe of Windham. She was born in that town May 21, 1778. She died here, greatly lamented, March 17, 1822, in her 44th year. In October, 1823, he married a second time, Mrs. Lucy Talcott, of Springfield, who survived him. Mr. Waterman's ministry in Windham was terminated in February, 1805. He was installed here January 1, 1806, and his pastorate ended only with his life. Very soon it was evident that a new era in the history of the church had begun. Locally it was the era of a transformation. The borough of Bridgeport was incorporated in 1800, with two hundred and fifty inhabitants. Its rapid growth gradually absorbed the life of the more ancient settlement. The future town, therefore, was taking on its proportions during this pastorate. It was incorporated in 1821. Parallel to this development was that of the church. August 6, 1806, it underwent a reorganization. The Half-way Covenant was definitely abandoned. A new confession of faith and covenant, and a code of standing rules, were adopted. In 1807 the new church edifice was completed, built by subscription on the site at present occupied. At first it was used two Sundays out of three, but after a short interval exclusively. In 1814 a Sunday School was organized by Mr. Platt Benedict, the first in town. It enlisted the pastor's sympathies and was ultimately taken under the care of the church, a supervisory committee being appointed. In April, 1821, the church purchased the land where the chapel stands, for a conference room and academy. A building was erected to answer both purposes, and was occupied as a conference room July 5, 1821. The title of academy had reference to the fact that Mr. Waterman was deeply interested in the education of young men. He more or less definitely projected a theological school. He did instruct a number of candidates for the ministry. This local and external development was only part of the interest of this pastorate. It covered a wonderful period. As many will remember, it was the time of the Evangelical Revival, the fruitage of which was so extensive, not alone in Christian homes and churches, but in the formation of the great beneficent organizations such as the American Board, the American Bible Society, and others. It saw the beginnings of the temperance reform in this state, in the action of the General Association in 1812. I need only remind you, moreover, that in the midst of it came the second war with Great Britain—a time of peril, of hardship, of impoverishment, in which all foundations were shaken, but out of which the country emerged without serious disaster. Afterward came the great contest which ended in the disestablishment of the Congregational churches of Connecticut—the overthrow of the Standing Order, as the phrase of the day had it. This event, in the time of it, seemed to many excellent men the triumph of the gates of hell over the Kingdom; but some of them at least lived to perceive that it was indeed what Dr. Lyman Beecher called it, "the best thing that ever happened to the Connecticut churches," their emancipation from civil control. I need only add that Mr. Waterman's ministry covered also the development of the Unitarian controversy. It is to be said to his credit that in all the excitements of this eventful period he commended himself to this church as a wise and trustworthy leader, and an effective helper of all that was good. He was a moderate Calvinist, and in the movements of his time sympathized decidedly with the progressive side. But he was a man of good sense and of tact. He kept his hold of men of different modes of thinking, and antagonized none of them. As a pastor, he was laborious and faithful; as a preacher, he was effective and acceptable. His style was perspicuous; his thinking was vigorous, and his manner was animated and earnest. His ministry as a whole was a successful one. The current of the church life flowed full and strong. Commencing with forty-seven church members, all told, he saw rapid increase almost from the first. The whole number added in his less than twenty years pastorate was about three hundred and sixty. In the autumn of 1825, while on a visit to Springfield, he was taken with typhus fever, and died there October 11, in his 56th year. The church sent a committee to bring hither his remains for interment, and thus ended his useful and honored ministry. He built and occupied the first house on Golden Hill, the one next west of the present parsonage. He was the originator of the first water-works in the town. He was a man of medium stature; very well built, and having the appearance of great physical strength ; and was a man of more than usual weight and influence. His countenance was amiable and intelligent, his movements quick and natural, his habits active. He had a high spirit, showed a keen sense of favors or injuries, and was liable to sudden flashes of temper. But he was placable, and soon recovered his self-control. He left behind him the reputation of a good citizen, and an exemplary Christian. The church venerates his memory, and his family is still represented in its membership.

In the settlement of a successor to this excellent pastor, in the year following his death, some difference of views seems to have arisen ; while it had no immediate results that were serious, it ripened into something quite positive a few years later. Prominent before the people as candidates were the Rev. Thomas T. Waterman and the Rev. Franklin Y. Vail. The former was a son of the late pastor, who since his fifth year had grown up in the parish. He had graduated at Yale in 1822 and then pursued his theological studies with his father, and was a young man of promise. He was a warm-hearted and earnest preacher, and had a useful ministry. He had strong friends here, and his claims were vigorously pressed. But for some reason the movement in his favor did not succeed and the choice fell upon Mr. Vail. The selection, however, seems to have been determined less by positive interest in him than by opposition to Mr. Waterman. He did not take a strong hold of the church, nor did he long retain his position.

He was born in Easthampton, Long Island, in 1797; entered Yale but did not graduate; studied theology in New York, and this was his first charge. He was ordained October 4, 1826, and his brief pastorate ended July 8, 1828. He was a man of small stature, of slender person, of amiable character. His home was on Water street just north of Clinton street, in a house now taken down. Neither his health nor his tastes fitted him for the work of a pastor, but he subsequently proved himself admirably adapted to work of another kind in which he was singularly successful. This was the raising of funds for beneficent purposes, in which he was engaged for nearly forty years. He was for many years the General Agent of the American Tract Society, which very highly appreciated his services. Later he was the principal agent in founding and endowing Lane Theological Seminary and the Ohio Female College. He died in Cincinnati, June 23, 1868. His wife was Catharine Matilda, daughter of Daniel Hawley.

It was more than two years and a half ere another pastor was installed in the First Church, and in that interval events occurred which resulted in the formation of the Second, or South, Church, and hence my history of the undivided church draws to an end. These events were accompanied by a good deal of feeling in the time of them, but from this distance we can speak of them dispassionately. I said a little while since that the movement to call Mr. T. T. Waterman was successfully opposed. It was the more conservative element of the church to whom he failed to commend himself, and their experience in the pastorate of Mr. Vail had strengthened those of an opposite tendency. It was a time of excitement in the theological world. The Unitarian defection in Massachusetts had no counterpart in Connecticut, but the fact of it awakened an uneasiness in our churches which rendered them abnormally susceptible to fears of erroneous teaching. Moreover, the controversies were already active which resulted in a second Divinity School in Connecticut; in the disruption of the Presbyterian Church in this country, and very likely would have disrupted the body of Congregational churches had there been any such body to disrupt. Good men honestly differed and honestly mistrusted the tendency of their opponents' opinions. In this sensitive condition of things it is not to be wondered at that a decided difference of sentiment arose here. We can speak of it without implying that anybody was blameworthy, especially as now nobody will claim there ever has been any real difference in the theological position of these two churches. When, in the autumn of 1828, the minds of the Society were directed to Mr. John Blatchford, the more conservative party in the church were not disposed to unite in calling him. In January, 1829, the church proved to be almost equally divided upon the question of calling him, and the call, issued by a majority of four only, he very promptly declined. It proved impossible to harmonize the antagonistic elements after this disturbance, and at length, December 28, 1829, a division of the church was resolved upon. January 24, 1830, three deacons, thirty-six other male members and seventy-eight female members were dismissed at their own request, to form the Second Church, the old church giving them one-half the church property and funds, and also contributing two thousand dollars toward the erection of a church edifice. The dissension between Paul and Barnabas resulted in the doubling of the missionary forces of the early Christian church. The division of the First Church, however regrettable it seemed, no doubt was overruled to the increase of the forces of the Kingdom in this growing community. The very honorable history of the Second Church bears witness that the good men who founded it, even if they were needlessly alarmed as to the tendency of the First Church, were men whose faith, whose loyalty to their convictions, whose prayers and sacrifices led them to accomplish a good work for Christ and His Gospel, in which both churches have reason to rejoice. It is with eminent fitness, however, that both have clasped hands to-day in commemorating the one hundred and thirty-five years' history which is their common inheritance. The separate history of this church since 1830 I shall pursue on another occasion.*

In concluding this review there has come into my thoughts a passage in one of Dean Stanley's Sermons at St. Andrew's. It is in the sermon on "Succession in Spiritual Life." It runs as follows: " The weary traveler in the south of Spain who, after passing many an arid plain and many a bare hill, finds himself at nightfall under the heights of Granada, will hear rushing and rippling under the shade of the spreading trees, and along the side of the dusty road, the grateful murmur of running waters, of streamlets whose sweet music mingles with his dreams as he sleeps, and meets his ear as the first pleasant voice in the stillness of the early dawn. What is it? It is the sound of the irrigating rivulets called into existence by the Moorish occupants of Granada five centuries ago, which amidst all the changes of race and religion have never ceased to flow. Their empire has fallen ; their creed has been suppressed by fire and sword ; their nation has been driven from the shores of Spain ; their palaces crumble into ruins; but the trace of their beneficent civilization still continues, and in this continuity that which was good and wise and generous in that gifted but unhappy race still lives on, to cheer and to refresh their enemies and conquerors. Even so it is with the good deeds of those who have gone before us. Whatever there has been of grateful consideration, of kindly hospitality, of far-reaching generosity, of gracious charity, of high-minded justice, of unselfish devotion, of saintly devotion—these still feed the stream of moral fertilization, which will run on when their place knows them no more, when even their names have perished."

Friends, it is not necessary to claim that our fathers and predecessors on this soil were in all things wise, or that their religious leaders were faultless men, in order to point to them as in many ways our benefactors. Their toils, their struggles, their sacrifices, their prayers, their counsels, their faith, their patience, entered into the long

* See p. 142.

process through which this community has become what it is, and have had their results in the material, the moral, the intellectual, the spiritual well-being which we recognize in our heritage to-day. "The *good* men do lives after them; the *ill* is oft interred with their bones." Honor to the men who planted the school and the church in the parish of Stratfield! Instead of their one church we see nearly fifty; instead of their one school a vast system; instead of their little hamlet this expanding city! Who will hesitate to believe that whatever there is in this grand evolution which is excellent or hopeful, is in some measure indebted to the beneficent influences by them set in motion two hundred years ago; or that those influences in their effects are still flowing, and will continue to flow perennially forever and forever more!

Dr. PALMER: Let us unite in singing, and afterwards I beg you to wait awhile till the photographs are taken.

Let us unite in singing the 1312th hymn—

"Oh God, beneath Thy guiding hand
Our exiled fathers crossed the sea."

Let us sing to the tune of Duke Street.

(At the conclusion of the singing, a view of the northerly portion of the church was taken by the photographer, chemicals being ignited which produced an instantaneous illumination.)

Dr. PALMER: While they are arranging for the other picture I want to say, having had occasion to refer to those churches that early went out from this, that this evening we are going to give those churches an opportunity to talk back. Our friends who represent those churches will speak to us to-night, I am anticipating, in such a manner as to be pleasing and profitable. Services commence at a quarter to eight.

To-morrow, the great day, the services will commence at 10 o'clock. We shall assemble, as the fathers were wont to assemble, by beat of drum. We shall have a full programme and shall be addressed by gentlemen who are well qualified to interest us in their commemorative addresses. We are especially happy in the presence of the Hon. E. W. Blatchford of Chicago, Illinois, who has come all the way from that city, in the midst of his busy life, that he might speak of the memories of his father and grandfather, and join in these festivities.

Respecting the plate before us, I must say that the cup that has been longest in the possession of the church was a gift to it in 1713. The donor was Matthew Sherwood, Jr. The other cup was a bequest to it at a later date, but is an older cup, having been brought here by a pioneer from England, Captain John Edwards, before 1700. The tankard was a gift of Richard Hubbell, and bears date a little later. They are the oldest pieces we have. I mention this because it may interest some to see them.

(The apparatus being arranged, a photograph was in like manner taken of the southerly portion of the church and the audience present.)

Dr. PALMER: My friends, you will be dismissed with the benediction. I thank you for quietly remaining.

"The love of God the Father, the grace of the Lord Jesus Christ, the communion of the Holy Ghost, be with all forever. Amen."

SERVICES OF
WEDNESDAY EVENING.

ORGAN PRELUDE.

ANTHEM, "Great is the Lord."

PRAYER,

BY REV. H. C. WOODRUFF, of Black Rock.

We invoke Thy presence and benediction, O Lord Our Heavenly Father, as we gather here this evening in this service of commemoration of the two hundred years of the life of this Church. We praise Thy name for all the memories of the hour, for the two centuries of Christian life and labor whose experiences crowd upon our thoughts, for the work and worship which have transpired within these walls dedicated to Thy praise. And we gather to-night especially to commemorate those who in the course of these years have gone forth from us to form new church homes for themselves. May they not feel that they have gone out from us because they were not of us, but may they rather realize that they are but members with us of that One family of which God is the Father and Christ the elder Brother. May they realize that we have a common Master and faith and life! And may their separation bring to them only a clearer and wider vision and a fuller experience of the Divine character and grace, and may they return to enrich us with the wealth of that which they have seen and experienced.

May this not be a period for retrospect alone. May our vision of the past make us also to look forward. May our memory be also an inspiration. And as we rejoice and are glad because of that which in the past Thy servants have been able to do, may we who are their successors address ourselves, with hope and courage and enthusiasm begotten of our experience, to the solution of those problems and the performance of those tasks which still await us.

We ask it in the name of Jesus Christ, Our Lord and Savior, and we would give all the glory to the Father, Son and Holy Spirit. Amen.

☦

WELCOME TO INVITED GUESTS.

By Rev. Charles Ray Palmer, D.D.

On the part of the First Church and Society of Bridgeport and the Committee of Arrangements, I heartily greet all who have assembled with us on this happy anniversary. It is delightful to see the old friends who have for the occasion returned to us, the kind neighbors and fellow citizens who enter into our joy, and those from every side who have lent us the encouragement of their presence and sympathy; and it is my special pleasure and duty this evening to welcome here the representatives of the Churches of the different communions who share with us the dignity of this occasion and who are of common descent from the old Stratfield parish, while no longer connected with it. The founders of St. John's parish, the founders of the original Baptist Church of this vicinity, the first nucleus of the oldest Methodist Church of our city, were originally members of the old Stratfield parish; they and their parents were most of them communicants in this church; some of the founders of the First Presbyterian Church also were baptized and brought up in this church. In celebrating the beginnings, their children have the same right here which we have ourselves. To my thought, the early history with all its treasured memories is the common heritage of the people of Bridgeport, and especially of the churches of Bridgeport. Brethren, although your fathers may have left the old church for conscience sake and you have churches organized to further convictions and preferences which the old church does not altogether share, she to-night accords to you the fullest Christian fellowship; joyfully welcomes you to the old hearthstone, and rejoices that each of you in your own way is serving with us the Kingdom of the Lord Jesus Christ.

Side by side we testify and toil that in the future this fair city of ours may be an orderly, an enlightened, a sanctified society; and so fulfill the aspirations with which our fathers began it. Thankful for your presence here, we shall be glad of any words of greeting with which you may favor us, but remember you are not strangers here but at home in this old household of faith.

Now, friends, we wish next to sing the 97th hymn, and we propose to sing it as the fathers used to sing. The minister will line out the hymn, and you will follow him. The organist will play the first line over to give us the pitch, then I will read the line and you will sing it, and so on with each line; but understand you are to come in very promptly at the beginning.

(The audience rose and Dr. Palmer lined the hymn, in the singing of which to " Old Hundred " all joined.)

Dr. PALMER: The first church organization which originated within the teritory of the old parish, of those who preferred to worship in some other way than this church did, was St. John's. We are favored with the presence of the rector of that parish, and we will listen to him, Rev. William H. Lewis.

The Rev. Mr. LEWIS said:

Dear brother and brothers of the household of faith, I think your pastor made a mistake when he began to-night by saying that these other ecclesiastical bodies within the limits of this city had broken away from the ties which interested you. I am sure it is not so, for as every one well knows who knows what the history of such a community as this is, who has traced its windings back and forth among the multitude of families which come in to make it up, every one knows that the lines of relation, the lines of interest weave themselves back and forth continually among the families of a place like this so that it is impossible except by death—and we do not recognize death except as an accident of life—to sever those relations; and in proof of this I will state a fact which is not perhaps known to all present here, namely, that one of those venerable vessels which lies on the table was given to this parish by an ancestor of my wife, and bears his name. And so I say we are glad to come here to-night—I am individually, having as a friend one worth having, your pastor, and as one interested in everything that concerns the religious life of this community, to come both individually and representatively and bring you my cordial greetings on this your two hundredth birthday; and when I was casting over in my mind what to say, the beautiful quotation with which your pastor closed his address occurred to me—I believe from Canon Farrar,—and instinctively I laid my hands on a little relic which has lain for some time on the mantelpiece in my study and I said "I will bring that." Our birthday is a birthday in a sense in the Kingdom of Great Britain, for that is a piece of an old Roman brick taken out of the wall of St. Martin's Church in Canterbury, whose history—you remember—Canon Farrar and other authorities in the Church of England have traced out to the last part of the first century; so that little edifice, with its walls built of Roman brick, of one of which this is a part, commemorates the beginning of the church, which I think Canon Farrar says was founded in the year 87, the records of which show that almost continuously, except through the vissicitudes of war in the kingdom, it has been open as a place of worship, and I had the pleasure three years ago of being taken into that venerable little building—for it will not cover one-quarter of the ground this church covers—and there standing on the very stone on which St. Augustine stood when in the year 597 he preached his first sermon to the Saxons. In front of me was the famous Saxon font; by the side of me was the tomb of Queen Bertha, in which her remains still rest, and on the left was a curious opening in the wall, known as the "Leper's Squint," something like a slit made in the wall through which those diseased and unfortunate people could look and see the praise and prayer and the sacrifice at the altar while not permitted to join the congregation. Such a bit of old material as that makes us all understand that age is relative. When we come to celebrate the two hundredth birthday of an ecclesiastical body and have present a memento from the eighteen hundredth birthday of an ecclesiastical body, we feel like children indeed; and yet on the other hand, when we come to measure the life of this body with the life of the community in which it has found its home, we feel venerable indeed—and so age is relative. As we look backward we see those older and older and older till memory ceases to work. As we look forward we see the great end to which we are all moving, and as God marks off our term of usefulness there is an age of light, and within that limit comes the counting of the birthdays, and we may, if we are working for Him and his Son's Kingdom, count every one which He gives us as a blessing direct from Him. I am sure that this old body of yours is venerable in the memories and minds and thoughts of all here gathered to-night, associated with a host of holy associations. It is no little thing that for even two hundred years there has been a body of Christian people standing up—whatever their mode of worship I care not; whatever their ecclesiastical organization may be I care not—we take this body of men and women whose lives are sacrificed to Almighty God, whose mission is to fight against the sin in the world, whose hope is in life everlasting, whose one name is the name of the Lord Jesus Christ, whose one desire in the world is to win souls for Christ and to follow in the example and footsteps of His most Holy life,—I say it is a thing to be proud of that for two hundred years this ecclesiastical body has stood for that in the community, and in the changes and chances and shifting and disappearings and reappearings of the life of this community there has been here represented a steady, wholesome, hearty influence for God and righteousness. I am proud to stand under that banner to-night, and I can stand and feel in my heart of hearts—as you have tried through your authorities here to gather up and bind together during these two days all those holy associations—I am proud to go back through the history of this church and see for what this church stood, what it has tried to do, what it has represented here; and then your duty is only half done, for there is no use whatever in any such commemoration as this if it does not bring with it an inspiration for the future; and if all of your preparations that have involved so much trouble and research shall count for nothing in the days to come except that you shall go right on the same old pathway and effort to improve, then you better not have celebrated—you should accomplish more in the future; but I am sure no such spirit lies here, that no such spirit will receive countenance here.

We are told by those who know that the two great signs of this last decade of the century are, first, a decided revival of religious feeling, a decided bent of the public mind towards religious research and religious truth. It is a most happy sign. I think it is Bryce, the author of the American Commonwealth, who says that sign is to be particularly distinguished among the American people and that they are known among scholars and are known among the nations as looking at the world from the standpoint of God and the people. I am sure if that is so that this church and every other church has its work laid out for it. And the second sign which he finds is the growing desire among all bodies of Christians for a true unity, and, dear friends, I venture to hope that from the exercises of these days there will come an impulse in the direction of the fulfillment of that desire.

Dr. PALMER: It is with great pleasure that we receive here to-night a representative of a body of Christians who went out from us nearly one hundred and forty-five years ago. We rejoice that for our part we have always dwelt with them in true fellowship, and it is a great satisfaction so to receive them on this occasion. We will now hear from the pastor of the First Baptist Church, Rev. George W. Nicholson.

The Rev. Mr. NICHOLSON'S remarks follow :
My Dear Doctor, sisters and brethren in the Lord, it is with great pleasure that I can return the compliment to the doctor and his people, and say that the Baptist Church has been in sympathy with him and the work for the Lord by every name in Bridgeport. I came down this afternoon to get acquainted with my mother (laughter). I was very glad to find, notwithstanding she was aged, that she was quite a fine-looking old lady, and it was with a great deal of pleasure that I formed her acquaintance through the historical discourse of Dr. Palmer. I once saw a group of five generations; it was a most beautiful picture; it has lingered with me ever since, and I can to-night, as I stand before you, bring before my mind the picture of that great-great-grandmother sitting opposite that great-great-grandchild with as much pleasure and delight as if it were her own child and she a mother of twenty years. The old lady was still fresh and full of vigor and full of interest in the affairs of to-day. I am delighted to be one of a group of more than five generations, to come and sit at the feet of her who bore us and gaze and admire and seek to learn, that we might imitate her good qualities, which are so evidently rich in themselves and numerous in their quantity. We congratulate you on reaching such an age so sweetly, so lovingly, so vigorously. It is one thing to grow old and quite another thing to grow old gracefully, and I congratulate you to-night, my beloved, that you have grown old so gracefully and that you show your grace in the figure and symmetry of your form. We congratulate you on rearing so fine and intelligent and numerous a family of children. I think I can say this without blush or hesitation. It so happens that I am only an adopted child, and for this reason I feel that I can the more freely and heartily congratulate you on rearing such a really magnificent family as is represented in this house this evening. Though some of the children

have independently chosen another way in some particulars from that taught by the mother—it is only natural at some times for the children to be a little naughty and a little independent and want to have their own way—she may regard them with pride in that we have tried to bring no dishonor upon the mother, we have tried to do the best we could in our way and not to hinder her in her way; and we come to assure you that though our ways have diverged a little we come around once in a while where we can look each other in the face, and as we do so we can see some features of resemblance and mutual recognition when we meet at the cross of the blessed Lord and Master from whence we have all derived our spirit and life and cheer and favor. I personally have shown my appreciation of one of the daughters of the church by linking my interests with hers, and I feel happy to assure you that I have had no cause for regret since the First Baptist Church and myself were married, nor have I any disposition to seek for divorce from her. We are glad that the opportunities are ours of calling upon our mother, especially as we find her in such good health and spirit and vigor, and our prayer is that she may be long spared to adorn the homestead and give pleasure to her numerous progeny all over this section of country. Some one has said we have millions of stars in the skies, millions of drops of water in the ocean and myriads of mountains on the earth's surface, but we have only one mother. How true! How glad we are to have her with us! How we dislike and regret the time of her departure when it comes in some of our homes! We feel we would hold her longer though age and infirmity were hers, and it is a matter of delight and great comfort when we feel we have our mother with us. So I rejoice with the daughter whom I represent to-night that we have our mother with us. What is home without a mother? We look with pride and delight upon the First Congregational Church as the mother of the following of Jesus Christ in Bridgeport, especially as we have our birth and name so closely connected with the free spirit of our country. It was a matter of information, and of very joyful information this afternoon when Dr. Palmer told us that a man who was pastor of this church was one of the signers of the Declaration of Independence. We believe in fore-ordination. Was there anything in this fact? If there is anything for which we have lived and labored and bled and suffered and died, it is religious liberty, and I thank God that we can come to-day after these years, representing so large a constituency of the country, and declare to you that religious liberty is still permanently ours as one of the bulwarks behind which we have lived and labored and for which we are willing to suffer and die in the days to come.

We congratulate you for your continued adherence to the old gospel, that though you had one contest between the ear and note, as we heard this afternoon, the contest between the ear and the Gospel has been successful, as it was between the ear and note; that you have not been allured from the old foundation by any of the sounds in the air, nor strained by the spirit of the world or rent asunder by the higher criticism or new theology; but like a rock in the weary land, a refuge in the time of storm for these two hundred years, through clouds as well as sunshine, through contests as well as conquests, you have stood firm, you have held out the signal of peace to the living, and held up the living Christ to the sorrowing and sick. One of the sublime mysteries of the day is the influence of the Christian church on the community in which it is planted. Estimating what you have done during these two hundred years for this section of our country by dates or figures or statistics can never possibly measure or reveal its extent; they are rather only like rifts in the clouds, through which you may glance at the immense labors you have performed and the success you have secured and the greater success beyond in triumphs for the Lord.

An island in the sea seems like an isolated field to an unknown voyager, but not to the old sailor. He looks at it with a different eye. He knows that beneath the surface of the water its roots are to be found piercing and penetrating in all directions, and the island is only one of the higher peaks of a range of mountains extending miles and miles in the distance, and in the storm the anchor is thrown overboard to grapple one or other of these roots for an anchorage till the storm be passed and the winds calm. So it is with the Church of Jesus Christ—it looks solitary and alone as here and there you see it pointing its finger to the skies like a lighthouse on the shore or an island in the ocean, but her roots are permeating this city of ours in all directions and its effects are felt in every department whether secular or religious. The old church has affected the vital interests of the section we represent.

We might congratulate you on the manifest elements of strength and prosperity which on every side are apparent; on the indications of spiritual progress, of growth in Christ-likeness; but we have come to congratulate you on reaching this birthday. We will pray God for yet a grander future for the First Church of Bridgeport than you have ever had, and though you have brought your thousands into the church, the day will come when the record will run up to hundreds of thousands enlisted for the service of God and the saving of souls and strengthening of everything which is for the good of us all. May the Lord bless you and abide with you and strengthen you, and may you come out and realize more success than you have in the past, until the day when the mother and daughters shall be gathered together and shall grasp hands cordially with each other over the differences as well as the mutual affections existing, and shall glorify God and bring the blessed Kingdom of Christ in all its glory!

Dr. PALMER: I remember having once had occasion to allude to the fact that the first Methodist society in New England originated in this parish, and that Dr. Pullman, being within hearing, said he didn't know of any organization in this world that he would rather make an improvement on than on the Congregational church. We are very glad to have him here to tell us to-night all there is in his heart.

Dr. PULLMAN spoke as follows: My dear brother, my only regret on this very memorable occasion is that the people called Methodists have not a better representative here, a more worthy representative than the speaker, but it is the accident of my life and the good fortune of my life to be at this time pastor of the First Methodist Church of this city, and I am therefore called upon to represent the Methodist community of the city. I join most heartily with the sentiments of congratulation that have been so well expressed by the honored clergymen who have preceded me. I was reluctant to appear here. I am always reluctant to assume to make an address, but finding myself among a lot of brothers—for we are all descendants of the same mother—finding myself surrounded by a band of brothers, I have been gathering confidence. I am glad to bring our congratulations because of your great history. May I allude to the fact that we are all delighted with the exquisite decorations of this temple of the Most High on this occasion? I thought I saw history before me and a vision of the growth of human society. We are glad also to congratulate you because the occasion illustrates the essential union of the Christian churches. I have looked through this book to find the bond or basis of church unity. I have not been able to find it in government nor in symbols nor in ritual nor even in opinions—for there were great varieties of opinion in the early churches, and yet there was the Holy Catholic Church in the first century, in the apostolic days, and I think I have found it in the new spiritual life of Jesus Christ. Whether Christians at Cyrene or Cappadocia, in Alexandria or in Rome, there was a unity that enabled them to walk and pray all together—all were included in a Holy Catholic Church. That unity is brought before us in the words of Paul where he said "created anew in Christ Jesus." There is a word in the New Testament that symbolizes this fellowship, a technical word, Koinonia, which translated means fellowship, communication. If we walk in the light as He is in the light we have fellowship with the Father and with His Son Jesus Christ, and I am proud to believe that this essential union exists in the Christian churches to-day. I know Dr. Palmer was sincere when he bade us all God speed; I know that this distinguished Baptist clergyman was sincere when he bade this great church God speed; and I know our honored brother of St. John's, whose honest words delighted us all, was sincere, when he congratulated us upon our union. Think of Martin, and Edwards, and Dr. Dwight, writing on the hill behind us, "I love Thy kingdom, Lord," Ray Palmer in New York, writing "My faith looks up to Thee," John Wesley talking to the colliers in England till their black faces were washed with tears—these men, the leaders of the Mighty Host of Jesus Christ, were sincere. I am glad that our distinguished founder, Wesley, said he wanted a league offensive and defensive with every soldier of Jesus Christ, and I think that I may say that that is the spirit of the Church to which I have the honor to belong. So far as I know, sir, we have no hobby of any kind that will prevent or hinder the most cordial co-operation and confederation and co-fellowship and work with any and all Christian churches. I do not believe in organic unity of the churches, but I do believe in the spirit of brotherhood and broad co-operation. A few years ago, soon after I left college, I went over to the old mother country. I was introduced to a distinguished English gentleman in Yorkshire. He was very courteous and very intelligent, and he kindly, like many of those foreigners, put his time at my service and said "I will take you and show you how a civilization grew," and he took me up to York and I saw the old walls where the followers of Charles the First had been within and Cromwell's troopers were without; he took me to the Minster, then to Beverly; then he said "we will run down to London," and we went to the room where Walter Raleigh wrote his History of the World, and we looked on the spot where the head of Thomas More fell in the basket. This afternoon, going among the relics of the church and hearing the historical address delivered here by Dr. Palmer, I felt that I was studying how a civilization grew. I looked yonder at the old log church, more significant to a student of human history than a collection of all the diamonds of the planet, and I was breathing once again the Puritan air, the air that Robinson and Brewster breathed and that the great Puritans breathed and that Cromwell at Dunbar breathed when he shouted to his followers "Let God arise and let his enemies be scattered!" I saw again the rise of one of the greatest epochs in the history of mankind, the old Puritan epoch.

Much is said over in England about the non-conformist conscience, and when the great leaders there have any great issue, such as the extension of the suffrage, the opening of the universities, home rule, the repression of the power of the distillers and brewers, education ; when they have any point, any great campaigns that have the element of progress, of democracy, of morals involved, they make their appeals to the non-conformists' conscience ; and the great leaders, Bright and Gladstone and the great Congregationalist, Dr. Dale, of Birmingham, and Hugh Price Hughes, when they make their appeal to the power of England make it to the non-conformist's conscience very largely, but that conscience is literally the Puritan conscience of an earlier age. It was a splendid outburst for manhood, that reach for liberty, that grand conscience-battle, that great Puritan movement in the mother country. I hardly know where my ancestors did come from. I am mixed up (laughter). I call myself sometimes an Irishman, but my forefathers fought with the Prince of Orange in the wars for the liberty of Holland, and from Holland they fought to liberate England and later on in other lands, but the blood of soldiers that struck for liberty in the days when the great churches were born is in my veins. In that epoch all the great churches, with the exception of the Episcopal Church, were practically born. The Baptist, the Presbyterian, the Congregationalist, the Quakers, and a little later, an offspring born out of due time, we Methodists came ; and then, sir, when I think of the migration in 1620 and of those who were in the Mayflower on that memorable voyage I begin to know how history unfolds and God's plans are developed. Virgil tells in the Æneid how Æneas, the son of Venus, brought the household gods or penates of Troy through many hardships over sea and land to the Lavinian shore and found room ; but in the Mayflower, in the spirit of Brewster and Robinson and Bradford, came the seeds of empires and civilizations that are transforming the world to-day, for on this fair land the world is gazing to-day. We would not be here but for that migration. The great Church would not be here but for that stroke for liberty by which the world was elevated. I have found this, sir, that the history of thought is the history of great men and great epochs. Copernicus elevated the level of men when he put the sun in the center of the solar system ; Newton elevated the level of the world's thinking men when he bound the universe together with the law of gravitation, and since then men have been thinking on a theory to elevate the universe. Darwin, I believe, has elevated the world's thinking by the great law of continuity of life, and great epochs lift the world's thinking and the world's learning. The reformation, the Methodist movement, but prominently as a movement of conscience, as a movement of conviction, as a movement of manhood, the great Puritan assertion in the sixteenth and seventeenth centuries stands out.

Now sir, I am talking too long. You kindly adverted to the fact that the First Methodist Church owes its original members to this church. They are not at all displeased with that relation. As you have intimated, we are not displeased, and I was wondering if we helped you any in return ; and I remembered your address to-day when you spoke of the time that distinguished man became pastor of the church, Mr. Waterman, and I think you told us that the church had only forty-seven members after a history of about one hundred and ten years, but after his pastorate three hundred were added. About the time that distinguished pastor came the Methodists came. You began to grow when Methodism came (laughter). After a hundred years and more you had only forty-seven members and you then leaped to the front, and that was cotemporaneous with the advent of Methodism; and I am not at all displeased to greet again and again brothers who were once Methodists in all these churches, and I love the Methodist Church and will remain in it, and God willing I will die in it, not simply on account of what we are ourselves but because we are also helping the great churches of the Lord Jesus Christ to do good in the world.

Some time ago I was in Melrose, Scotland. I was looking at the Abbey. I spent the night there and going in the morning of the day I had to leave I was taking a last lingering look—and I can see those delicate, exquisite arches and columns still as they stood out in the beautiful morning light—and turning to leave I saw a great tall Scotchman at my elbow, and I said "What a pity to see such a beautiful structure in ruins!" "Ach," said he, "what does it matter about the structure so long as the truth remains," and I thought it was a great sentiment. We had no such structure in our fair land, but we could say, as George W. Curtis said, that the New England communities furnished the highest average of well-doing in the history of the world. We can point to Massachusetts, we can point to Connecticut, we can point to the old Pine Tree State and, let me say, to the great Congregational churches, for it was your impulse and high idea of civil and religious liberty that laid the foundations of these New England communities. We pulled apart; we are coming together.

With a prophecy I would like to close. I had a sort of dream this afternoon of what would be two hundred years from now. All the churches will remain I think. The Methodist Church will be there two hundred years from now, the Congregational Church will be there, the Presbyterian Church will be there, the Baptist brethren will be there, the Universalists will be there, the Unitarians I believe will be there, the great Roman

Catholic Church, the Greek Church, they all will be there, but they will be softened, they will make less of non-essentials and more of love to the great Head of the Church. In that better day there will be no sectarianism —no strife whether we shall sing by ear or note, but one spirit uniting the band of Christian hearts.

You have seen a composite photograph. I saw a little while ago a composite photograph of Gladstone's cabinet; the great Premier was in it; John Morley, with his intelligent face, was in it; the great public leader, now premier, Lord Roseberry, was in it, but the ultimate effect was a refined, intelligent, spiritual, elevated being. The churches will remain, but they will come into such unity of spirit that there will be the effect of a great composite photograph in which will be distinctly seen the features of the Lord Jesus Christ.

I wanted to tell a little about the child that you have referred to, but must not detain you. Out in a Kansas conference a year ago Chaplain McKabe was on the platform beside one of our Methodist bishops—we call them bishops. The roll was called of the old preachers. The name of Allen Butner was called. An aged veteran of the war rose up and made a little speech and said in closing, "I am a veteran of the war and a worn-out Methodist preacher." Chaplain McKabe knew his early record and leaped to his feet and said "That is the man that led the assault up Missionary Ridge," and the bishop reached out and grasped the man's hand, saying, "Give me your hand." The audience leaped to their feet, somebody struck up "My Country, 'tis of thee," and the voice of the great assembly went out while tears fell everywhere, and McKabe said that Butner led the advance and shouted through the shrieking bullets and piercing shell and said "Come on, come on." Grant was looking on, and Sheridan. Grant said, "Sheridan, who ordered that attack?" Sheridan said, "Nobody ordered it, they did it themselves." That, sir, will be the spirit of the great churches of Jesus Christ in the years to come. Filled with loyalty to Him, they will march forward a band of brothers, bringing this world to the feet of our Blessed Lord and Savior Jesus Christ.

Dr. PALMER: We can hardly claim a parental relation as to the First Presbyterian Church. It was an offshoot from the Second Church and not from the First, yet many of its original members were born and brought up here. We are glad to see here its pastor, Rev. Henry A. Davenport.

Mr. DAVENPORT'S remarks follow:—My dear brother and Christian friends, "Behold how good it is for brethren to dwell together in unity." We come with cordial greetings, and it is pleasant to see so many dear people here attesting to the heartiness of the appreciation of this unusual and so significant occasion. Of the pastors of native or English-speaking churches who greeted me when I came here, the pastor of this church is the only one that remains; one whom in these years I have learned not only to esteem but to love ardently, and you must allow me to say to-night, because it comes from my heart, that a service of this character as well as the work of a man like him, standing in one pulpit for twenty-three years, is as impossible of calculation as the drops that flow from the perennial fountain.

In relation to the local churches it is rather a pleasantry, it stirs a little mirth when we think we are not offspring but offsprung, yet imitated our mother and considered ourselves justified by her example: that having asked for the portion of goods that were falling to us we acted in our own independent way, and we appreciate the cordial welcome we get here. We bring our hearty congratulation to Dr. Palmer and our Christian friends for the reason that this church has been true to the orthodox symbols of faith through all its history. Among all the tangent movements of the passing days this church has held to the main road, and one could but be impressed when the roll was called of the faithful men of God who have ministered here, men whose lives were the best comment on the gospel. Carlisle says history is the lengthening shadows of the world's great men, and we cannot help but be impressed when we think of the heroic members of this church. Strong were they. Nature made them heroes. Grace made them kings to reign forever. We give you our congratulations because it seems to me, my dear sir, that we claim a little interest after all, if not from the point of view of the local church, yet from the point of view of the Presbyterian denomination. This infant church leaned back on the old Saybrook platform. As we heard this afternoon, some of the pastors of this church were educated in Presbyterian institutions of learning and some of them came from or went to Presbyterian churches, and thinking of this occasion I was recalling a little history—I was thinking of the time when there existed a plan of union, when committee men were eligible to the General Assembly of the Presbyterian church, of the time when there were more Presbyterians in the field of foreign missions than there were Congregationalists, of the interest we had in the Home Mission Society, and I was thinking of these things with something of complacency. I was encouraged when the preacher of that notable historical sermon announced his text in these words, " Remember the days of old, consider the years of many generations; ask thy father, and he will show thee ; thine *elders*, and they will tell thee," but that was all taken out of me when he went on in the course of the service and revealed the fact that there was great uneasiness on the part of the independent portion of the church, and it was rather a blow to me ; and I recall how Dr. Dexter in his work seemed to be annoyed that in whatever angle he looked he was running against Presbyterians (laughter), and yet if the lines of ecclesiastical cleavage have been more sharply drawn and denominationalism has been more thoroughly crystalized, it is pleasant to remember that then and now there is the spirit of true fellowship to which the brothers have referred. There is a legend that tells about a brave prince that cut his way through a dense forest to find a castle, and when he found it there was revealed to him a maiden who had been waiting a hundred years for his coming and there was a union of their lives for time to come; and even as the prophecy just made, may we not think that the work we have accomplished in the years gone by will be more than ever realized in the years to come?

I have been trying to make it real to myself what it means to be two hundred years old. Seventeen years ago in the providence of God I came to this city. Do you realize that it is within that period of time that half of our churches have come into being and that most of the permanent institutions of benevolence and charity have come into existence? At that time the church I have the honor to serve was about twenty-five years old, and twenty-five years before its mother was about twenty-three years old, and from that point you would have to go back fifty years to get to the American Revolution, and then this church was hale and stalwart and strong and old. Two hundred years! We don't think of it, we don't realize it. The great institutions of to-day belong to the decades, and this church stands as a monument of the centuries. And especially our young people do not realize it. With reference to these great parish institutions, they are like the boys who go under the apple tree and pick the fruit and swallow it thoughtlessly and thanklessly. I am glad of an occasion like this that will call a halt and cause people to think and consider the heritage that has come to them, and I have been trying to think here to-night about the great constituency of this church during two hundred years. Oh, the praises that have gone hence in that time! Is church life and church work a thing of to-day? No, it links eternity.

> "One family we dwell in Him,
>   One church above, beneath,
> Though now divided by the stream,
>   The narrow stream of death.
>
> One army of the living God,
>   To His command we bow;
> Part of the Host have crossed the flood,
>   And part are crossing now."

And these pictures bring it back to me. The people who have gone out from this church have gone into that. Christian friends, I had thought of what a splendid argument we have here for Christianity in the two hundred years of the life of the Church. The Christian religion is not an experiment, it is no longer a novelty to be scanned with curious and skeptical eye, and God gave his revelations not so much through acts as through events. We are scanning events which are the finger-marks of God. In all the relations of the Church, its relations to religious and civil life, like the two sides of the one fabric, the Church brought the power of Heaven to bear on earthly things; and one of the great lessons we learn in all the differences and disagreements amongst men is that while men come and go and theories fall and rise, God stands within the shadow watching over His own.

Just one thought and I will leave you. On looking back to the beginning of this church and following it on with its various achievements, I am saying to myself what a vantage ground it has to-day for bringing about unparalleled achievements. I noticed an athlete the other day down at the Park and I said to him, "Don't you run too far before you jump? It seems to me you lose your strength." "No," he says, "it is indispensable, we must get the momentum." Think of the momentum this church has got in two hundred years with which to grapple the problems of this nineteenth century. When it began, what were those days? Days of acts of toleration, days of the Indians, days of the pirates, days without any such facilities or means of Christian work as you and I enjoy to-day. When this church began Wesley was not born, Edwards' thought had not entered upon its high career. And what was the site of our fair city? In those days it was comparative nakedness to what you and I see to-day and enjoy, and yet from that point the fathers advanced, and as we look back and scan their bravery and valor, you and I ought to be inspired as we come into touch with the devotion and consecration of the two centuries. And while we bring our congratulations, we bring our best wishes for the future of this grand old church. Gladstone said that the decade from 1875 to 1885 witnessed greater triumphs for Christianity than all decades of the ages preceding. We are living in a grand and glorious time. It is a grand day in which to live and work, and may the significant services of this occasion bring new life to this church and gird it with new strength that every year to come may be more splendid than the years that are gone. There are difficulties still before us; in the face of them let us recall that brother of your faith over in the land of Turkey when the command of the Sultan went forth that within a brief period all of his order must be exiled. That man of God said, "Friends, the Sultan of the universe can change all that." Oh, for a living faith in the sovereign God who rules in and over all! May it possess and control us, every one; and may it be said concerning this church, as the bishop said of Washington, "in youth true, in manhood brave, in age wise, in memory immortal." (Applause.)

Dr. PALMER: Now we are going to give you a little ancient psalmody, "The Lord descended from on High," to old "Majesty." That does not go back two hundred years, but more than one hundred years. The choir will render the old tune, which you will be glad to follow—if you can.

The psalmody was then rendered by the choir and the benediction was pronounced by the Rev. Dr. Russell.

SERVICES OF
THURSDAY MORNING.

✠

Drum Prelude.

✠

Organ Voluntary.

✠

Anthem, "Send Out Thy Light."

✠

Prayer of Commemoration,
By Rev. CHARLES RAY PALMER, D.D.

Dr. Palmer: Christian Friends and Fellow Citizens, we have met this morning to commemorate the Founders of this ancient church, the Fathers of this community. We endeavor to revive in some measure the men and their ways. We have assembled as they were wont to assemble, by beat of drum. We have set sentinels at our door with weapons of defense because they did it. We have placed above us not only the flag of the United States, but the Colonial flag of 1686, bearing upon it the Red Cross of St. George, the crown royal and the cipher of King James, and also the British Ensign in memory of the later colonial days. We have set here our ancient plate, nearly as old as the church. All these are suggestions of the past, as are our models of the churches, from the most ancient on your extreme left to the latest upon your right; the present which has been evolved from the past speaks for itself. I wish to remind you, that the fathers deserve our veneration for what they were, and what they purposed and what they wrought. They profoundly believed, as their petition to the General Court shows, in their responsibility to God, and their dependence on his protection and favor. They cherished for themselves and for their children the aspiration to be a religious and an enlightened community. They built their school and their church almost as promptly—quite as resolutely—as they set up their own habitations, and armed to defend them. In all the disabilities of an infant settlement, and not unconscious of peril from their savage neighbors, they encouraged one another and took courage from their ennobling aspirations to lay the foundations, and accomplish the tasks, in the abiding results of which we as their children and successors rejoice at this late day. It is fitting that we recall their toils, their ventures, their sacrifices and their deeds, and keep their memory green. I invite you to join with me in a prayer of commemoration and thanksgiving. Let us pray.

Almighty and Everlasting God!—the Father of our Spirits, the dwelling place of Thy people in every generation, the confidence of the ends of the earth—we look unto Thee and desire to worship Thee in spirit and in truth ; in devout and grateful affection to call to remembrance all Thy loving kindness, all Thy faithfulness, and Thy great deliverances in the past. We thank Thee, as we gratefully make mention of the fathers who planted this community. We thank Thee that Thou didst enable them to plant it with the right seed ; we thank Thee that the work of Thy servants has from a humble beginning grown into so great proportions as it reaches to-day. Our Father in heaven, we give Thee thanks that their aspirations have been so largely exceeded ; and that there has grown up here a Christian community, strong in many respects, strong most of all in its purposes and its expectations of the future ; looking with hope unto the best ends for which society is organized, and seeking the favor of Almighty God unto the remotest generations. We thank Thee, O our Father and our God, that so many of us are assembled on this occasion, and we pray that as we are talking together of the past we may be very mindful how entirely we depend upon Thee in the present, how manifold are the possibilities of the future and how faithful the promises on which our hearts have taken hold. Assist us in the services of this hour and grant unto us and unto our children that, walking in devoutness before God, loving righteousness and pursuing the ways of peace, we may continue to make increase in all that pertains to a Christian church and a Christian community, and that we may see this Commonwealth and this great Nation more and more manifesting the spirit of a Christian people, a great and glorious people, who have a mission from God to be a light unto the nations of the earth.

This and every needful blessing we ask through the riches of Thy grace, through Jesus Christ our Lord. Amen.

Dr. PALMER: My friends, the senior deacon of this church will present a paper on the "Limits of Stratfield Parish as Originally Constituted." He is himself, as I said yesterday, a descendant of the first deacon of the church, Deacon Rowland B. Lacey.

[The address of Deacon Lacey was delivered from manuscript at this point.]

✢

PAPER OF DEA. ROWLAND B. LACEY.

It is said when the distinguished Roger Ludlow of the Connecticut colony, having started with his company of followers from Hartford to occupy and hold Uncoway (Fairfield) against the encroachment of the Dutch of New Amsterdam, as they came to Pequonnock he here paused to rest and refresh his tired flock and jaded animals. The Indians had long had their corn fields on the extensive plain now known as our "west end," and on Golden hill plateau. Ludlow was charmed with the location—its fine groves—the beauty and fertility of its open fields, and would gladly have located his settlement here—but this he could not do, as before his start his company was bound to settle at Uncoway—and that was his objective point. The settlement of Stratford was made at about the same time—both as a result of the successful expedition of Captain Mason against the Pequots, leaving the shores and fair fields of Pequonnock in the partial occupancy of a remnant of the conquered Indians.

The enchanting vision of the beautiful harbor and lands of Pequonnock remained in the minds of these adventurers—was rehearsed abroad, and later some of the more enterprising sons of Stratford and Fairfield families were joined by others from the Connecticut river settlements and from Massachusetts bay in acquiring titles to Pequonnock lands—and the Indians were restricted to Golden hill and the fields and shores immediately south, where they long remained a menace to the infant settlement of Stratfield.

The division line between the two ancient towns (of Stratford and Fairfield) was the wide street identical with the present Park avenue, commencing near tidewater at a point near Park place and extending northerly about eighteen miles on a line slightly divergent westerly from the meridian. The territory occupied was about equal in area on either side of this center line, or in other words one-half in Stratford and one-half in Fairfield—the outer limits for some years remaining rather indefinite. Two other roads were opened into the interior, one substantially identical with Main street north of Newtown pike and the other with Clinton and Brooklawn avenue and the Easton road.

The main east and west road of the settlement was the old New York and Boston stage road, otherwise called "King's Highway," the present North avenue. On the east was Pequonnock river, forming an excellent harbor, lying close upon the bosom of Long Island Sound, yet with tide water of good depth, extending by a somewhat winding channel between wooded bluffs far inland, so landlocked as to be protected from the storms and enemies that swept and infested the inland sea. From this territory a North society was improvised which became with contiguous territory North Fairfield parish (now Easton), and Stratfield was confined to an interior depth of a little more than four miles.

It is not my province to rehearse the history of the settlement. Suffice it to say it had the elements of growth and made such progress that the General Court recognized the propriety in May, 1701, of defining its limits, more particularly its western boundary, as follows:

"May, 1701, this assembly having heard and considered the petition or request of the inhabitants of Fairfield village—presented to them by Lieut. James Bennett, desiring that the court would state and settle for them a line for the west boundary to their plantation, etc., do order and enact that the line to be the west boundary of the said plantation shall run so that it may take in and include within their bounds one Moses Jackson Miller, his housing and lands, and run on the west side of old Jackson's lots (viz.), pasture, building lot and long lot upwards to the northern end of the bounds of the town of Fairfield, and that all such person or persons as have built or shall build and inhabit on the east side of the above said line, and on the west side of Pequonnock river, shall pay to all public charges that shall arise in the said plantation his ratable part thereof, provided always—That this act shall in no wise hinder or abridge the inhabitants of said plantation of using and holding the privilege of feeding sheep to the westward of the above said line, as it was granted to them formerly by the inhabitants of the town of Fairfield; and further it is enacted by the authority aforesaid: That the said plantation (formerly called Pequonnock and Fairfield village) shall for the future be called by the name of Stratfield.—Col. Rec. iv, 356.

October, 1752—by act of the General Assembly—on a memorial of the Society, these limits were enlarged on the north and west, and further defined at the southwest border, near the present Burr road so-called. Later New Pasture Point,—the present East Bridgeport, was included. The new west line was in part the Morehouse highway, being the second highway west of the Division Road. The special features of the present site of the City of Bridgeport on the west side of Pequonnock river, was the commanding eminence of Golden Hill, with excellent springs of pure water (well known to the Indians) and its beautiful wide expanse for an upper town; now so well utilized with elegant villas and happy homes of more modest size and architecture. On the east side was the fine plateau between the Pequonnock and Old Mill stream, its extensive fields of fine pasture, its groves of timber and high wooded bluffs overlooking the harbor—of which the elder President Dwight (of Yale College) thus wrote in the 3d vol. of his travels, in 1822:

"A more cheerful and elegant piece of ground can scarcely be imagined than the point which stretches between the Pequonnock and the Old Mill brook (East Bridgeport), and the prospects presented by the harbors at the mouths of these streams, the Sound and the surrounding country, are in a fine season gay and brilliant, perhaps without a parallel."

Of Bridgeport at this period he wrote: "There is not in the State a prettier village than the borough of Bridgeport. The style of building adopted is unusually happy. None of the houses are large or splendid, but almost all of them, together with their appendages, leave upon the mind an impression of neatness and cheerfulness, not often found elsewhere. There are two churches in this village; an Episcopal and a Presbyterian (Congregational); both respectable buildings,—appearing like twins on the opposite sides of a small green. The two parts of Bridgeport are connected by a bridge, ninety rods in length, which crosses the Pequonnock in the center of the village, and was the origin of its name."

The fertile plain across the southern border of the territory at the distance of from one to two miles, rises into hills and thus continues gradually twelve or fifteen miles, affording fine agricultural possibilities, which were early utilized to a greater extent than to-day. Old Mill hill on the east, Grover hill and Holland heights on the west, with the intervening Beardsley park and Spooner park, with concourse and observation points, attest the beauty and grandeur of the scenery, while the rural drives and walks with their shades and seclusion possess an unfailing charm.

Time has demonstrated the beauty and excellence of the water front with its series of harbors, charming Seaside park and its boulevard.

The Newtown and New Milford turnpike, and later the Housatonic railroad, by their immense traffic, demonstrated the central position of the settlement, and the results have been the fulfilment of the prophecy made by the tarry here of Ludlow, and his evident appreciation.

✣

ROLL CALL OF ORIGINAL MEMBERS OF THE STRATFIELD CHURCH.

RESPONDED TO BY THEIR DESCENDANTS.

Dr. PALMER: Our fathers made much in their religious faith of the covenanted mercies. They rejoiced in the Old Testament promises. They believed that their seed should continue, and instead of the fathers should be the children. It has occurred to us it would be a fitting service this morning to call the roll of the original members of the church and see how far every one of them is represented by a descendant. To that we now propose to address ourselves. Naturally the first name to be called should be that of Charles Chauncey, the minister. He is the only one, so far as I know, who has no representative to-day. It is our disappointment because we expected Dr. Chauncey M. Depew would be here to respond for his distinguished ancestor. He himself desired to do so, but other duties have prevented him, and so far as I am aware we are not prepared to present a representative of Charles Chauncey, but this church is his memorial, and his name is identified with all that is good among us.

Richard Hubbell, Sen. "*Present.*"*

Responded to by Major Howard Gregory Hubbell, a descendant of the eighth generation.

Isaac Wheeler, Sen. "*Present.*"

Responded to by Robert E. Wheeler, a child of this church and descendant of the seventh generation.

James Bennett. "*Present.*"

Responded to by Clarence H. Kelsey in accordance with an unbroken family tradition.

Samuel Beardsley. "*Present.*"

Responded to by Samuel Fayerweather Beardsley, a descendant of the eighth generation.

Samuel Gregory. "*Present.*"

Responded to by Hon. Morris B. Beardsley, who represents Samuel Beardsley in his own right, and Samuel Gregory in the right of his grandmother.

Matthew Sherman. "*Present.*"

Responded to by James Eaton Beach and by David Sherman Beach, descendants of the seventh generation.

Richard Hubbell, Jun. "*Present.*"

Responded to by Captain H. W. Hubbell of the United States First Artillery, a descendant of the sixth generation.

David Sherman. "*Present.*"

David Sherman had no son. From one of the daughters Deacon R. B. Lacey descended and makes a response.

John Odell, Jun. "*Present.*"

Responded to by Henry R. Parrott, Chairman of the Society's Committee, descending from John Odell through his grandfather's mother.

* Each representative, as he responded, came forward and took his place in a line from right to left.

The first members have thus demonstrated their right to be regarded as the fathers of this church. We might place here many more descendants from the original nine, some descended from two or more of them. We have been most careful to place those only whose descent we could verify, except in one instance, where we have been obliged to rely upon tradition. These are the indications of the faithfulness of the God who remembers mercy unto thousands of generations. (Applause.)

We will unite in singing the 1046th hymn.

The hymn was rendered by the choir.

Dr. PALMER: Our friends who have just appeared, as they represented the original members, have a right to be heard for themselves, and the Hon. Morris B. Beardsley has now an opportunity to respond for them.

Hon. M. B. BEARDSLEY: Ladies and gentlemen, I confess to a feeling of great pride as I arise to respond on behalf of the descendants of the original members of this grand old church whose Bi-Centennial we are to-day met to celebrate. I have never entirely forgotten an incident of my early career in this city. I was a candidate for political office, and my opponent, who had himself come from a distant State shortly before, deprecated the fact that a new comer in the city—as he styled me—should so far presume as to contend with him! To-day, standing here, tracing my pedigree back directly to that William Beardsley who was the first deputy to the General Court from Stratford, and who gave its name to the old town, and down through Samuel Beardsley and Samuel Gregory, two of the nine original members of this church, and asked to speak for all of them, I have my vindication.

It is a felicitous as well as noteworthy feature that at a roll call we are able to muster unbroken ranks; that after the lapse of two centuries in the same church there could be found members of each of those original families; that they are members in good standing and active—one of them, the senior deacon of the church, representing the first deacon of the old church; and another, Mr. Parrott, after a third of a century of service, still the honored chairman of the Society's Committee.

Surely it shows sturdiness of race, loyalty in church affiliations and no evidence of family deterioration.

How worthy of our respect and grateful remembrance are those pioneers!

I would that one of them could stand in my place and could tell you their story; that he could tell you of the causes which led them to separate themselves from the older villages of Stratford and Fairfield, of their aspirations and of the difficulties which beset their path; how coming into this comparative wilderness they built their homes, and then to meet the requirements of education and public worship erected the school house and the church; how, unterrified by hostile Indians and undaunted by the opposition of their former white friends who disliked to lose them as taxpayers, and in the face of obstacles which we their descendants would consider insurmountable, they laid the foundations of a new community.

Our pastor in his masterly historical address has given us the fruits of his researches, and has laid before us all that has been preserved in the records of those years. With rare eloquence he has pictured to us what manner of men they were and enumerated their difficulties, their triumphs and their failures.

They seem to have been fair samples of that noble race of men whom God raised up to accomplish his work in these New England states—having high aims, indomitable perseverance and lofty character.

They held together this little community for a century and made it the nucleus around which gathered that which in time became the borough and then the city of Bridgeport.

From the first the influence of these early settlers has been felt, and their history and that of their descendants is largely the history of Bridgeport.

Neither the First Church nor the Congregational denomination can monopolize this occasion. We are commemorating the natal day of this community, and it is not the fault of those in charge that the entire city is not participating in them, as they were invited to do.

These men did not come here to form a church, but to make homes, and the school house and the church came afterward to meet their growing necessities. They were first of all citizens who had separated from the communities in which they had lived and came here to form one for themselves.

The records tell of their struggles, and as each emergency arose they met it.

During the Revolutionary war they formed a company and took the field, and in each stirring epoch they played well their part.

Stratford learned that they had outgrown her leading strings when, wearied of going over there to vote, they adjourned the town meeting to meet here, and, as Pharaoh of old, was then moved to "let them go." How well they have succeeded let this fair city attest. Let me repeat it. This is more of a city than a church anniversary. It should be a civico-religious holiday, and enlist the interest of every one.

We hear many pessimistic utterances regarding our cities, and I am aware that Bridgeport in common with her sisters has and will have difficulties to contend with which our ancestors never dreamed of, but I have faith in the American people, faith that as they have overcome dangers in the past so they will outlive greater ones even if they must come in the future.

I believe in another century we shall find the old church at her post, and in the midst of a greater Bridgeport, that there will be then a tri-centennial celebration, on broader lines, wherein city and church shall have equal parts.

We can only hope when that day comes that we may be able to receive from those having that in charge a little of the respect and esteem and gratitude with which we look back on our predecessors; and that we may feel that though it was not for us to found the city, it was for each one in his own line, and in his own humble way, to contribute all that lay in his power to beautify and enlarge and develop our city. (Applause.)

✢

THE SAYBROOK CONSTITUTION AND THE CONNECTICUT CHURCHES.

PROF. GEORGE P. FISHER, D.D., LL.D., New Haven.

Dr. PALMER: Charles Chauncey, the first minister of this church, preached the Gospel to his people here, and did service in the colony of Connecticut. Among other things he was a prominent member of the Saybrook Convention called to frame an ecclesiastical constitution for the churches of Connecticut by the authority of the General Court. I felt that the best commemoration we could make of Charles Chauncey was to ask Dr. Fisher, the Professor of Ecclesiastic Divinity in Yale Divinity School and a scholar of world-wide fame, to tell us in a familiar talk something about the true significance to the State of Connecticut of the Saybrook Constitution. I am very glad to introduce Professor Fisher to you.

Prof. FISHER: Brethren, ladies and gentlemen, I sympathize with you all in regret at the absence of the Hon. Chauncey Depew, who was once a pupil of mine at Yale College and whose career I have always followed with interest. It is some consolation to me, however, to reflect that the theme assigned to me is a different one from that which he would have taken up and that Mr. Depew is more familiar with many other platforms than he is with the platform framed at Saybrook (laughter). I feel honored at being appointed to take part in this most interesting anniversary; for there is no church more deserving of respect than the First Church in Bridgeport. I design to make a few simple statements respecting the ancient constitution of the churches of Connecticut, which Mr. Chauncey took part in framing. You will remember that Diedrich Knickerbocker, in his history of New York, begins by saying that, in order to get a fair start, he will go back to Adam. I do not propose to go back quite so far; and I trust I shall not transgress the limits of time appointed to me; for I must go back a little way, to remind you of some circumstances connected with the early settlement of New England.

There were, as you all are probably aware, two very distinct classes of settlers, and two settlements, on the shores of New England. The first settlers at Plymouth were out-and-out Independents, who had renounced the established Church of England, and all its ways. The settlers, or great body of settlers, who founded Massachusetts and Connecticut were non-conforming members of the Church of England. When, however, they found themselves on these shores, and framed their own organization to suit themselves, they found themselves substantially in harmony with the Pilgrims at Plymouth. There was always developed, however, a more conservative type of Congregationalism among the Puritan settlers of Massachusetts and Connecticut than characterized the Pilgrims. In fact, among the English Independents there were two types. There was Brown, the founder of the Brownists, the class under which the Plymouth settlers may be reckoned; and Barrow—a martyr, an early martyr to Congregational principles—who was of a much more conservative turn. Further, among the settlers of Massachusetts and Connecticut there appeared in process of time two tendencies; a more conservative spirit, and a tendency to democracy; and these tendencies came on occasions, especially as you draw near the close of the seventeenth century, into conflict. The organization of our churches throughout New England was Congregational, and each church had a pretty complete control of its own affairs. The powers of the ministers or elders were very great compared with what they are possessed of at the present, in relation to the body of the church members; but each church elected its own minister and selected him without any aid from abroad in that matter. Towards the end of the seventeenth century there appeared in Massachusetts a strong conservative feeling and movement, and in 1705 a convention of ministers met in Boston, the Mathers being among the leaders in this movement, who drew up certain proposals for an alteration in the constitution of the Congregational churches. There were two principal measures which they recommended. The first was the establishment of an association of ministers for the licensure of candidates for the ministry; and the second was the forming of a standing Council to take part in the ordination and installation of ministers.

This proposal, although it was favored and urged by powerful influences, was not agreeable to the Massachusetts people. While one of these measures was adopted and associations of ministers were formed who licensed candidates for the pulpit, the second measure, which was the recommendation of a standing Council, was not adopted.

But in Connecticut, about the time of the organization of Yale College in 1701, the conservative feeling grew quite strong, and there was a desire to carry out those measures in regard to the church organization which were agreeable to the mass of the people. In 1708, largely through the influence of Governor Saltonstall, who was of that way of thinking, the Colonial Legislature took the first steps that led, during that year, to the assembling of the Saybrook Synod, which met in connection with the meeting of the Corporation of Yale College at Saybrook, and framed the ancient constitution of the Connecticut churches.

Now one of the members of that synod—I suppose the youngest—was the Rev. Charles Chauncey. He must by that time have become a conservative—in case he had ever been anything different. The tradition respecting the Rev. Israel Chauncey, his father, was that at his ordination the laying on of hands was by a Mr. Brinsmade, a lay elder, who, it is said—and I believe the tradition credible—wore a leather mitten on the occasion, and hence it was called a "leather-mitten ordination." It was thought a very loose and objectionable method of ordaining a minister.

The Rev. Charles Chauncey was, however, a conservative and took part in framing the Saybrook synod.

Now the Presbyterians and Congregationalists in England in 1691 had formed a confederacy or union together, and drawn up certain heads of agreement to determine their relations to one another. One related to the licensing of ministers, and the other to the calling of councils, which were, however, to be advisory councils. The Saybrook Synod adopted the heads of agreement, which had been framed in the manner I have stated; and they also drew up a platform of their own.

These two parts of the Saybrook constitution were not strictly consistent. There was a compromise, and therefore a conflict arose on the interpretation of the document composed by the delegates at Saybrook and sanctioned by the legislature. They established the associations of ministers, meeting to license candidates for the ministry; and in the platform they departed from the provisions of the heads of agreement by saying, or appearing to say, that the standing council which they established, or the consociation—which was a council—should have *authority* to decide questions in dispute, and questions relating to the settlement and dismissal of ministers. Therefore there were two interpretations from the beginning; a strict interpretation — a more Presbyterian interpretation—and a more free interpretation, which followed the substance of the heads of agreement adopted in England.

In Fairfield County the strict interpretation—that which gave to the standing council of the Consociation of churches the power to determine questions in dispute—was adopted and carried into effect. It found approval also in some other counties. Whereas in New Haven County the Saybrook constitution was accepted only with such appended interpretations,—appended to the act of acceptance—which were on the side of a free Congregational system. We may say the upshot of the whole matter was, that a constitution in a degree Presbyterian was adopted for the Congregational churches of Connecticut, and sanctioned by the Legislature. When the great revival broke out there was occasion for further legislative interference owing to the zeal of the revivalists and the measures which were adopted by them looking to the separation of churches. The laws were very strict in regard to what were called "separatists." Thus the Colonial legislature ordained that no minister should preach within the bounds of any parish in Connecticut without the consent of the minister thereof, a penalty being attached for any violation of that law. The Rev. Dr. Finley, who was afterwards president of Princeton College, was arrested in the town of Fairfield, by a sheriff, for preaching within the parish of the minister of Fairfield. He was taken to New Haven, where he was compelled, on the Lord's day, to attend a regular Congregational service; and the next day was set by the sheriff beyond the bounds of the colony. Those were the "good old days" when the conservatives ruled. Such was the origin of the Saybrook platform, in the framing of which the Rev. Charles Chauncey took part.

Now, a few words—for I must not take up your time with these reminiscences—respecting the working and operation of that constitution. Well, it is the old conflict between conservatism and democracy. The tendency of Congregationalism has been sometimes towards aristocracy, but more and more towards democracy. For a century after the settlement of New England the elders and ministers of the church had concurrent jurisdiction with the members. No important measures, except in great emergencies, would be passed without the concurrence of the senate and house, the minister and the church members.

Were there time, I would speak of what is called "the half-way covenant," which was an attempt to turn the Congregational church into the likeness, so far as practicable, of the English parish. These questions were not theological, they were ecclesiastical. The churches were pretty well agreed for a long period, certainly for a century, in regard to their theological opinions.

As to the general effect and influence of the Saybrook platform on our Congregationalism, I myself am inclined to take a favorable view. There was some friction no doubt in connection with it; some oppressive measures no doubt were taken. But these were aside from the main drift of events. One effect of that constitution, by which the Consociations were created, was to bring the churches of Connecticut into closer relation with the Presbyterian church, than were sustained by Congregationalists elsewhere in New England. Generally one consequence of this fact was that as our people went out into New York and into the states further West, they affiliated easily with the Presbyterians, and a plan of union was established somewhat after the fashion of the heads of agreement which were framed at an early date in England between the Presbyterians and Congregationalists. The effect of this plan of union was that the Congregationalists and Presbyterians were united in maintaining and diffusing the gospel. No doubt the results were strongly in favor of the spread of the Presbyterian polity. Presbyterianism, therefore, prevailed very extensively in New York and the states farther westward. This concession was made by the New England Congregationalists in the interest of peace and fraternity.

I am aware that in modern days our Congregational writers have generally held that the plan of union was a mistake, and that it contributed to the building up of the Presbyterian church to the detriment of Congregationalism in this country. But for one I am not sure that this is the correct view to take. But for some arrangement of this kind the Presbyterians and Congregationalists would have been rival and conflicting sects, whereas this for the time was avoided.

Then from another point of view the fact should be noted that New England principles and New England ways of thinking have largely leavened the Presbyterianism of New York and of the western states; and had there been from the beginning an antagonism between these two parties, then the Presbyterian church would be —well, be worse than it is now (loud laughter)—would certainly have been quite different from what it actually is.

Now I have made statements such as I have made to my class at home, and I will not prolong them. I will simply say that this semi-Presbyterian arrangement in Connecticut—which in 1784 came to an end by legislative measures—so far as it resulted in the closer fellowship of the churches here, and in the effects which I have described, worked by no means badly. This conjunction of the Congregationalist and the Presbyterian is an example of that influence which New England has exerted through this land. It has not gone out as the champion of small things or of ecclesiastical bigots. It has contented itself with being the nursery of men and the nursery of principles. (Loud applause.)

✛

THE MEMORY OF THE FATHERS THE INSPIRATION OF THEIR CHILDREN.

HON. ELIPHALET W. BLATCHFORD, Chicago, Ill.

Dr. PALMER: One of the most significant gifts ever bestowed upon this church was that of the Rev. Samuel Blatchford, whose pictures hang in the middle of that side of the church; who came here towards the end of the last century. We are happy in having with us to-day the Hon. Eliphalet W. Blatchford, of Chicago, a grandson of that pastor, and the son of another pastor, whose pictures hang nearer the rear of the building. He has come in filial affection to speak to us to-day; has come all the way from Chicago, out of a very busy life. I know you will be glad to hear him. I have the pleasure of presenting to you Mr. Blatchford, a business man of Chicago, President of the Board of Trustees of the Chicago Theological Seminary, and Vice-President of the American Board of Commissioners for Foreign Missions.

Hon. ELIPHALET W. BLATCHFORD: Members of the First Congregational Church of Bridgeport and the other churches who have united in this celebration, ladies and gentlemen—While realizing that the invitation to address you at this time is due only to my being the son and the grandson of two of the honored pastors of this church, I am still deeply sensible of the honor conferred. The request to speak, with the programme already printed, came to me as a surprise shortly before leaving home. It was accompanied by a letter from your pastor indicating the attractive place assigned me between the eminent Professor of History and the President of Yale University. With all deference to your pastor's judgment, I may confidentially say to you that while the honor is great, the trial to a simple layman is somewhat appalling.

The thoughtful and scholarly historical address to which we listened yesterday has given to the theme assigned me—"The memory of the Fathers the inspiration of the children"—a new and deeper meaning. While listening to the simple records of the successive pastorates, I was deeply impressed with the power of the work of a Church of Christ continued steadily through two centuries. No great achievement, as the world calls greatness, but a persistent holding up through poverty, trial, self-denial, opposition, political exigencies, national revolutions, foreign and civil war, of that banner which is one day to float victorious over a world redeemed. My brother, and members of this and affiliated churches, in rescuing from the mist of time the facts which outline the life of this Bridgeport church for two hundred years, you are doing a work whose influence extends far beyond this place and time; you are bringing to many who are battling for the same truth in this and other lands, courage, cheer, faith in the promises of God, and recognition of His guiding providences.

I feel the topic of the hour suggests my presenting facts connected with the life of my grandfather—Rev. Samuel Blatchford, pastor of this church from 1797 to 1804, and also of my father—Rev. John Blatchford, also pastor of this church from 1831 to 1836. I am indebted for the facts relating to my grandfather to an autobiographical sketch, privately printed by my cousin, Samuel Blatchford, late Associate Justice of the Supreme Court of the United States.

Samuel Blatchford was an Englishman, born at Plymouth Dock, now Devonport, opposite Plymouth, 1767, of parents "both of whom were eminent for piety." "By them," he writes, "I was early devoted to the service of the sanctuary, should it please God to make me a subject of divine grace, and my studies were directed with special reference to that object." His studies in the ancient languages were pursued with special thoroughness, thus laying the foundation for his prominent and successful career as a classical teacher.

In the autobiography some facts are stated, which, as they touch upon national as well as personal interests, I will read. They occurred when he was about ten years old:

"About this time the American Revolution commenced, an event which excited the interest of all Europe, and brought forward, even in England, many open friends to the claims of America, and the rights and liberty of the Provinces. Among these were my relatives, who distinguished themselves, as Providence gave them opportunity, by manifesting the sincerity of their zeal. This was particularly the case with the Reverend Robert Heath, my mother's eldest brother, who, together with my mother, essentially ameliorated the suffering of the American prisoners who were confined in Mill Prison at Dartmoor. From their own resources they advanced considerable sums, until, at length, a benevolent association was formed in London, for this purpose. On referring to a letter which I received from my uncle Heath, dated February 13, 1797, I find that the Marquis of Rockingham, the Duke of Richmond, and several other conspicuous characters were at the head of this noble institution."* "It

---

* These facts were corroborated by the testimony of Lord Houghton, given to me personally.

was at the request of these noblemen," writes Mr. Heath, " who formed the committee of this society, that I undertook to distribute such subscriptions as might be raised for this purpose of benevolence. That which I was privileged in doing afforded me sincere pleasure, for they were in a state in which they could not help themselves." " The assistance was sometimes conveyed by Mr. Heath's direct agency, and sometimes I was employed, as being by my youth less subject to suspicion. In consequence of this, I was compelled to spend portions of several days in each week in that prison where our American brethren were treated rather as rebels against the government than as prisoners of war. The kindness with which I was received by these poor fellows, and the frequent conversations which I held with them relative to their country and their homes, awakened within me feelings by no means transient, and led me, at that early age, to determine that, when I became a man, I would choose my residence in America. I well remember their expression of gratitude; and their sincerity was testified by the numerous little presents which I constantly received from them, consisting of carved boxes, box inkstands and miniature ships, beautifully rigged.

The spiritual wants of these poor fellows were not neglected, Bibles and hymn books were distributed among them, and Mr. Heath would frequently address them on the subject of religion. Nor did the charities of these benevolent individuals stop here. Retreats were provided for such as fortunately should make their escape. Among these happy few was the late Captain Smedley, collector of customs at the port of Fairfield, in Connecticut. He was concealed in the house of a Mrs. Chenough, whither I have often been sent with means of relief for him and others.

Before an opportunity arose for forwarding those concealed at Mrs. Chenough's to Holland, on their way to America, the following circumstance occurred : A gentleman, captain of a vessel of war, but whose name I do not recollect, had been secreted at my father's until the search after him was supposed to be over. To effect his return, it was determined that he should accompany my uncle and my mother to London. A post-chaise received them about three o'clock in the morning, and they traveled unmolested as far as Haldown Heath, an extensive common of flinty soil, between Plymouth Dock and Exeter, when, hearing the trampling of horses, my uncle perceived, from the glass in the back of the chaise, that a company of horsemen was pursuing them. In this extremity, the expedient was adopted of placing the fugitive on the bottom of the carriage and concealing him with their cloaks. The company, having overtaken them, caused the postillion to stop. Observation was made by the officer, and the company passed on, after having made an apology for detaining them. They now hoped to meet with no further molestation, but soon perceived that the horsemen had halted, and were waiting the coming up of the carriage. The postillion was again ordered to stop, the former process was repeated, and they then passed on towards the city. Whether the fugitive was really being pursued or not, could not be ascertained. My uncle thought it prudent, instead of going to the city, to enter the lower suburbs and proceed immediately to the town of Collumpton, about twelve miles distant, on the Bristol road. At Collumpton they changed carriages, and reached London in safety. My mother, who was a woman of timid make, although not apprehensive at the time of suffering any evil effects from her fright, underwent, in consequence of it, a severe attack of illness. She was removed from the carriage to her bed at her brother's, Mr. Richard Heath's, and was unable to leave it for a space of six weeks."

I will not longer linger over the details of the early life of Dr. Blatchford. His first distinct religious impressions commenced when, between eight and nine years old, he listened to a sermon from the words, "The Master is come and calleth for thee." "About the age of twelve," he writes, "the Lord was pleased, as I humbly hope, to further by His own spirit the word of grace. It was under the preaching of a colleague of Mr. Kinsman's, a Mr. Dunn, from Psalm 80, verse 19, "Turn us again, O Lord God of Hosts, cause Thy face to shine, and we shall be saved." My distress was very great, and my affliction called forth the solicitude of my parents. My father urged upon me the great truths of the gospel, as the claim which God had upon the hearts of His creatures, the necessity of regeneration, and the certainty of salvation to all who should obtain reconciliation with God through the merits of the sacrifice of Christ. These prayers and exhortations were, I trust, instrumental in causing me to seek, and, as I trust, to obtain a hope which will never make me ashamed. Now was I peculiarly delighted with the idea of being, at some future time, honored of God by entering the ministry."

He pays a beautiful tribute to this Christian father:

"Previously, however, to my removal from Willington, it pleased God to visit my dear father with a disease which terminated in his death. He was a rich partaker in the grace of God, lived much in the fellowship with the Father and with his Son Jesus Christ, and, in the sixty-third year of his age, terminated his earthly pilgrimage, and entered into that rest which remaineth for the people of God—an inheritance incorruptible, undefiled, and that fadeth not away. He was a most affectionate parent. My last interview with him I can never forget. He took me with him to Mount Batton, a favorite retreat, about half a mile from Plymouth Dock. After having spent a considerable time there, during which we experienced mingled emotions of pleasure and pain, we set out on our return. Having reached a retired field, I received his last advice, and, while we knelt down together on the sod, he renewedly dedicated me to God, and solemnly implored the blessing of a covenant God and Father to rest upon a beloved son whom he expected never to see again in this vale of tears, this land of separation."

Time forbids dwelling on his student life, his entering on the ministry, his faithful labors at places in Devonshire, and finally his call to the work in this country. A passage from the autobiography, of historic interest, as illustrating British ecclesiastical and colonial expedients, I will read. Whether such illustration forms part of the Church "history" of your honored guest, I know not:

"Previously to our marriage, an invitation was presented to me, through the Rev. Dr. Lake, of London, to accompany Lord Dorchester to Canada, to the governorship of which he was appointed. The design, which was originated by Charles James Fox, was to establish, under the patronage of the British government, a Presbyterian Church, with privileges equal to those enjoyed by the Episcopal Church, in order to induce persons to emigrate from the United States to Canada. The salary offered was £300 sterling per annum, with other emoluments, and I was to be returned at the expense of the government if dissatisfied with the situation. This offer was declined, on account of the opposition of my intended wife's friends. After this, a second proposition, of a similar nature, was made to me, but, for similar reasons as before, I again declined, and Lord Dorchester sailed without me. The design of countenancing Presbyterianism in Canada, with equal privileges with those enjoyed by Episcopalianism, has, I believe, from that time, been abandoned."

On the nineteenth of June, just a century ago next week, Dr. Blatchford set sail from Exmouth, Devonshire, for New York, which they reached after a voyage of forty-three days.

After various experiences, strange, some of them painful to one who had been familiar only with the settled customs of Old England, he found his first settlement at Bedford, New York, whence in 1796 he was invited to Connecticut. The interesting and important relation subsisting between the parish of Stratfield, to which Dr. Blatchford was called, and the Bridgeport church, as presented at this celebration, as also the references to the distinguished ancestor of the honored President of Yale University, who graces this anniversary with his presence and words, prompts me to read one more passage from this autobiographical sketch :

"Early in the succeeding year, 1796, I received an invitation to spend a Sabbath at Greenfield, Fairfield County, Connecticut, where was settled the late Reverend Dr. Dwight, who, by a display of talents of the very first order, diligence, a fine and cultivated taste, and an untarnished character for piety and zeal in his Master's cause, had secured to himself a high reputation. My preaching in this place elicited from the church and congregation an invitation to preach for them, and the following communication was forwarded to me: "At a meeting legally warned and held in the parish of Greenfield, the 1st day of April, 1796—Daniel Sherwood, Moderator. Voted unanimously, to invite the Reverend Mr. Blatchford, for one year, to preach for said parish. Voted, to give Mr. Blatchford £160 currency, for his services for said year. Voted, to give Mr. Blatchford $20, to defray his expenses in removing to Greenfield. Hezekiah Bradley, Society's Clerk." After taking the advice of my brethren, and spreading the whole affair before the throne of Divine Grace, for direction in the path of duty, I came to the resolution of accepting their invitation, with the privilege of being bound by this agreement no longer than six months, if any circumstances should occur to render my removal desirable. During this period, I was introduced to my excellent friend Dr. Dwight, who requested me, whenever I came to New Haven, to make his house my home. I was present at the Commencement of Yale College next ensuing, and, at the request of gentlemen belonging to the United Society of Whitehaven and Fairhaven, which pulpits were then vacant, I preached for them a few Sabbaths, in exchange. An intimation was then given that it would be desirable, if it might be done consistently, that I should yield my engagement in Greenfield, and take into consideration the wishes of the people thus informally expressed. This request I thought it my duty not to comply with. I accordingly continued at Greenfield.

Early in the year 1797, I received the following extracts from the records of the proceedings of the Presbyterian Society at Stratfield, Connecticut: "At a meeting of the members of the Presbyterian Society at Stratfield, Conn., legally warned and held at their meeting house, February 15th, 1797, Joseph Strong, Esq., Moderator, a motion is made, whether the society wish to call a candidate for settlement in the ministry. Voted, they do. Voted, that Richard Hubbell, Deacon Seth Seelye, Stephen Summers, Aaron Hawley, Benjamin Wheeler, and Lambert Lockwood be a committee to look out for a candidate and make report. Voted, this meeting adjourn until Monday next, at 4 o'clock, P. M." "February 20th, 1797. Met again, agreeable to adjournment. Moderator being absent, voted, that Capt. Amos Hubbell be Moderator pro tem. Motioned, that, from specimens we have had, we admire the Reverend Mr. Blatchford as a preacher, and wish for further opportunity to determine whether it may not appear for mutual good that he take charge of this church and society as pastor. Voted unanimously. Motioned, that our committee for the purpose of looking out a candidate be, and they hereby are, recommended to said Mr. Blatchford, with directions to offer him at the rate of $500 for one year, commencing his labors with us next spring; and, further, we agree, that if, after his being with us six months, we do not mutually covenant with him on some more permanent footing, he may either leave us then or continue through the year. Voted unanimously. Meeting adjourned without day. A true copy from the records. Lambert Lockwood, Clerk."

Of his ministry here statements made indicate a life of labor and enjoyment. He writes:

"I had also succeeded the Reverend Dr. Day, the present President of Yale College, as instructor in an academy at Greenfield, and, previous to my formal acceptance of the invitation from Stratfield, I made some stipulations with the committee from thence, other than those expressed in the call—such as, building an edifice proper for an academy, as I was desirous of instructing some youth in classical literature, as an additional means of support for my numerous family. These arrangements being made, I removed to Stratfield. I succeeded in my plans, and the school flourished. I was installed by the Association of Fairfield East, and we all felt happy in our new situation. We occupied a house situated in the western part of the town, commonly called Stratfield or Pequonic."

In January, 1804, Dr. Blatchford received an invitation to take charge of the Presbyterian churches of Lansingburgh and Waterford, New York. After much consideration he accepted the call. He writes:

"The field of usefulness was more extended than the one in which I was then laboring, and the means of support more ample, which, on account of my large family, was exceedingly desirable." (He was the father of seventeen children, of whom twelve reached mature years.) In this sketch he speaks warmly of his relations with this church, and the Associations of Fairfield East and West, making affectionate mention of "Drs. Edwards, Trumbull, Ely, and Ripley, together with Messrs. Eliot, Stebbins, Pinneo, Rexford, and Huntington (of Middletown), also Drs. Perkins, Lewis, Burnet, Shea and many others, and among those toward whom the sense of obligation must remain, while kindness can make any impression on my heart."

After an honored ministry in the churches of Lansingburgh and Waterford, of twenty-four years on March 17, 1828, Samuel Blatchford went to his eternal home, dying as he had lived, in the firm hope of a triumphant entrance upon a blessed immortality. He was honored by the church, of which he was the faithful pastor, by the academy, of which he was the able and successful principal, by Union College, of which he was an instructor and head of the Examining Board, and by the denomination, from which he received the highest tokens of respect and regard.

My father, John Blatchford, who filled this pulpit from 1829 to 1836, was the sixth son and tenth child of Samuel Blatchford, and was born at Newfield (now Bridgeport) on May 24, 1799, during his father's pastorate here. At the age of seventeen he was converted and united with the Presbyterian Church of Lansingburgh, under his father's ministry. He graduated from Union College, Schenectady, in 1820, and in '23 from the Seminary at Princeton. After brief pastorates at Pittstown, and Stillwater, New York, in 1829 he accepted a call to this church in his native place, twenty-five years after his father had closed his ministry here.

Of the six years as pastor of this church I have no written records. My boyhood memory, however, brings before me many a picture which throws a halo about persons and places associated with this life. These memories, fragmentary though they be, are summoned back by many names familiar to me on the long roll-call of this church. Hubbell, Hawley, Beardsley, Sherwood, Sterling, Thacher, Wheeler, Wordin, Burton, Burr, Thompson and Baldwin.

Up to the end of their lives, my father and mother ever cherished tender memories of their Bridgeport life; and the kindness ever experienced was often the theme in our family circle.

Permit me two reminiscences of these early years, first the death of a beautiful brother, next me in age—my first grief—the mystery of death—death entering our own little nursery. And with it too, assuaging its bitterness, the memory of tenderest sympathy poured out like a benediction by the members of this church.

The second—a grief too, but different—a parting with an infant-school teacher, tenderly loved—who was married in this church to Rev. Mr. Armstrong, then under appointment of the American Board as Missionary to the Sandwich Islands. How my young heart swelled almost to bursting at that parting! It was a memorable gift Christianity gave to Heathendom in Armstrong. You all remember the glorious work he did in those islands in church and state, and the noble gift—a gift no words can measure—sent back by those parents to their native land—the patriot soldier, the devoted philanthropist, the friend of the negro and the Indian—General Armstrong of Hampton.

In 1836, after a successful pastorate of about seven years, the state of my mother's health rendered a change of climate imperative. The physicians recommended Southern France for her difficulty, which was of a pulmonary character, but she was judged too feeble to endure the voyage across the Atlantic, consequently a change to the West was decided upon, where for forty years, sheltered by the care of husband and children, she lived a life of activity, usefulness and happiness.

It was in its early formative period that my father removed to the West. He carried with him the training, discipline, and practical power obtained during the pastorates of his early manhood. And he made them operative and fruitful in ministerial and educational work, as the first installed pastor of the Presbyterian Church in Chicago, as acting president of Illinois College, the oldest college in the State, and later as President of Marion College in Northern Missouri. His genial, sympathetic nature attracted to him friends wherever he lived, and his persuasive power in the pulpit was marked. Overwork, during a revival in Chicago in 1839 and '40, protracted during many weeks, seriously impaired his health. His nearest ministerial neighbor was ninety miles away, and the burden of the frequent services on Sabbath and during the week was too severe. He never fully regained vigorous health, though he was able to accomplish much during many succeeding years. He died at the home of his daughter in St. Louis, on April 8, 1855. His remains rest in the beautiful cemetery at Quincy, Illinois, overlooking the Mississippi's mighty flow.

I read the closing passage from the discourse preached at my father's funeral by the Rev. Dr. Post, of St. Louis: "The painful malady of which he died was of two months' duration. Its course was marked by the most intense suffering to which disease can expose man. But, through all, his faith, his patience, his trust and submission, through Christ we believe, that strengthened him, never failed. The Angel of the Covenant, 'one like to the Son of God,' went through the furnace with him. His mind was perfectly tranquil, perfectly at rest. All was peace. On Sunday, the last day of his life, a few hours before his death, he followed through the reading of the twenty-third Psalm by his son, with much manifest comfort, and, with frequent responses, indicated his appreciation and enjoyment of it. A short time before he died, the spirit that seemed to have gone far down the dark valley, never to return, came back once more, and looked out in clear intelligence from that eye which then was closing forever. In the stillness of that awful moment, I said to him, 'Brother, do you feel the Savior near you? Does He sustain you?' He answered, with a most meaning look of the eye, a repeated pressure of the hand, and attempted murmurs from his palsied mouth, 'Yes, yes.' This, friends, was the last testimony of our beloved brother—the last words of John Blatchford to this world, till the heavens and the earth be no more. Ages shall not add thereto, nor can they substract from it."

Truly, "The Memory of the Fathers is the Inspiration of the Children."

"Great is the Lord, and greatly to be praised ; and His greatness is unsearchable. One generation shall praise thy works to another, and shall declare thy mighty acts."

✢

THE SERVICE OF LEARNING, THE SERVICE OF THE CHURCHES.

REV. TIMOTHY DWIGHT, D.D., LL.D., New Haven.

Dr. PALMER: My friends, it is remarkable that while having a long list of ministers upon our rolls, we have no living ex-minister here to-day. Only one is living and he too feeble to be here. But there is a tradition which I am going to tell you. After Dr. Towne ended his ministry here, the church were looking for a new pastor, and there was a young man of great promise who bore an honored name, whom it was understood might be available, and the church set their hearts upon him, and he, I am told, was quite willing to come, except that, just at that moment, the Corporation of Yale laid hands upon him for a professorship in the Divinity School.

Now I remember in the burying-ground of the town in which several of my ancestors originated a monument with this inscription, " Sacred to the memory of "—giving a lady's name, date, and so on—" who ought to have been the wife of Thomas Palmer." It is understood that the stone was erected by the gentleman, and not by the friends of the lady. I am going to borrow that quaint phrase and introduce Dr. Dwight as the man who ought to have been the minister of this church. But you will appreciate how much more extensive and valuable have been the services to this church and to the churches of the United States which he has rendered in the position to which God called him. Yale men honor him as the beloved head of their University; a large number of ministers honor him as a teacher and counsellor, and we all honor him,—for what he is and has done; and I especially from my heart honor the beloved friend of more than forty years, who has consented at a great sacrifice to be here to-day, to speak a few words to us. I will introduce him. (Loud applause.)

Dr. DWIGHT: Dr. Palmer, ladies and gentlemen of this church and of this city—One of the most striking exhibitions of the business capacity and power over men possessed by your pastor, which I have in my mind, is the fact that I am here. (Laughter.) In some unguarded moment, a few months ago Dr. Palmer informed me he and you were to have this celebration, and said he hoped I would be a participator in it. As a friend, I told him I would endeavor to be here. I had no expectation of being called upon to address you. At the close of last week I received a note from him saying that I was the only surviving predecessor of his with the exception of one, who was unable to be present; and that he had concluded to put me upon the programme; and I wrote back that with the immense pressure of duties devolving upon the president of the university, it being just before Commencement, that I could not be here to take any part in these services. The next morning I received the programme printed with my name on the list, and I am here. This looks to me more like Presbyterianism, or the historic Episcopate, than democratic Congregationalism. (Laughter.)

Dr. Palmer told me I was the only predecessor of his, with one exception, who is now living. Allow me to say a few words on this subject. In the first place, I have been casting about in my mind on one side of the matter to know which of his predecessors I was. (Laughter.) It has been a peculiar experience of mine in my life that I have been mistaken for many eminent persons; and I came to the conclusion, after much thought, I was the Rev. Charles Chauncey (laughter), but that was dissipated and my hope was broken from its foundation by hearing Prof. Fisher was the Rev. Charles Chauncey. (Renewed laughter.)

The succession of your ministers, one after another, I do not know, but I would say that I came here, so far as my recollection goes, after the sentinels at the door had been dismissed, and after these muskets had been removed (laughter), and so it was not in the earliest period of the church. If I may look at another side of my relation to this church I would say that my pastorate here commenced on Saturday evening, in the year 1858, and terminated to the satisfaction of the congregation on Sunday evening (laughter), and so far as I was myself concerned, I had one happy deliverance (laughter). I expected to come to this church with the sensation and feeling of a candidate. I was invited to be here on a particular Sunday—by reason of an engagement elsewhere I was unable to come on that Sunday, or else by reason of some other arrangement here the engagement for me was postponed till the next Sunday; and I was elected to an office in the Yale Divinity School, in the intermediate week between the two Sundays, and I concluded to accept that offer and election; and I have therefore never had,—though I came so near having them,—the sensations which belong to a candidate for a pastorate.

This church was one of those who have sought my services to which I would most gladly have come at the time, but I was called into another service; and Dr. Palmer has assigned me some words on "The Service of Learning, the Service of the Churches" to address to you this morning. I will only say that the relationship between the churches and the school of learning, in our country, in our New England especially, from the beginning has been a very close relation. Our fathers and their descendants had no thought of the churches as fulfilling their duty without the establishment of the school of learning; and they had no thought of the schools of learning except as operated and influenced by the churches; and they committed the care of their education largely to those who were the ministers of the church; and the glory of our New England colleges has been largely connected, in all periods of the past, with the fact that the pastors of these churches—like your present pastor—have been connected with the administration and government of our New England colleges.

The service of the University which I represent this morning to the churches, and in an humble way my own service to the churches, I may say has been manifested in this place. The number of ministers who have come to this place, and to the towns which really are closely connected with this church, is very considerable. Dr. Palmer was made by me largely, excepting so far as his father and mother had a slight influence upon him; and the honored pastor of the South Church, who has recently left you, was one of those whom I sent here, as a partial fulfilment of my duty to this church, and there are others here in whose labors I have rejoiced, and certainly the city of Bridgeport has been closely related in these past years with the school of learning in which I have had a small share. I trust that the Institution and the churches of Connecticut will continue in the same happy relations in the future; that the churches will supply to the Institution of learning their sons and their kindly influences in all coming time; and that the institution of learning will do for the churches and the State what it has done in the generations past.

I express my thanks to Dr. Palmer for insisting upon my saying a word to you, for it is very pleasant for me to recall the incidents of my short pastorate here, and very pleasant to see the church in the flourishing condition in which it now is; and I wish to assure you of my kindest personal feeling to you all, and to assure Dr. Palmer, though he does not need it, that the friendship of forty years is as strong on my part as it is on his. (Loud applause.)

✣

THE DEBT OF A COMMUNITY TO ITS FOUNDERS.

Hon. Joseph Hawley, LL.D., U. S. Senate.

Dr. Palmer: President Dwight called me up a great many times in earlier years. I did not feel it to be very presumptuous to call him up when I got a chance.

Brethren and friends, when we originally planned this celebration, we were made very conscious of the riches of this church in the way of biography, and a number of illustrations of it came to our knowledge, but in the maturity of our arrangements we have given less attention to that than we originally projected. Samuel Sherman, who came here about 1685, was an ancestor of Gen. Sherman and of the Hon. John Sherman, U. S. senator from Ohio. We had hoped to have him present to-day among others. We have a letter of regret from him, other engagements having prevented his coming.

Among the early settlers of this locality was Joseph Hawley. The second deacon of this church was Deacon Hawley. There is no family who has contributed more largely, contributed more generously, to the history of this church and the South Church. There is no family which is more numerously represented here, or which was connected more honorably with the trying times in the history of the community than the families descending from Joseph Hawley. And above all we have present with us to-day a man whom Connecticut always delights to honor, and we are glad he is here as the representative of his family and has consented to unite with us in this celebration. I have the pleasure of presenting him to you at this time. Senator Hawley will now address us.

Senator HAWLEY: Dr. Palmer and fellow-citizens— The manner of Dr. Dwight's impressment here is exactly mine. I received a suggestion concerning a great celebration—like his very much; and then I received a notice that I was down for a certain subject, and I am here; and pay my willing tribute to the power of Dr. Palmer in addition to Dr. Dwight. I knew it would be interesting, but it is a great deal more than that. It is inspiring, when a man has any pride in the history of New England and this beloved State of Connecticut. I have seen in much more ambitious celebrations nothing more inspiring than the sight of the representatives of nine of the original colonist families. Mr. Beardsley, I think it was, is perfectly right in saying that this is a celebration of the two hundredth anniversary of the city of Bridgeport. Your beginning was like that of the great majority of the New England towns, especially the Connecticut towns. There were three men especially known. One was the pastor, another the school teacher and the third the Militia captain; and in all the days of trouble, when the great Brother Jonathan desired to retain the hearts of the people, he reached them, perhaps more easily than in any other way, through the pastors of all these scattered towns and country churches. They were men of very considerable education, men of strong character, of marked and positive characteristics, and didn't have a doubt about what was right and wrong respecting their country or their God. Then they had not heard of the word "agnostic"; and when Brother Jonathan wanted the people he reached them through the school master, and the militia captain, and the pastor—and through the pastor most of all.

I think it is Macaulay—I have read it somewhere lately —who says that the people who do not honor the noble deeds of their ancestors will leave no record of deeds of their own that their posterity will care to honor. It is to our honor that we honor the men who founded Connecticut. A young Grecian, who afterwards became a famous general himself, passing over some battle-field where heroes had once contended, said, "Every young man should come here!" If it were possible, what a joy it would be to have all the young men and the young women just coming into maturity in this State hear and read these inspiring records. Yes, these anniversaries ought to be observed by every community in the State. I rejoice to have seen several such celebrations; I rejoice over the monuments they have put up, and the volumes they have printed, giving a history of the early settlers. These celebrations are of great value in that respect; and let us feel encouraged by them. Sometimes we are discouraged a little and think that the old-fashioned Americanism is getting out of fashion. We look at the census and find more than half of our people here are either foreigners by birth or the children of one or two foreign parents. It is not to be endured that the ancient spirit, the belief, the earnest belief in something, the absolute, unquestioning devotion to one's country as well as one's God—it is not to be endured or allowed that these things shall fade away. Let us feel encouraged by many things. The Daughters and the Sons of the Revolution, the Colonial Dames, the other Colonial organization, whose name I do not recall at this particular moment, are movements in the right direction. The monuments they are putting up in various places, the investigations of these ancient historical matters they set on foot—these are great reminders of the old Puritanism and the old Colonial and Revolutionary patriotism—and there has been no reason within the last thirty or forty years to think any less of our country than we did before. (Cheers and applause.) The Puritans were not a race of people nor were they a religious faction. Puritanism is not any particular class of men, it is a type of character. Puritanism is a character. These men were mostly of fine old English stock, mingled, I think, to some extent with the good Dutch stock that came over into the eastern counties of England, but it was not because they happened to be Englishmen that they were Puritans. There have been Puritans essentially elsewhere; the Huguenots, the Quakers, or Friends, and many more. What finer illustration could there be of an absolute devotion to God and to the love of country and of right than we see in Luther? Luther was a Puritan in this sense of the word; so was Loyala the Jesuit, the founder of that great order. He was a reformer, as he thought, in the Catholic Church, and a man who had the most absolute devotion to the highest ideals of right. How beneficial, or how mistaken he was, it is not necessary to say. You do both men only justice if you consider their fidelity and their belief in something outside of and above and beyond themselves. It seems to me that in respect of their high sense of duty, the Mahommedans, in their days of purity and glory, were one class of Puritans.

There is a good deal in these latter days to make one uneasy and critical; the large class of men who are cosmopolitans in every country but their own, who are very much at home abroad, always thinking that things are better done over there; and who in the great struggles going on here are saying, political or ecclesiastical, or whatever it is they may be, "I don't think much of this thing," "I doubt the wisdom of that matter," "I think it is largely a matter of interest with them all whether in church or in state"; and "on the whole I take no part in these things." "I never meddle with politics, I don't meddle very much with religion, and there is nothing new, and there is nothing true, and it does not matter anyhow."

There is a great deal of that sort of agnosticism in political and church affairs which does not come from the Puritans. When they believed, they believed in their very bones. It was like fire in them. They were not long in doubt, either, whether there was an Omnipotent and Eternal God and Father, who invited them to be His children, but who commanded them to fight, who sent them into the world to do something and to be something, not to be sitting on the fence listless, but to grapple in with their sleeves rolled up, taking their share in all the magnificent work that was going on.

This is a glorious age. There never was one like it. There never were so many demands for industrious men and women; and I add again that there never was a time when so many of them are realizing the fact. It is a great realization of a glorious time. Our boys should be faithful to the ancestors whom we honor, and imitate their example, and make their stay in the world worth something. I believe with Macaulay, if we don't respect and love our ancestors for the work they did, we will leave nothing behind us that the people hereafter ought to respect. (Applause.)

My record in Connecticut is a modest one. I am descended from Samuel Hawley of Stratford, I am not certain whether of the seventh or eighth generation. The Hawleys have been all about Fairfield County. They are still, I am happy to say, about here; and we are all cousins in some degree or other, I never inquired, for it is a very serious job; but I am not ashamed of the name, straight down yeoman in the English sense, the owner of lands and the cultivator of lands, except my father, who was a modest preacher of the gospel and a member of the General Assembly for a long time. I am very glad to be with you to give, if it be possible, even a moment of satisfaction. (Loud applause.)

Dr. PALMER: Now, friends, before any of you leave, I wish to say that over in the incomplete Masonic building, yonder, there is a luncheon provided, and when we are through with the exercises of this morning, all will be fed who find it convenient to go thither.

There is a point of considerable importance to which I wish to direct attention at this moment, namely, the relation of this Ecclesiastical Society to the city in which we live.

The erection of the Parish of Stratfield by the General Court instituted the first independent authority within the limits of this city. In it began the organized community which in due time was to take the now familiar name of Bridgeport. For more than one hundred years the form of the authority was unchanged. Then there was evolved from the Parish of Stratfield the Borough of Bridgeport, in the year 1800. Out of this grew the Town of Bridgeport, in 1821; and out of this the City of Bridgeport, in 1836. In the beginning there was no separation between Civil and Ecclesiastical jurisdiction—the authorities of the Parish exercised both. After 1818, the two were of course entirely separated. Since then the town or city has been one thing, and the First Ecclesiastical Society another thing. But each of them legitimately represents, in its own line, the ancient Parish of Stratfield. We of the First Church and Society have invited here to-day the official Head of the City, as one to whom we sustain a special relation. Not merely as one of the "powers that be," whom we are bound to honor, and do honor, in our place, but also as one equally with ourselves standing upon the ancient foundations laid two hundred years ago. We hope that His Honor has a word of greeting for us, to which we will now listen.

Hon. FRANK E. CLARK: On behalf of the City of Bridgeport, I extend to you most hearty congratulations. To the founders of this church and to their descendants, the citizens of Bridgeport are greatly indebted; through their efforts and examples our prosperity has been largely made possible.

Our local, state and national history glistens with the names of Sherwood, Sherman, Wheeler and Beardsley.

Two hundred years ago, when that little band congregated for divine worship in the little village of Stratfield, they marked the beginning of our prosperous city.

From a sparsely settled community, through the age of boroughhood, up to the full bloom of a magnificent city, can we trace the noble work of the First Congregational Church and Society.

Without resorting to the sensationalisms of to-day, your ministers have accomplished a vast deal to be proud of, in their plain, simple way. Under their guidance, citizens of whom we all feel proud have been reared. The lessons which they instilled into the hearts of the young have borne fruit a hundred-fold. You have an abundance of reasons for rejoicing on this, your two-hundredth birthday. I feel that I would be derelict in my duty as Chief Executive of this city, should I fail to express our thanks to you, to rejoice with you and to thank the Almighty for the many blessings which He has bestowed upon us all. (Applause.)

Dr. PALMER: I have here a list which I am going to read. I hold in my hand a bundle of letters from those who would have been glad to be here, but for various reasons were prevented from coming. I wish simply to mention some of them in order that it may be truthfully said the letters were presented here, and they will be printed in the official account of this meeting. The list comprises the following:

Hon. John Sherman, U. S. S.
Dr. Chauncey M. Depew, New York City.
Dr. John W. Sterling, New York City.
Rev. Dr. Joseph H. Towne, New York City.
Rev. Dr. George Leon Walker, Hartford.
Prof. Henry A. Rowland, Johns Hopkins University.
Rev. Alfred T. Waterman, Michigan.
Rev. Charles H. Peck, No. Bennington, Vt.
Rev. Dr. Horace C. Hovey, Newburyport, Mass.
Mr. David Sherman Lacey, California.
Mrs. Mary Dudley Wilcox, Lawrenceville, N. Y.

Miss Julia E. Hunter, New York City.
Rev. J. J. Wooley, Pawtucket, R. I.
Mr. Joseph D. Bartley, Bradford, Mass.
Prof. Arthur M. Wheeler, Yale University.
Mr. Walter Hubbell, New York.
Rev. Dr. Henry Blodget, Missionary to China.
Dr. Gerald H. Beard, Norwalk.
(For the letters see p. 157 and following.)

Dr. PALMER: I feel very thankful to all the gentlemen who have taken the pains to speak to us this morning; and certainly feel gratified by the interest which has been manifested in this celebration. I hope that this afternoon we may again assemble, for the remainder of the programme, in which I expect to find great satisfaction and enjoyment. After the singing a recess will be taken, that all may refresh themselves, and I renew the invitation to all present to avail themselves of the luncheon. It is in the incomplete Masonic Building opposite.

The choir will now lead us in singing hymn 1019, " O, where are kings and empires now?"

BENEDICTION.

The love of God the Father, the grace of the Lord Jesus Christ, the Communion of the Holy Ghost be with you forever. Amen.

SERVICES OF

THURSDAY AFTERNOON.

✣

"Should Auld Acquaintance be Forgot?"

✣

ORGAN PRELUDE.

✣

ANTHEM, "Praise the Lord."

Dr. PALMER: Before resuming our exercises I am going to give a brief notice. The collection of relics in the chapel has excited so much interest and is really so well worth seeing, that arrangements have been made to keep it open this evening. So far as any may feel interested in extending this information I wish it might be done. I repeat, the room will be open this afternoon after service, and also in the evening till 10 o'clock.

While speaking of relics I have been asked to state a fact, which is known to some but not to all. The flag which is over this pulpit is the one which was used in the unveiling of the John Robinson Memorial at Leyden four years ago. It is thought some would be interested to know of that connection. I brought out the fact yesterday that the beginning of this settlement was in a movement of Fairfield and Stratford families towards this locality; and I showed that the First Church was formed of men who came from the Fairfield and Stratford churches. We are this afternoon very glad that representatives of the Fairfield and Stratford churches are here; and we are going to hear from them. I am glad to

introduce my brother, for whom I have the highest esteem
—the pastor of the First Church in Fairfield—as the first
speaker this afternoon.

✛

WORDS FROM THE MOTHER CHURCHES.

(1) First Church in Fairfield.

Rev. Frank S. Child.

Rev. Mr. CHILD: Honored shepherd of this flock, members of this and other flocks—I cannot follow the example set us by the rector of St. John's Parish and bring you a brick from St. Martins-in-the-Field. Did every traveler carry away a brick from so small a shrine, what would become of St. Martins-in-the-Field?

But I do bring you a treasure which centres in itself associations and memories sacred to the mother and the daughter church. It is this silver cup which has been used for more than two centuries in the celebration of the Holy Communion in old Fairfield Church. The name inscribed upon this vessel is that of the Rev. Samuel Wakeman, pastor of your ancestors as well as of ours. He it was, you remember, that favored your first school enterprise. He it was that abounded in helpful counsel and tender sympathy when this parish was set off from Fairfield and Stratford.

Many of the first settlers of this place, and their immediate descendants have, doubtless, pressed their lips to this memorial cup and received strength and inspiration through such a service for the toil and burden of those early days.

When Garfield was inaugurated president of the United States, his venerable mother was present to witness the ceremony. The oath of office had been administered, the address given; then the loyal son turned to his mother and imprinted a kiss upon her brow. It was a memorable scene. Who doubts that the mother's heart swelled with honorable pride and generous affection, as she recalled the great work achieved by her famous son!

—III—

It is with sentiments akin to these that the Prime Ancient Society of Fairfield, the two-thirds mother of the First Church in Bridgeport; (for in the original members of the new parish thirty-three families came from Fairfield and thirteen from Stratford;) it is with sentiments akin to these that the First Church of Fairfield, the two-thirds mother of the First Church of Bridgeport, sends greeting and congratulation on this anniversary.

We have listened with maternal interest to the narrative of church-life flowing like a strong and grateful river through two hundred years of time. Just as the great streams of earth bear refreshment to the land, adorn and exalt nature, serve many practical ends and scatter benedictions all along the way, binding times and interests and events into a kind of noble oneness; so has the stream of life named the First Church of Christ in Bridgeport pursued its path through the generations, yielding refreshment, beautifying character, diffusing blessings, making the past an inspiration, filling the present with the fruits of righteousness and quickening great hopes for the future, binding fast, present and future into the oneness of the Kingdom.

The ministers serving this people have been marked by a rare spirit of fidelity. Growth and expansion have ever been dear to the church; so that when another daughter has gone forth, she has gone forth with sweet memories and happy encouragements. Beneficence has been woven into the texture of your history. Spirituality has been an abiding characteristic through these decades of activity. Splendid leadership in affairs has also been manifest. Now all these things belong to the mother not less than to the daughter. The story has oft been repeated that when the people of Stratfield applied to the General Court for the transfer of their taxes to the support of a church in this part of the parish, the Prime Ancient Society of Fairfield set forth her opposition with remarkable force and perspicuity. It has been said, on the other hand, that Stratford showed a conspicuous willingness to contribute her smaller proportion of people to the new parish. So the reluctance of Fairfield to lose her good people was strikingly offset by the eagerness with which Stratford apparently desired to get rid of hers. It is not for me to speak of this as a virtue on the part of the two-thirds mother on this side of the waters, or to speak of it as a vice on the part of the one-third mother on the other side of the dividing waters. But this is certainly a condition of things which admits of favorable interpretation, so far as Fairfield is concerned. In fact, the ties which bound the Prime Ancient Society of Fairfield to Bridgeport, Greens Farms, Greenfield Hill, Southport and Black Rock were always so strong and tender that it required all the grace which the mother could command to permit these daughters to shift for themselves.

There are, as you know, cases of family affection where separation is almost fatal to continued peace and happiness. When Elizabeth Barrett left her father's house and made a home for herself with Robert Browning, it broke the tender ties that had formerly existed, and she was never permitted to enter the father's home and look upon his face again. Now there was not such a break as this between mother church in Fairfield and daughter church in Bridgeport. The strained relations which existed for a very brief time were lovingly adjusted, and there speedily manifested itself a spirit of helpfulness and sympathy. The Prime Ancient Society takes increasing satisfaction in the progress and achievement of this beloved daughter. For the mother has given much of her best blood to the Stratfield Zion. The original members of this church were among the most worthy, devout and hopeful of our people. It was not alone that the mother lost a portion of her taxes, but it was also that her strength was taxed to a measure, and a good portion of her spiritual life was made to run into another channel. But when once the thing was determined the mother was generous. The departure of these good people meant a good deal to the parish. It was like the dividing of one's farm; it was like a cutting down of the King's territory. But Fairfield gave the territory, especially since she was compelled to do it; and as always, under such circumstances she made the best of the situation. But the matter did not rest at this point, for I find, just as good parents continue their kindness and liberality to their children when they have made a home-roof for themselves, so Fairfield continued her manifold gifts to Stratfield or Newfield or Bridgeport.

A cursory view of our church records and our town records reveals the fact that when the male members of the daughter church wanted life-companions they had a way of coming to the mother church and winning the hearts of the maidens. And not satisfied with this kind of contribution, I find also that the fair ladies of the daughter church captivated the sturdy gentlemen of Fairfield and time out of mind persuaded them to come over into the latter settlement and make their home.

We cannot claim the first minister, Mr. Chauncey, although he was made a freeman of Fairfield, but his first better-half was a Fairfield product. These were days when people devoutly believed that they should marry and give in marriage. The indebtedness of Bridgeport's first church to one of our families cannot be measured. Fairfield had a way of putting the Burrs into all sorts of responsible positions. Was a colonel or a general wanted, did Princeton desire a president of the college or the United States a vice-president for the senate, there was a Burr for the position.

But these are not the only honors which came to the family. Now and again some Burr man was made judge, sat upon the bench and pronounced sentence upon prisoners; while ever and anon some Burr woman was made judge, sat upon another kind of bench and pronounced sentence upon a more agreeable sort of prisoner. The pastors of the Bridgeport church were repeatedly brought into this latter court before different Burr judges and sentence pronounced upon them was ever the same. And the sentence was always executed.

When Lyman Hall discovered that preaching did not agree with his mental health, he left your parish and came to Fairfield. The natural thing for him to do was to court and marry a Burr, daughter of one Thaddeus and sister of another Thaddeus. And when Mr. Lyman discovered that teaching in Fairfield did not agree with his mental health he wisely emigrated to Georgia. He found his sphere and made an immortal name. But it is not too much to say that both these parishes shared the training of this eminent man and directly contributed something toward his power. Doubtless, the instructions in penmanship which he gave and practiced while teaching in Fairfield, had much to do with that characteristic signature appended to the Declaration of Independence. It is proper to note in passing that Mr. Lyman did not have the same inducements to teach school as did one of your pastors. Mr. Blatchford, with his seventeen children, was always sure of a full session, no matter what the weather. And however much the various pupils might object to his methods of teaching and his peculiar discipline, there were seventeen pupils, or thereabouts, whose parents never made complaints and were inclined to make the best of the instruction.

Coming down to later times, I find that the indebtedness of this church to the mother assumes a new form. Having given good men and women, having supplied the ministry with notable helpmates, having passed over more or less of territory, the day comes when Fairfield prepares a preacher for this parish and sends him forth to stamp his individuality upon the people.

Mr. Hunter was a man of certain remarkable gifts. Judge Sherman was his intimate friend and loving counsellor. The young preacher had his wits sharpened by many a tilt with the famous statesman, who was a deacon in the Fairfield church and always present to give his pastor the benefit of his generous criticism and his loving inspiration. But with all his helpful intentions, the judge was not able to curb Mr. Hunter's impulsive spirit. So that it was not many years ere this minister graduated from the schooling of the mother church and Judge Sherman. His spicy wit left a pungent odor which still lingers in Fairfield. When this brilliant, eccentric man came to the North Church of Bridgeport, he brought with him a fine and commanding intellectual equipment. But there interblended with such equipment those peculiarities of constitution which time had emphasized rather than softened, so that like unforgetable impressions were made upon the daughter church not less than upon the mother. His ministry in the two parishes, remembered with mingled emotions of laughter and tears, approval and condemnation, is an interesting and suggestive bond between mother and daughter.

Along the same line of generosity it is fitting to say that the Prime Ancient Society of Fairfield extended her favor to your daughter and her granddaughter, the South Church. Dr. Hewitt came to Fairfield fresh from the School of the Prophets. He spent ten years of splendid, consecrated service among us, learning those important lessons in preaching and shepherd work which a man ought always to learn in his first parish. When he had developed his masterful resources and finished a very faithful apprenticeship, he entered upon the delicate, onerous task of shaping the life of the young South Church. Again there were formed ties indissoluble, which bound the old and the new into oneness of sympathy and experience. So pleased and helped by such gifts was the city of Bridgeport, that she finally sought, not only the strength of the mother church, but the presence of our law and justice in the form of court house and jail. The same sort of reluctance featured the gift of these institutions as was manifest when the old parish was compelled to pass over thirty-three families to the new and form the North Church. But the mother, with her accustomed wit and grace, observed complacently, after the thing was done, that it was precisely the thing for her to do, so that she again accepted the inevitable with a dignity of submission both exemplary and beautiful.

It was natural to think that relations being so intimate and the daughter continuing to draw upon the vitality of the mother, a period would be reached when a sense of grateful indebtedness must develop and some conspicuous liberality express appreciation of such long-continued indulgence. But wherein do we discover the signs of gratitude? Is it when more territory is demanded? Is it when the old parish again and again shares with the new the sacred associations of the past? Is it when one after another of our people become absorbed into the busy life of the growing city? Did we look at the matter from this narrow and selfish point of view, small signs of gratitude would be detected. But we are fain to confess that such is not a fair way of putting it. For we observe that there has existed and there continues to exist a beautiful spirit of generosity on the part of this First Church of Bridgeport. She gathers strength unto herself, she draws upon the resources of the mother, she looks to the Fairfield parish for various kinds of substantial encouragement, simply that she may multiply her own daughters, enlarge her growing usefulness, give the first mother the dignity and happiness of granddaughters, quicken into a more expansive life among us the kingdom of our Lord Jesus Christ. This is a form of gratitude most precious and ennobling. The mother rejoices that the daughter abounds in the many generous sacrifices and happy reduplications of life manifest in the spiritual history of Bridgeport. And that which has been is interpreted as an earnest of that which is to be—years and generations of an illustrious past to reproduce themselves though coming time in work and character instinct with the Spirit of God.

Daughter Church of Bridgeport, grown like your mother to be the honored mother of many churches, the mother church in Fairfield extends her hands above you in loving benediction. That same uplift and outlook which she craves for herself she craves for her eldest child. The two hundred and fifty-six years of the one church-life are almost equaled by the two hundred years of the other. It has been an eventful and sublime epoch. During these two centuries, which have changed the face of the world and wrought for the triumphs of liberty, intelligence, righteousness, as have no other centuries, mother and daughter have stood side by side in all honorable purpose, theological expression, sincere consecration, free-hearted gift of men, devout co-operation for the good of humanity and the exaltation of Christ. Into these supreme tasks have been compacted infinite love, zeal, faith, joy, hope. And the fruition has appeared in Christian manhood and womanhood, rich and enduring contributions to the worth of the world.

Daughter Church, the Fairfield mother greets you with affection. She counts your achievements as witnesses to the fidelity and sacrifice vital to the triumphs of our common Christianity. Eminent and consecrated ministers have served your parish with notable success. The people have responded to wise and loving leadership with significant unanimity. The church has entered into the development and prosperity of city and state with an energy, hopefulness, inspiration, enthusiasm known alone to the Great Head of the Church.

May coming days bring you larger opportunities and richer powers. May the precious old-time associations serve to broaden and deepen new-time currents of spiritual activity. May the works of generations gone be like seed falling upon good ground, bringing forth some sixfold and some an hundred-fold. May this venerated Zion continue to shine with multiplied splendor and glory amid the galaxy of churches which begem this busy, fruitful city by the sea!

Dr. PALMER: It is not everybody that has two mothers. We, as a church, rejoice in the fact that we have two, and having heard from one, we now propose to hear from the other, the First Church of Stratford, represented by its pastor, the Rev. Joel S. Ives.

(2) FIRST CHURCH IN STRATFORD.
REV. JOEL S. IVES.

Rev. Mr. IVES: Venerable Daughter, Christian friends of this North Church and the other churches of this vicinity:

It was said last night that a child can have but one mother. To-day, we make real the anomaly of a daughter with two mothers, unless it be said that Fairfield, in this case, inasmuch as she permitted those thirty-three families to pay taxes for the support of the churches both in Fairfield and in the new enterprise, may be called a mother-in-law.

The date from which we, as Congregationalists, date our American history, is 1620, when our Pilgrim Fathers landed on the shores of Plymouth bay. It was a little company, which the first winter decimated by privations and disease. It would seem that their first effort would be to strengthen their stakes and deepen their foundations, through the consolidation of all their interests. But instead, they followed the example of the first Congregationalists on the western coasts of the Great Sea. They went everywhere from Plymouth bay, carrying their Puritan conscience and their Congregational liberty of worship and their Pilgrim love of learning. It was sturdy stuff that pushed out into the wilderness, making settlements through Massachusetts, even to the banks of the Connecticut river and the shores of Long Island Sound, until there was formed this

> " Pure republic, wild, yet strong.
> A 'fierce democracie' where all are true
> To what themselves have voted."

The first Englishman who came to the charming haven formed by the incurving lines of Milford Beach and Stratford Point, found here an Indian clan called Cupheags, which seems to mean "a place shut in." But for untold years it was the favorite camping-place of Indian tribes. The Mohicans appear to have come from the Hudson to the Housatonic, camping first near the falls at Kent and thus naming the river Pootatuck. What attracted the Indians attracted the white man also, as he looked upon the beauty of the situation, as the broad Housatonic swept out into the Sound.

And there are records that, in 1637, the Connecticut colony conquered the Pequot and Pequannock tribes.

Thomas Stanton, for many years the Indian interpreter at Hartford, writes, that in March of 1637 there was found in Milford " only one house or the karkise of one." John Winthrop came with his company to Saybrook in 1635; John Davenport to New Haven in 1638, and the following year a church was organized in Milford, with Mr. Prudden as the first pastor, while during the same year Rev. Adam Blakeman had come down the river from Wethersfield, and, together with those already on the ground, formed the first church in Stratford, two hundred and fifty-six years ago.

This date cannot be assigned from documentary evidence, as the records of the church previous to the year 1675 have been lost. But upon the records of the General Court is this: "Sergeant Nichols" is assigned "to train men and exercise them in military discipline," in this plantation; and they were also given power "to choose seven men from among themselves," who should decide "differences and controversies under 40s." There was, therefore, town government at the mouth of the Housatonic in 1639, and as the late Professor Johnson says, " it would hardly be too strong to say that the establishment of the town and of the church was coincident."

Except for the company who came with the Rev. Adam Blakeman from Massachusetts after a brief stay near Wethersfield, your mother church seems to have been organized from individuals who had gathered here and not by an organized company, as was usual. Mr. Blakeman's pastorate continued till his death, September 7, 1665, at the age of 67 years. Thomas Hooker says of him: " For the sake of the sacred and solemn simplicity of the discourse of this worthy man, if I might have my choice I would choose to live and die under Mr. Blakeman's ministry." His will makes plain that he was a member of the Cambridge Synod. His home was at the corner of Stratford avenue and Elm street, west of the site of the first meeting-house. In 1651 it was voted, "by the town in public meetings," that " Mr. Blakeman shall have sixty pounds and pay part of his own rate."

Five months before the death of Mr. Blakeman the town voted to call Mr. Israel Chauncey "to help Mr. Blakeman in the ministry for a year," and in June, 1666, there was a "mutual agreement" for his settlement. He was the son of the Rev. Charles Chauncey, president of Harvard College, and father of the Rev. Charles Chauncey, the first pastor of this church. He was born in 1644, and was actively engaged in the founding of Yale College, being chosen, November 11, 1701, as the rector of the college, but declined the honor, probably because of failing health, as he died March 4, 1703. Nathaniel Chauncey, his nephew, and the first graduate of Yale College, in 1702, was called to the vacant pastorate, but he declined the call.

Israel Chauncey was an honored name in the colony. His ministry of thirty-eight years in Stratford, marked by great wisdom in affairs and dignity of character, means much, both to the mother church and to this daughter church as well. His studies included medicine in addition to theology, and during the troublous times of the Narragansett war he was appointed one of the council of the army, and by this council ordered to "go forth with the army as their chirurgeon."

During Mr. Chauncey's pastorate the differences of opinion resulting from the half-way covenant, together with other causes, brought about the formation of the Second Church in Stratford, almost thirty years before the date which we celebrate to-day. This movement resulted in the migration to the "wilderness of Pomeraug," and the formation of the First Church of Woodbury.

The first house of worship in Stratford was probably like the picture yonder, except that there must have been a place for a bell, probably in the lookout on its top, as a means of safety from the skulking Indians. This bell was the first of which there is any record in the colonies.

In 1661 "it was agreed that there shall be a gallery builded in the meeting-house in the convenient place." This building was torn down in 1681, and some of the materials of its construction are in existence.

The second meeting-house was built in 1681, near the present soldiers' monument, on what was then called "Watch Hill," its dimensions being "48 feet in length, 42 feet in breadth and 16 feet between joints." By vote of the town this building was seated in accordance with the amount paid toward its construction, the amount voted being one hundred pounds. In 1689, it was voted to fortify the house, so that it could be used "as a place of security for women and children."

Dating thus from the beginning of Stratford and Fairfield, we are contemplating the history of two hundred and fifty-six years. It was one hundred and thirty-seven years from the founding of the mother churches to the Declaration of Independence, and only one hundred and nineteen years since that date.

Who can measure the meaning of these figures?

But there is a wider sweep of historic forces—it is the universal Church of God. Our Congregational church has a larger place in the kingdom of God on earth. Our freedom of worship, our liberty of thought, our protest against hierarchy, "the common priesthood of believers," our zeal for the kingdom of righteousness and truth, these are our heritage and these are the things we would bear onward to the church universal.

The mother church of Stratford gives to-day to her second daughter her warmest congratulations upon this two-hundreth birthday and her assurances of co-operation, both with pastor and people, in the work which God gives us to do.

> "Hail ancient church! Lift high thy voice,
> Through centuries yet to come rejoice,
> The church triumphant waits, and we
> Shall join the immortal company."

Dr. PALMER: Let us unite in singing to one of the old tunes, in which we can all unite, the 329th hymn.

HYMN 329. "Ye tribes of Adam join."

Dr. PALMER (after singing the first verse): Let us do better than that on the next verse, all sing; (after singing the second verse) that is better, now better still.

Dr. PALMER: Sixty-five years ago, friends, to-day, strange it may seem to you, there was not a store or a shop upon Main street; it was full of residences, and so were the cross streets; State street, Wall street, Bank street and John street, all this part of the town was a residential section. The stores were all together in Water street. There was a house and garden where the Atlantic Hotel stands, there were houses and gardens extending to the water on the shore where now the Consolidated Road's freight houses are. It is difficult for us to conceive how different a locality this was then, from what it is now. This church was in the center of the population. Now, I suppose, there came to be so many people in need of church privileges that there was a reason for a division. At any rate a division came about, a division which at that time was regretted here, but doubtless proved to be for the good of the community.

When that division originated the Second Church, I believe that the people who stood by the old church were sorry to see them go; but they are exceedingly happy that in the preparations for this occasion and in carrying on the arrangements of this occasion they came back here and are here with us on the same footing with ourselves.

Now we are going to hear from the pastor of the Second Church, the Rev. Dr. Russell.

✥

WORDS FROM THE DAUGHTER CHURCHES.

(1) THE SOUTH CHURCH.

REV. FRANK RUSSELL, D.D.

Dr. RUSSELL: Christian Friends of the North Church, and of the other Associated Churches and of all the Churches:

I feel very happy indeed to be able to stand here and give my testimony to the greatness of this occasion. When I first contemplated coming to Bridgeport I knew nothing about Bridgeport. I knew something about two men in Bridgeport; they were very attractive. One of them had had quite a career and has gone. His name was P. T. Barnum. The other was having his career, and that was Dr. Palmer; and those two names were very significant in my first acquaintance with Bridgeport.

I little thought that within a year and a half I should be ushered into such a celebration as this, the sacredness of which has not yet been half told. It is more significant than we think. Our fathers, whose careers have been enumerated here, builded, as we see now, wiser than they knew; and I feel like saying that the projectors of this commemorative occasion were building a great deal wiser and greater than they knew. There were giants in those older days; we have had them named, we have had the roll call. We have found their descendants still here. We have gathered in these great congregations—this is the fourth and the last, and some of us begin to feel this ought not to be the last. We would stay in such a frame as this, and we would keep this decorated tabernacle awhile. It has been my thought to-day that it is most too bad to go down from this mountain top without the Sunday school children of Bridgeport coming in here and into the adjoining building, and have the significance of these things explained to them; yea, every school child in Bridgeport, boy or girl, should be permitted, as we have been permitted, to have realized before them the commemoration of this great scene. I know some of them have been taken out of the public schools to-day for that special purpose, that they may have a sight at the relics, the decorations, in order that they may be instructed more appropriately as to what this gathering means. Emphasis has been given to the leadership and the great instructors which this church has had from its beginning. But I think it is worth while to mention the years of humble common ministry of a church, not of a pulpit merely, but of the membership of the church, the ten thousand instances of kindly sympathetic attention to the sick and the poor, the greetings of new comers, the cordial affiliations and sympathy with those who were in trouble, the unnumbered instances of counsel given and received; all of this permeating the life of the community, strengthening and blessing it, till after the two hundred years of the outpouring of such streams we are enabled to sit here and say to each other—what a congregation of faces, mature, strong, showing great character!

Then we remember how it is in the Western churches, that ministers are told of all new comers—"family moved in over on such a street. Where did they come from? Well, they came from Illinois, Indiana, came from Ohio, came from Pennsylvania—well, I will get around in a few days and try and make their acquaintance."

But told that a family has moved in at such another number. "Where did they come from?" "They came from Connecticut." "Where is my hat?" They only lose ten minutes before they see that family. (Laughter.) And they will testify to you personally the reason for these different acts. When we find a New England Congregational family we know generally they have their letters with them or they will come very soon, and go right into the church with the family, ready at once for services. He will not board around for two or three years before he finds a boarding-place, but will attend to his church duties as he attends to his ordinary duties, in a clear, good, prompt manner. And he will be in his place in the church at work right off; because he is accustomed to it. He has borne burdens and he expects to enter into that church-life in his new place.

Now that will hardly be matched by families commonly, on an average, moving from other states. It is that training in this land of steady, strong habits. I confess personally that I was proud to have my own lineage familiarly mapped out so that some of these scenes seemed very familiar. Well, I came from England in 1638 and landed with John Davenport's congregation in the first ship that touched at New Haven or Quinnipiack harbor, and under the Center Church was buried both the father and the son who came over. The first one born in this country graduated from Harvard, a tutor there for a time, one of the founders of Yale, pastor of Middletown for twenty-six years, and his son in Rocky Hill, then Wethersfield thirty-four years, each of them buried at the close of their pastorate, and so on till they come down to me, the eighth. I was very glad also to hear about the Saybrook platform and the scenes of the settlement of the territory and the establishment of the churches about here. It was expected, I suppose, that I should speak something about the South Church. It is only for the purpose of representing it that I am here at this time with these remarks. I thought, when it was suggested to me that the children of this dear old mother church should have something to say respecting each family, that it would be rather a difficult matter for me to say anything on that point; but the more I looked into it the more I found it a very pleasant message that I should bring. When I first began to inquire about it in the South Church, I said, "You say we separated from the North Church?" "Yes—but it was over sixty years ago." Well, that sounded better. "Then there was some unpleasantness between the North and the South? we hear it spoken of sometimes." O yes, but there is an abundance of peace now. Well, I think there ought to be, there are strong members in the South Church that united with it before I was born. Then I said to one and another, "What was the cause of the division between the North Church and the South Church?" The first one said, "Well, it was something about theology." Then I asked the next one, "What was the cause of the separation of the South Church from the North Church?" "Something about theology." I asked the next one, and he said something about theology, and I never got further than that, excepting in one case. One of them said, "It was something about theology, I believe, New Haven theology;" and that is as far as I have ever had any explanation given to me.

I was reminded of the man who bestowed a great deal of his attention upon his theological convictions, so that he might stand up to them. "Now, I believe," he says, "that God foreordained, or else that he had foreknown

—well, whichever way it is I don't know, but I believe in it." (Laughter.)

As to any modern difficulty or difference between the North Church and South Church, I never found a single glimmer, or look, or tone that had in it any lack of perfect harmony between the two bodies. Indeed, they are not very far apart, five hundred feet; they didn't go very far South to get the name of the South Church. I have tried to read up the history about the circumstances when they did go. And I found that when the separation commenced and one hundred and seventeen wanted to go and form a new church, here was the mother that followed them with love and with gifts, and when they talked about building a building, handed over $2,000 to help them. That don't look like any great degree of unpleasantness between the North Church and the South Church. And then right away, before they had their wooden building built that cost $5,000, they had a revival of religion in which it is on record that both churches heartily joined and reaped great fruits. Well, that first year of division seems to have been a glorious year; and then Dr. Hewitt was called; he stayed just as long as dear Dr. Palmer has been in this church; and I cannot find a single glimmer of any difference between the two churches.

I find traces of a great deal of heroism that belonged to the South Church. I read in their records with absolute amazement that they commenced the burden of building the present edifice just at the beginning of the war, and that in 1862, right in the midst of the conflict that was draining the very life out of communities, they completed it for liberty and the Gospel. (Applause.) I say that was grand and it was wonderful; and I rather fancy there must have been a good deal of sympathy, active and valuable sympathy, from the brethren of the North Church when that was done.

I have no particular occasion to pursue the details of the history. That has a more substantial record, for there stands the building which represents the South Church. I have one more thought that has been uppermost in my heart in all the sessions of this gathering; and that is the purpose, the common purpose which is before us and before all of the churches of this cluster of churches in this city—the promotion of the same Gospel; there is no new Gospel. If sixty-five years ago there was any exploited in the minds of any at the time of the division it certainly must have been given up, because it has been the same Gospel ever since which the two churches have proclaimed, the everlasting Gospel of the forgiveness of sins through our Lord Jesus Christ; and the churches are sent to push that Gospel into the homes and into the hearts of all who dwell around about them, and into the regions beyond to the remotest parts of the earth.

The churches that have been formed in Bridgeport have been missionary churches. They have been missionary churches at home, as well as abroad; they would not be missionary churches abroad had they not been missionary churches at home. So my thought to-day is that we are here in a common warfare; our methods almost exactly the same, yes, exactly the same; our purposes the same, our gospel the same, our songs the same, our prayers the same, our prayers in behalf of each other the same and constant; and the work that comes before us to do is to minister with all the churches upon every street, and in every home in this community, that people may be brought into some of the churches in proportionate numbers to recognize the kingship of our risen Christ, and to follow Him in activity of purpose, in humility of life; recognizing Him and walking to the same church with His people, alike in their activity to spread the Gospel in this region, and extend it to many others. May this be our prayer, may this be our purpose, may this be our hope, that the generations of children yet to come may at the end of another century have to enumerate that on the latest of the then three centuries there has been great activity and great presence and power of the Holy Spirit in the hearts of the people, in the enlargement and furtherance of our common Gospel. God bless the churches of this city, God bless this North Church, the original church of this city. (Loud applause.)

Dr. PALMER: The next movement growing out of the abundance of life in the First Church was a mission school. There was a new community beyond the river. When I came to this city, Park St. Church had grown out of that mission school and was, for the first time, trying to get on without missionary help. It was feeling its feet beneath it, it was beginning to walk, it was gathering strength. I have watched its growth from that time on. I have been extremely interested in seeing its progress; some of its pastors have been very dear to me. It has grown to be one of the largest and strongest churches in the city and we have rejoiced in its growth. It has shown a commendable spirit, not only in bearing its own burdens, but in taking the lead to further church extension. We rejoice to see that; we rejoice in its present prosperity, and are extremely glad to welcome here to-day its gifted pastor, from whom we hope to hear at this time.

(2) THE PARK ST. CHURCH.

REV. EDWARD GRIER FULLERTON, PH.D.

Rev. Mr. FULLERTON: Dr. Palmer, ladies and gentlemen—I am sure that we all feel like extending our sympathies to Dr. Russell for having had a relative in Wethersfield for thirty-four years. He was certainly very honest to tell us about it, and I know we would all be glad to sign an application for the estimable gentleman's pardon if he were still alive. (Laughter.)

A story has gone the rounds of late which tells of a little girl who was very proud of her family ties. She was once watching her mother, who was more than usually well dressed at the time, and, after a few moments of silent inspection, said, with a satisfied sigh: "Oh, mother, how sweet you do look! I'm *so* glad you married into our family!" I know that to-day these assembled churches are saying the same thing, from the bottom of their hearts, about their mother.

A clerical friend in an adjoining parish told me of the shrewd saying of a child that he and his wife had adopted. The little one did not understand, of course, the legal measures it was necessary to go through before she became really theirs, but she knew something was going to happen, and looked with great eagerness for the papers to come. When at last they arrived, her new mother threw them down before her and said: "Now you are as much my little girl as though you were born in this house." To this the child responded pleasantly: "Yes, and you are just as much my mother as though *you* were born in the house,—aren't you?" There is an excellent application to that story, but it has slipped my mind just now. Never mind. Let it pass. (Laughter.)

There is no need of extended remark from me at this time. You naturally expected lengthy speeches from the old mother churches of us all,—Fairfield and Stratford, for when mothers get to talking of their children, they never *do* know when to stop. You naturally expected, too, to hear something good from the big sister, the South Church, and you were not disappointed. By the way, I have never been quite able to make out the relationship of my church and the South. Is she partly a progenitor and partly a contemporary? I usually have to satisfy myself by saying: "Well, as she is a block or two more distant from us than the First Church is, we can just call her a *step-father*." (Laughter.)

You also look for a good deal from the younger children—Olivet, West End, and the baby, the King's Highway Chapel. You are waiting now, I know, to hear their innocent and merry prattle, and I shall not detain you long.

The gathering of this afternoon is in some respects *the* feature of the whole celebration. This is true, not because we have superior talent to display, for the meeting yesterday afternoon, with your pastor's scholarly and accurate historic address; of last night, with the greetings from brethren of other denominations; of this morning, with its array of distinguished speakers, it would be hard for us to compete with. But you must remember that this is distinctly a family gathering, in which the mother, the grandparents, and the children, have come together to felicitate each other on this interesting period in the career of one of our number. As such, an interest attaches to this meeting that is peculiar, and all its own.

Well, we are very proud, I can assure you, of our heritage. I speak, I know, not only for my church, but for all the rest as well. We were glad to learn, yesterday afternoon, of the close relationship there was between us and old Stratford and Fairfield,—glad to know that the ties that bind us are stronger and closer than railroad ties. It is comforting to be assured of the exact statistics of our heritage—thirteen of our forefathers coming from Stratford, and thirty-three from Fairfield. Inherited tendencies are hard to trace with any degree of exactness, but from the mystic thirteen of Stratford we have all perhaps inherited the go-ahead spirit, the tendency to "make things hum" that is such a feature of the insect life at least of that pleasant suburb of ours. Possibly, also,—for there is nothing more contradictory than different traits in the same character, we also have from her that sleepiness, that unwillingness to do church work that a scattered few of our number show. For Stratford is an intensely soporific spot, you know. Brother Woodruff, of Black Rock, has in fact evolved from his witty consciousness a conundrum regarding the beloved pastor of Stratford Church. "Why is Brother Ives like Shakespeare?" "Because he is buried in Stratford." From Fairfield we probably inherit our pride, our satisfaction with ourselves, our firm belief that "we are the people," or at least a very important part of them. Why, Fairfield is so content with herself that she didn't even want the trolley, and the trolley retaliates by shaking off the dust from her wheels upon poor Fairfield every time she goes through the town.

I think especially at this time, however, of what my own church, in particular, owes to her mother, the Old First. It is familiarly said, you remember, that the training of a child should begin two hundred years before it is born, and ours has begun two hundred, or nearly, before that—to us—interesting event. One of the marked features in the life of this church, as you noticed all through the history of yesterday afternoon, has been her courage, her steadfastness, her indomitable spirit in the face of obstacles. I look back at the first beginnings of Park Street, a quarter of a century ago, and, seeing the same traits strongly marked there, realize that she came honestly by these first requisites of success.

Then, too, our Mother Church has been very fond of children. Her bump of philoprogenitiveness has been strongly marked. She has constantly been sending out infant churches, until quite a "quiver full of them" have sprung up around her. We have tried to be true to our heritage in this respect, also. and, though little past our majority, have a flourishing child in the King's Highway Chapel, that has recently begun life of its own account. It seems a little dreadful that thirty or forty of the members should suddenly become "highwaymen," but those things will happen sometimes. (Laughter.)

And now I trust that we may be true to our mother in other respects, and as we inevitably must grow old, do so as gracefully as she has done. It is our hope and prayer that our children may rise up and call us blessed, as hers have done for her to-day; that our history may be as brave and noble a history as that which she looks back upon; and that when we leave the church militant on earth to join the shining ranks of the Church Triumphant in heaven, we may have as many stars of rejoicing as we know will glitter in her crown. (Applause.)

Dr. PALMER: This morning, owing to the fact that President Dwight was anxious to take a train, and his time was getting a little short, an interlude was left out of the programme, which I want to have introduced at this time, the choir leading. Perhaps you will be refreshed if you rise while singing.

INTERLUDE, "The breaking waves dashed high."

Dr. PALMER: It is in the neighborhood of twenty-five years ago that certain members of this church felt that something must be done with the northern part of the city. And one member of this congregation became responsible for the renting of a hall, for the furtherance of church work in that section. The memory of one of those who survives testifies that at the first service there were five persons. There were three teachers and two pupils. That was the beginning of the Olivet Church, a church which has now become one of the strong and hopeful churches in the city, but which, for a great while, had a painful struggle to make good its right to be. We are proud of the eminence which it has reached, and its promise for the future, and we greatly love the man who ministers to it and who has done so much to make it the exceedingly alive and prosperous church it has become. I am glad to introduce the Rev. Edwin K. Holden.

(3) OLIVET CHURCH.
REV. EDWIN K. HOLDEN.

Rev. Mr. HOLDEN: We are glad to recognize to-day the truth of the Proverb (17:6), that "The glory of children are their fathers." The daughter for whom I speak is most happy in this anniversary of her mother. She bears to you congratulations, gratitude and affection. She congratulates you on your venerable years, on the magnificent service which you have rendered the community in particular, and humanity in general, through the long period of your ministration.

As I listened to that splendid discourse by Dr. Palmer, yesterday afternoon, and saw this panorama on the wall marking so suggestively the advance of our civilization, and heard the names of those eminent men, some of whom we have listened to to-day, whose roots run back to this church, I venture the statement that among all the forces that have combined in the last two hundred years in shaping and realizing the best institutions and life of this entire community, not one has been more potent than this First Church of Christ.

But this fact is so prominent that it has been emphasized in the thought of all who have spoken upon this occasion.

I would have been glad to hear some one speak upon the relation of this church to the great missionary work of our societies. It gives a fine opportunity to discover the spirit of the church. Its zeal in this direction has been most marked. I took occasion to look back over her records and I found, as I expected to find, that she has been among the foremost in missionary enterprise.

It was natural, therefore, that this missionary zeal should show itself in its own city. In church extension in this city, this church has taken the lead. It is for me to speak only for one child of her love and fostering care.

The records of the Olivet Congregational Church begin as follows: "About the year 1868, a mission Sabbath school was established in the northern part of Bridgeport, under the auspices of the North Congregational Church." November 16, 1870, a church was organized. You will observe, therefore, that on the 16th of next November, this daughter will celebrate her twenty-fifth anniversary, to which the mother church will have a most cordial welcome. I have felt that this church must have a great deal of affection for Olivet Church, if for no other reason than on the principle that parents always feel a little more tender towards a child that has been a great deal of care to them and has caused them much anxiety and solicitude. Olivet Church certainly had a struggle for existence. But this church never forsook her. It was your money that kept her doors open, when other resources failed. I have heard the story of how the pastor of this church, with one of his saintly members, who is still spared among us a benediction to all who know her, met together to see what could be done to keep the doors open for another year, and solved the question by each pledging $500. From this time her steps began to be more firm; slowly but surely she has been making her way. Her history for the last three or four years is well known to you, for you have been in it, you have largely made it. Your money has been largely instrumental in giving us a habitation in which we all take delight. So we come to you to-day from a good, beautiful and commodious home, happy in our work, not only to congratulate you, but also to express to you our gratitude and our affection.

I should not be true to myself to-day, if I did not express my high regard for, and my personal indebtedness to Dr. Palmer. If it is not in good taste to speak in this personal way in Dr. Palmer's presence, then I know of no other way but to consider him for a few moments as absent.

Perhaps you are familiar with the story told of the Rev. Thomas Williams and Dr. Emmons. Each wrote the funeral sermon of the other with the mutual understanding that the one who should survive the other should read at the funeral of the deceased the discourse as previously prepared. They lived on to advanced years, when Dr. Emmons, being the older, and thinking he might die first, wished to know what his friend would say about him, so he asked him to read to him his discourse. Mr. Williams consented, and during the reading Dr. Emmons interrupted him with some remarks or criticism, when Mr. Williams said, "Be quiet, sir, remember that for all the purposes of this discourse *you are a dead* man." So "for all the purposes of my words," Dr. Palmer is not present.

I want to say frankly, that I have counted the friendship of Dr. Palmer as one of my best blessings, since I have been in Bridgeport. I will tell you what has made me esteem and honor Dr. Palmer. I came here ten years ago last spring from the Seminary to engage in Christian work in the Olivet Mission. Ten years ago last Sunday I was ordained to the Christian ministry. The ordaining prayer was made by Dr. Palmer. By him I was formally set apart to the Christian ministry. I was without experience, and in a strange land, and from that day to this he has been to me counsellor and friend. His home, in which at that time was that noble woman, whose name and great kindness will never be forgotten by those of you who knew her, has been so cordially open to me and mine, that I regret that there should be even a rumor that his residence will soon be transferred to another city. Hence my esteem and affection.

Again we all know that this community is more indebted to the twenty-three years of service of Dr. Palmer than any of us can realize. The ministry is indebted to him. He has done much to divest our sacred calling of everything that is patronizing and unmanly and imparted to it the wholesome flavor of Christian manliness.

Fred Douglass, commenting on the parable of the Good Samaritan, said of the priest who passed by on the other side, "He was all priest and no man."

Dr. Palmer, without ever sacrificing anything of the dignity of his calling, has shown himself at all times a man.

This city is indebted to him. It is worthy of recognition and of profound gratitude that such a man with high attainments, with the most wholesome ideas of humanity, and religion, whose zeal has been marked with sobriety and sound judgment, has stood in your midst for twenty-three years.

God be praised for his work here! For the generous gift of himself and his means to this community. For the saintly memory of her whose influence lingers with us and will to the end of time. I bring the hearty congratulations of Oliver Church, I bring her gratitude, I bring our tribute of honor and love. (Loud applause.)

Dr. PALMER: One bright, sunny morning, about ten years ago,—a little more, I went with the superintendent of our Sunday School to the West End. We learned that the city had pre-empted a certain piece of land for the school. We remembered that in New England school and church were apt to go together. We decided that the City Fathers had thus indicated where they thought the center of population was to be in that rapidly growing suburb. We had the pleasure that day of deciding the question of location for a future church. Knowing that the standing committee of my church was behind me, with their cordial approbation and consent, I bought the land, and from that beginning there has grown up a very vigorous and interesting young church, with a fruitful present and an exceedingly promising future. We look upon that church with a great deal of affection. We welcome its new pastor, who will speak a few words to us at this time. As he is little known to you all, personally, I am all the more happy to present to you Rev. Cyrus F. Stimson.

(4) THE WEST END CHURCH.
REV. CYRUS F. STIMSON.

Rev. Mr. STIMSON: Rev. Doctor and Christian sisters and brethren of all denominations:—I am in the peculiar position at this moment of the proverbial gosling. The First Church we acknowledge as our common mother, and so I recognize in you all sister churches, but since I have not yet been ordained and installed I am not yet a bird of like feather. But, nevertheless, I have been long enough connected with the West End Church to have caught its spirit of devotion and loyalty to its mother, and of affection and reverence for that mother's able servant, *our* dear Dr. Palmer; and I therefore can speak for the West End Church, and, I believe, can give true though inadequate expression to its feeling. I could not write what I would speak in the name of our church, for I needed the flavor of the occasion to fill me; and as we have listened to one after another of the great men who have graced these days of celebration as they have made the past live again—I have been filled again and again with the martial spirit which has made kingly and loyal servants in all times for the service and advancement of the kingdom of our Lord Jesus Christ. Perhaps, therefore, the best thing I can do will not be to give the history of the little nursling which has developed so precociously into an awkward maid of somewhat uncertain promise, but who is now showing form and comeliness which warrants your support—the best thing from the West End church will not be the rehearsal of familiar history, but a pledge of our church's purpose and spirit for the future. She gives her warmest greetings to the First Church, to the Rev. Dr. Palmer and to all who are assembled here, as she unites to the fullest in their congratulation to our goodly mother church. For the future our West End Church desires to attest and illustrate its heroic blood. We tremble, as the Roman youths and maidens did of old, as we feel our ancestral dignity. We come from that Romulus and Remus seed of immortals, suckled by a wolf and cradled by hardship into heroic manhood.

Our mother is of divine lineage; her ancestral tree reaches Christ as its root. Hence we give you, Rev. Dr. Palmer, and all our friends, the pledge that we will give proof of the great blood that lives in us. We will not forget that our church rests where Indian corn fields were but a little time ago. We will emulate the noble Blatchford, whose aspirations and achievements have inspired us all. You remember the account of his toils by night to help the American prisoners, and how by perils and self-sacrifices he was filled with the zeal of a hero and came to the new world to sow that we might reap. Our ancestors, whether Englishmen, Scotchmen, Germans or Irishmen, were educated not in our public schools, but in the clan and tribal-meet, where ancestral songs were sung, where bard and minstrel heralded the deeds of the unforgotten dead. Thus the glowing memories of past greatness inflamed the zeal of our fathers to new works of heroism. So it has seemed to me that Dr. Palmer and the First Church and its friends have prepared a great folk-meet of the churches, that here we children might all be inspired by the celebration of the ancient works of our fathers, and add new lustre to their fame by our recognition of their worth. We gladly join in the songs of celebration, in the words of encomium, and wish our mother many days of jubilee to come.

Let us close with the promise that we of the West End Church will fight and work, toil and sacrifice, laying yonder the foundations of a church, asking for no nobler hope than that our church may prove a true daughter of its most noble mother. (Applause.)

Dr. PALMER. I am not going to try to define exactly our relations to the King's Highway Church. It is not necessary. The actual beginning of it was a movement by one member of this church to establish a mission school in the locality, but with our cordial approbation it was taken under the fostering care of the Park St. Church but the Park St. Church asked our help and we cheerfully gave it; and so it is a sort of joint child of the First Church, and its daughter, the Park St. Church. But it is a very dear church. It is the baby. We think extremely well of it; we had just got it started and built a house when some incendiary burned the house down. We rebuilt it quicker than it had been built before and it has nearly doubled its membership since its organization a year ago. It has a very promising future before it, we hope. We thought we would like to have a message from it this afternoon. We should like to hear a few words from its pastor, the Rev. Wilson R. Stewart.

(5) THE KING'S HIGHWAY CHURCH.

REV. WILSON R. STEWART.

Rev. Mr. STEWART: Dr. Palmer, members of the Mother Churches and all the Sister Churches, and others—

> "The baby, new to earth and sky,
> What times his tender palm is pressed;
> Against the circle of the breast
> Has never thought that this is I."

These words of the poet seem to me to express the feeling of the baby church. While she was nurtured by her mother she did not realize the greatness of her ancestry, did not realize the purity of the blood which coursed through her young veins. The story is told of two children who were taking an outing in one of the city parks with their nurse. A very elegantly-dressed woman passed them. The children turned around to the nurse and said, "Nurse, who is that lady?" and the nurse replied, "That is your mother, children."

Now this is not exactly *our* relation toward the mother church. We know our mother church, we realize all that she has done for us, but not until the last two days has the baby church realized her true position or fully realized the greatness of her mother, and the dignity that has surrounded this church from her earliest years. As Dr. Palmer has remarked, we can claim two mothers. The baby church is the offspring of the Park St. Congregational Church and also of the First Church; our territory being on the East side, the work naturally started under the care of the Park St. Congregational Church. I hardly feel that it is necessary for me to describe the history of our church, for in comparison with our mother we have no history worth mentioning.

As I sat here this afternoon and listened to the remarks that were made by our grandmothers, by the parent church and by our big sisters, I began to think what is there left for the little baby to say. We cannot look back over into the past and tell you of grand achievements. We cannot peer into the future, we know not what it will bring forth; and it seemed to me that our voice this afternoon would be that of

> "An infant crying in the night,
> An infant crying for the light;
> And with no language but a cry."

And yet I would have you understand that we are a very healthy child, and the cry we shall give you this afternoon shall be a most lusty one; there is nothing sick or puny in this baby. How could she be otherwise than a healthy baby with such royal, such blue blood coursing through her veins!

About five years ago a Sunday School was started on Old Mill Green. On the first Sunday there were present twenty children, gathered in the house of one of the members of this church. In five weeks from that first

Sunday the membership of that school numbered one hundred. In this way did the King's Highway Church start from the Sunday School. There was no thought when that Sabbath School was organized that it would soon become a church.

In 1893 through the help of the Park St. Church, and through the help of good Dr. Palmer of this church, a building was provided for that Sunday School; but as the doctor has told you, that building was destined to be of short duration. In less than a year it was burned to the ground.

I am reminded of a remark of the good doctor's, when the members of Old Mill Green assembled to see what could be done to furnish another building for this school. The doctor said, "Ashes make a good fertilizer," and they proved to be in this case. In three or four months from the time that building was burned to the ground there stood on the same spot another building, more complete than the first, furnished throughout. In one month from the dedication of this second building, which occurred on May 22, 1894, a church organization was completed. On June 28, 1894, fifty members organized the church now known as the King's Highway Church; thirty-four of those members, I believe, coming from the Park St. Congregational Church, and eight or ten of them coming from this church. While the number was not so large from this First Church, I assure you that the quality was most excellent. We have on our church roll the names of some of the descendants of the founders of this First Church, illustrious names in the early history of the city of Bridgeport. We are proud of them, we are proud of them because they are active, because their souls and their hearts are in the work on Old Mill Green.

Good Brother Fullerton, a few moments ago, styled us highwaymen; we shall permit you to look upon us as highwaymen, if you consider the name in the right sense. You know highwaymen are those who go out and get others sometimes to join their band. This is what the highwaymen of Old Mill Green are doing. They are going out into the highways and hedges; they are beseeching others to come in and join their band, to become highwaymen in the sense that they are followers, soldiers of Jesus Christ, and are willing to do all in their power for the furtherance of His Kingdom.

I bring you then this afternoon the congratulations of the baby church—the King's Highway Church. I, too, stand under the peculiar relation to our good Dr. Palmer. Only four months ago was I ordained to the Christian ministry. On that occasion, the most important in my life, it was the good Dr. Palmer who laid his hands upon my head and consecrated me to the Master's service. I shall never forget that occasion. I shall never forget the prayer uttered by the good doctor on that occasion.

I said a few moments ago we had no history to speak of; but when I sat here yesterday and to-day and listened to the grand history of this old church, I thought, on the one hand, that there was very little for me to say for the infant church; and yet, on the other hand, I was impressed with the fact that with God there is no such thing as time, and all through the exercises of the last two days, in the history of the mother church and in the greetings of the grandmother churches, there seemed to be one glad refrain, one message of cheer and hope to the young churches. It was this:

> "Grow old along with me!
> The best is yet to be
>   The last of life for which the first was made;
> Our times are in His hands
> Who saith a whole I planned,
> Youth shows but half;
>   Trust God; see all, nor be afraid."

You know it is considered very often an honor to be considered the baby in the family, for the very reason the baby receives more caresses than any other member of the family. It is nurtured with the most tender care. We are proud this afternoon to be considered the baby church and yet we shall be willing to give up this coveted position as the baby church for the sake of the growth of the Kingdom of God. We doubt not but in a very short time there will spring forth another new church which shall be known as the "baby," and we shall gladly make way for all the little strangers that shall come in time.

Again I extend congratulations to our mother church on this joyous occasion. (Loud applause.)

Dr. PALMER: It is proposed to close these services by singing the 854th hymn, "Happy the souls to Jesus joined."

Before we sing I wish to say that I am very thankful to all of these good brethren for what they have brought here, their loving words and best wishes. I am very thankful to all who have taken part in this joyous commemoration, and when the commemoration is over new service is the next thing to think of. We will address ourselves to the work in the future of this good city of ours—hoping that when another century has passed away there may be fresh rejoicings over the progress of the kingdom; and that those who have been here so deeply interested at this time may be succeeded by their children and their children's children in the rejoicing of that joyous occasion. (Long-continued applause.)

SINGING.

"Happy the souls to Jesus joined."

BENEDICTION.

✣

SERVICES OF SUNDAY, THE 16TH.

On the Sunday following the anniversary, the 16th of June, the Bi-Centennial decorations still in place, and the spirit of the great occasion unabated, commemorative services were continued. In the forenoon Dr. Palmer took up the dropped thread of his historical discourse, and in the afternoon, following out the suggestion of Dr. Russell, there was a great gathering of Sunday-school children, which filled the church. The latter occasion was very enjoyable, the children's singing and the ministers' familiar addresses filling an hour and a half very agreeably. The schools of the First Church, the Second Church and the Presbyterian Church came in a body. Other schools were numerously represented. And thus the bi-centennial celebration was fitly concluded.

The second part of Dr. Palmer's historical discourse treated of the First Church after the division in 1830. Announcing the same text which he used on the 12th, he proceeded as follows:

The withdrawal of so large a proportion of the First Church was to those who remained a matter of sincere regret. But they by no means lost heart. They were about one hundred and seventy in number, and on January 31, 1830, with entire unanimity renewed the call to Rev. John Blatchford, then of Stillwater, N. Y., and he promptly accepted it. He was born here, May 24, 1799, during his father's pastorate, but was removed before he was five years old with the rest of the family to Lansingburg, where his boyhood was spent. He graduated at Union College in 1820, and studied theology in Princeton Theological Seminary. He was ordained pastor of the Presbyterian Church in Pittstown, N. Y., in August, 1823; and in April, 1825, he was installed over the Presbyterian Church in Stillwater. He was installed here February 10, 1830, and continued until July 26, 1836, when he was dismissed at his own request, the health of his wife obliging him to change his residence. She was born May 12, 1805, the daughter of Eliphalet and Martha (Herriman) Wickes, of Jamaica, N. Y. His home here was on Golden Hill street, on the north side near its present intersection with Harrison street. He removed to the west, and resided successively at Jacksonville, where he was Acting-President of Illinois College, and Chicago, where he was pastor of the First Presbyterian Church, and at Wheeling, Va. From 1841 to 1844 he was connected with Marion College, in Missouri, the latter part of the period as President. Thence he removed to West Ely, Mo., and thence in 1847 to Quincy, Ill., where he died in April,

1858. He received from Marion College, in 1841, the degree of D.D.

Mr. Blatchford was a man of medium stature, in figure well-proportioned, cheerful in his habit, of a genial spirit, and of frank and pleasing manners. His appearance was attractive, and he was an acceptable preacher. He had a bright and ready mind, a somewhat effusive style, spoke in a sympathetic and winning way, and with a good deal of unction. He was a particularly effective preacher in revival seasons. He came from beyond the limits of New England, and did not enter into Connecticut controversies, yet his sympathies were decidedly with the more advanced party. The church quickly felt his influence, and before much above a year had elapsed nearly as many as had withdrawn were added to its numbers, and its strength was restored. He took an active part himself, and was skillful in enlisting others, in all kinds of Christian work, and was heartily in sympathy with missionary operations. He organized here a Young Men's Temperance Society, into which were gathered nearly all the choice youth of the town. A copy of the constitution is still extant with nearly two hundred and twenty-five names annexed, of whom some are here to-day. It was an interesting and a sanguine time, and he was in touch with it. A great advance in religion during the half-century since the Revolution was recognized, and there were happy auguries of coming progress. His removal was greatly regretted. The church in parting with him testified strongly to his faithful, acceptable, and successful performance of his ministerial duties.

There succeeded to him a man of a very different type. The Rev. John Woodbridge was the son of Sylvester and Mindwell (Lyman) Woodbridge, and was born in Southampton, Mass., December 2, 1784. He was of Puritan descent, and himself a Puritan of the Puritans. He reckoned among his ancestors not only some eminent divines, but Governor Dudley, and the apostle Eliot. He fitted for college at Westfield and Deerfield Academies. He graduated at Williams in 1804. He studied theology at

Goshen, Conn., with Rev. Asahel Hooker, and was licensed to preach at Sharon, June, 1807. Soon after he was called to Woodbridge, Conn., but declined the overture. He then labored for some months in the Black River country, in New York, as a missionary. Later he was called to a church in Philadelphia, but did not accept. Toward the end of 1809 he began to preach in Hadley, Mass. Here he was ordained June 20, 1810, and fulfilled a long and honorable pastorate. He married May 4, 1814, Mary Ann, daughter of Major Thomas Seymour, and his second wife, Susan Bull. She was born June 16, 1789, and died in Hadley January 16, 1858. In 1825 he received from his Alma Mater the degree of D.D. Early in 1830 he was called to Bowery Church in New York City, and declined. Later the call was renewed and accepted. He was dismissed from Hadley, September 15, 1830, and installed in New York October 1. In 1836 he was dismissed from the Bowery Church, and a new enterprise was commenced by his friends in the Chapel of New York University, but the financial crisis of 1837 led to the relinquishment of the enterprise, and he accepted a call to Bridgeport. He was installed here June 14, 1837, and continued some seventeen months. He was dismissed November 20, 1838. In the following April he was installed over the North Church in New Hartford, where he remained until January, 1842. Thence he returned to Hadley, where he was installed February 16 over a part of his former church, organized as a new one. Here he remained until the autumn of 1861, when he went to Chicago to reside. He died September 26, 1869, in Waukegan, Ill., at the age of eighty-five years.

Dr. Woodbridge was beyond question a man of very unusual powers—of a vigorous mind, a strong will, of warm affections. His personal presence was commanding, his courage unquestioned, his integrity recognized. He was of scholarly habits, and considerable learning. He was an aggressive and stalwart controversialist in the realm of theology. In the position here, he was doubtless a misfit. He came here from a Presbyterian pastorate in the year in which the Presbyterian Church was divided. His sympathies had been with the Old School party. He was extremely staunch in his conviction that the theological views which he had received were the very substance of the Gospel. He encountered here very strong prejudices against the views he held, and was conscientiously the more strenuous in urging his opinions because aware of their unpopularity. The contrast of his sentiments and of his manner with those of his predecessor operated unfavorably for him. His biographer describes his pastorate here as "indeed stormy, but happily for him short." He had warm friends, and hearty admirers, but there was a general acquiescence in his resignation. He retired, not without honor, from a conflict he could not maintain

He was succeeded by Rev. John H. Hunter in about three months. Mr. Hunter was born in New York City, in March, 1807. He graduated at Union College in 1825, and studied theology at Princeton Seminary. He was ordained over the church in Fairfield, December 17, 1828, and continued until January 15, 1834. He was installed pastor of the North Church in West Springfield August 24, 1835, and dismissed thence February 16, 1837. He was installed here February 27, 1839, and continued until November 13, 1845. Mrs. Hunter was Julia Maria, daughter of Daniel and Sarah (Plant) Judson, of Stratford. She was born July 11, 1811. Both were favorably known here at their coming, and the church increased under his ministry. In 1844 some twenty-five were added at one time. He was a brilliant, but eccentric man; a man of genius, but of that type of genius which is often erratic, and which, in its decadence, sometimes approaches the borderland adjacent to insanity. He was of medium stature, of good appearance, but had a way of carrying his chin low, and far forward, so as to give his shoulders the look of one who stooped. From this position of the head, he looked over his glasses with a penetrating eye, in a way to be very definitely recollected. He was not eminently a student; was fond of out-door life, of walking excursions, and especially of fishing. He spoke with a tone strongly nasal, from the presence of a polyp in his nostril. He had a grotesque humor about him, which sometimes appeared in his religious services, and always made him an agreeable companion. His style was singularly unstudied and pure. Without apparent effort, in speaking or in composition, he seemed to abound in matter. His thoughts were for the most part pertinent and often valuable, but there was a constant scintillation of sharp, or fanciful, or striking suggestions, which was a kind of by-play of his mind. This excited and fastened attention, while it somewhat detracted from the directness of discourse. Sometimes, in this sidewise fashion, he would hit or thrust rather hard. His theological opinions conformed to the prevailing orthodoxy, but he was not much given to expounding them. He aimed rather to give men impulses in the direction of the practical life than to quicken their thinking, and he seemed less careful to hold up to men the highest moral ideals, than to set before them a reasonably high and yet manifestly practicable morality. The action upon his resignation was accompanied by considerable excitement. A financial difference between him and the Society occasioned not a little heated feeling. But he left strong friends, and an impression of himself in the life and the traditions of the church which only a man of very decided character could have created. After leaving here he went west to look after some lands which his father had acquired, and was not again settled in the ministry. He spent the remainder of his days in a somewhat wandering life in the west and southwest, preaching, teaching, trading in land—miscellaneously employed. He died in Texas, February 22, 1872.

His successor was the Rev. Benjamin St. John Page. He was born in Northford, July 18, 1815. He graduated at Western Reserve College in 1834, and studied theology in Yale Divinity School. He was ordained by the Grand River Presbytery, at Painesville, Ohio, February 10, 1839. His wife was Emily Benjamin, daughter of Samuel and Charlotte A. (De Witt) Maltby. At the date of his ordination he was supplying the church in Chester, Ohio. In

1840 he came to New Haven and spent a year in study. He returned to his father's home in Euclid, Ohio, and for some years was unable to assume a permanent charge on account of invalid health, but served temporarily several churches acceptably. He came here from Euclid. He was installed February 10, 1847, and continued until August 30, 1853. After leaving here he was located as stated supply, in Durham three years, in North Haven six years, in Durham again two years. Subsequently he resided at Winsted, without charge, a year or more; then two years or less in Milwaukee, Wis., and then he became stated supply of a Presbyterian church in Warren, O., where he died November 9, 1868.

He was a plain, somewhat angular and ungraceful man in appearance, but by no means without abilities. He would not be thought remarkable for refinement of mind or manner, but was industrious and studious, and labored hard to meet the demands made upon him by his charge. Many of his sermons were unusually well written, close, vigorous, and well-applied; full of earnest, fresh, and even powerful thinking, in well-chosen speech. But his average of performance was hardly of this high character. His preaching was not always acceptable in matter or style, and sometimes went aside from what good taste requires, in pursuit of originality. He was very much indebted as a man and as a pastor to an eminently judicious and helpful wife, who was much esteemed in all relations, and whose influence over him was most happy. He had very little to do with the churches around, with the churches at large, or with enterprises of beneficence, but kept himself very much within his own field of labor. He was in many respects a fairly capable man, but could not easily adapt himself to circumstances or to others' tastes, and hence failed somewhat in the delicate relations of a pastor. His soundness of character and general fidelity to his convictions were undoubted.

In the course of his pastorate the present house of worship was erected. It was built by subscription, and the paper bears date June 1, 1848. The previous house on

THE FOURTH EDIFICE.

this site was removed a short distance northward, and occupied while the new one was building. It was used for the last time April 7, 1850. It was sold for the use of Christ Church, and removed to a site on John st. west of Broad, where it was accidentally destroyed by fire in 1851. The new edifice was dedicated on Thursday, April 11, 1850, and opened on the following Sabbath. Messrs. Freeman C. Bassett, Ira Sherman, Hanford Lyon, and Sherman Hartwell were the building committee, and Mr. Thomas Dixon of Stamford was the architect.

It was nearly ten months after Mr. Page's dismission before his place was filled. His successor was the Rev. Joseph Hardy Towne. He was born in Salem, Mass., May 27, 1805. He was the son of Solomon and Lydia (Goodale) Towne. He was fitted for college at the Salem Latin School. He graduated at Yale in 1827, where he was the class-mate of Dr. William Adams and of Dr. Horace Bushnell. Soon after his graduation he entered the law office of Messrs. Pickering & Otis, in Boston, whither his parents had removed. He remained in this office three years, with the intention of following the legal profession. His purpose was changed, however, and he commenced the study of theology, residing with his parents and pursuing his studies under the direction of his pastor. He was licensed to preach by the Suffolk South Association, September 6, 1831. He preached for a while at Fitchburg, but declined to settle there. Later he was called to the Pleasant St. Church in Portsmouth, N. H. This call he accepted, and he was ordained there June 13, 1832. Just previous to this event, May 1, 1832, he married Eliza J., daughter of Caleb and Eliza (Childs) Wiley, of Lynn, Mass. She was born December 11, 1815, and continued the beloved companion of his life until September 18, 1894.

It was the testimony of one of his contemporaries whom I knew well, that the young pastor excited large expectations of his future usefulness, and was everywhere most favorably received. In the autumn of 1836 he was called to Salem Street Church in Boston, to succeed the Rev. Dr.

Blagden, and he was there installed June 2, 1837. He continued in this relation until December 27, 1843, when he was dismissed at his own request. A new enterprise was set on foot in Boston known as the Leyden Chapel, in which a new departure was taken in the order of worship. Here a church was organized February 7, 1844, and he was installed pastor just three weeks later (February 28). The new church seemed a promising movement, but failed to fulfil the expectations of its promoters, and was disbanded in July, 1847. He was called thence to High Street Church in Lowell, where he was installed December 15, 1847. There he continued until May 22, 1854, when he was dismissed to accept a call to this church. He was installed June 14, 1854. His home was at 232 Main street.

His reception here can be best described in his own words,* written after fifty years. "After my installation I found myself the pastor of a united, affectionate and generous people. The years of my pastorate in Bridgeport are a sunny spot in the landscape of my ministerial life. I was then in the vigor of my days; all my children were growing up around me, for death had not then invaded the happy circle; my wife, in the full bloom of her womanhood, gladdened my home with the sunshine of her presence and love. My parish was one great family. A wide and most inviting field of usefulness was open before me." Under such happy auspices commenced a ministry still pleasantly remembered here.

The most noteworthy event of it perhaps was the deep religious interest in the winter of 1857-8, in which the church was greatly blessed, and received large accessions. Thirty-eight were added at one time, seventy-four during the year. His preaching was extremely acceptable to his people. He acquired in college the reputation of a graceful and effective writer. His study of the law lent to his earlier style an increase of vigor, and the habit of constructive reasoning. During his residence in Boston he added to his general culture. He had also engaged in literary labors there, jointly with Dr. Parsons Cooke. He

* MS. Letter.

was conservative in his theological views and sympathies, but never a controversialist. He had a rich vein of sentiment, and not a little of poetic feeling. One of his discriminating hearers left on record the testimony that "many of his discourses were rewritten, and worthy of any pulpit in the land." He was specially gifted in prayer, and endeared himself as a sympathizing pastor. He resigned his charge after four years and was dismissed June 29, 1848. On October 28th of the same year he was installed pastor of St. Peter's (Presbyterian) Church in Rochester, N. Y., and continued there until March 9, 1860. In 1859 he received the degree of D.D., from Marietta College. From June 1, 1860, to October 1, 1861, he was stated supply of the Westminster Presbyterian Church in Buffalo. Thence he was called to the First Presbyterian Church in Milwaukee, Wis., which he served for four years. After this he rendered occasional services, but was not again a pastor. By a regretable misfortune his voice became impaired, and finally the disability became permanent. After leaving the west he gave himself to other pursuits, and for many years has resided in Andover, Mass., spending tranquilly the afternoon of life.

After six months' interval he was succeeded by Rev. Matson Meier-Smith. This gentleman was born at Harlem, N. Y., April 4, 1826. On his father's side he was of Connecticut descent, and had in his veins the best of Puritan blood. The founder of the Mather family was one of his ancestors. On his mother's side he was of purely German extraction. He was the son of Dr. Albert Smith and Emily Maria, daughter of Casper Meier, a native of Bremen. He graduated at Columbia College in 1843, and studied theology in Union Theological Seminary, with the class of 1847. He was ordained by the Presbytery of Geneva, October 23, 1849, pastor of the church in Ovid, N. Y. In the same year, November 14, he married Mary Stuart, daughter of Norman White, Esq., of New York City. He resigned his charge in September, 1850, on account of apprehensions concerning his health. In the spring of 1851 he was called to Brookline, Mass., where he was installed June 5, succeeding Rev. Dr. R. S. Storrs. This pastorate he fulfilled until November 23, 1858, when he resigned to accept a call to this church. He was installed here January 5, 1859. He was dismissed June 6, 1865, and at once entered the Episcopal Church. March 6, 1866, he was ordained deacon, and April 20, priest, by Bishop Eastburn of Massachusetts. May 6 he became rector of Trinity Parish in Newark, N. J., and continued there until April 16, 1871. During the year following he travelled in Europe. December 1, 1872, he became rector of St. John's Parish in Hartford, and continued until May 1, 1876, when he resigned to accept the Professorship of Homiletics in the Divinity School in Philadelphia. In this chair he continued until his decease, March 26, 1887. He received from Williams College, in 1856, the degree of M.A., and from Columbia College, in 1863, the degree of D.D.

Mr. Meier-Smith's home here was at 276 Washington avenue. He came hither in response to urgent solicitations and with the hope of large usefulness. But he was early made conscious of an element of opposition, which proved a serious annoyance, all the more that the expressions of it were somewhat petty, and persistent to a degree that was unusual. The intense political excitements preceding and accompanying the outbreak of the Civil war added to his discomforts, his patriotic sympathies leading him to the utterance, in a manly and outspoken way, of sentiments not welcome to all his parishioners, and most unwelcome to some elements in the community. It is evident from what his biographer records that while he had warm friends, and for the most part a loyal support from the church, he felt his position here to be something less than comfortable. His experience brought to its consummation a process which began at a much earlier date. He wrote to me some years later in the following words:* "If you refer at all to my defection, it may be as well for you to know that it was no sudden movement, but the result of some ten years of earnest thought and painful perplexity. The real reason why I gave up my pastorate when I did was that I might

* MS. Letter.

enter the church of my convictions." Of course such an event could not take place without exciting much feeling, and much comment, but the church he left took as kindly a view of his conduct as could reasonably be expected. His ministry here was blessed to the church; he received one hundred and seventy-six to its membership, and won the friendship of many who tenderly cherish his memory. He left behind him here the reputation of excellent abilities and an amiable character. His discourses were thoughtful and well-reasoned. His subjects were well-chosen. While his German extraction appeared somewhat in his looks, his manner, and his habits of mind, and he often indulged in sentences of unusual length, no one complained of obscurity in his style, and he was regarded as an instructive and interesting preacher. He was remarkable for his earnest and reverent prayers, and made himself much beloved in his work as a pastor. It was certainly from no want of facility in the devotional exercises of the pulpit that he chose to make the transition from the Congregational to the Episcopal ministry. During his pastorate, and largely through his efforts, and personal sacrifices, the existing Chapel building was reared, and it was first used at Christmas, 1860.

Before the end of the year in which he was dismissed, the thoughts of the church had been directed to another minister. Rev. George Richards was born in New London, November 2, 1816. He was the son of Peter and Ann C. (Huntington) Richards. He graduated at Yale in the class of 1840. After teaching for a time he entered Andover Theological Seminary. In 1843 he became a student in the Divinity School at Yale, and in 1844 a tutor in Yale College. He was ordained October 8, 1845, as associate pastor of the Central Congregational Church in Boston, Mass., the colleague of Rev. Dr. W. M. Rogers. In 1851, by the death of the latter, he became sole pastor, and continued in that relation until April 20, 1859. After a foreign tour he became acting pastor of the church in Litchfield, Conn., commencing in December, 1860. He closed this engagement after five years, to accept a call to this church, and was installed January 3, 1866. In

1868 he was elected a member of the Corporation of Yale College. He was dismissed from his pastorate August 24, 1870, and died October 20, in the same year. His wife was Anna M. Woodruff, to whom he was married in Philadelphia, September 29, 1846. Mr. Richards was a man of refinement and excellent scholarship. He cultivated while in college facility in extemporaneous speaking. During his tutorship he enjoyed among the students the sobriquet of "the Mouth of the Faculty." He always spoke easily and felicitously. He was in appearance slight, neither tall nor stout. He was extremely neat, almost to the point of fastidiousness, in his person and apparel. He was somewhat precise also in his manner. But he was highly gifted as a preacher, and a lover of his work. The style of his written discourses was faultless, remarkable for lucidity, elegance and grace. Nor were they wanting in force of argument or urgency of appeal. His extemporaneous discourses were equally acceptable in their way. In his weekly lectures he never used notes. He had a firmness of voice which, without apparent effort on his part, carried every syllable to his remotest hearer. His ministry began with the most favorable auspices, and was increasingly acceptable for two or three years. But to the sorrow of all who loved him, he became the victim of a disease of the cerebellum, occasioning loss of vision, and impairment of faculty, which resulted in increasing disability and distress, and finally in his death. Moreover, after the impairment began, but before it was understood, certain actions of his occasioned comment, mistrust, and in some instances accusation. Not altogether unnaturally, perhaps, his character was called in question. But as time went on, and his true condition became apparent, the opinion prevailed that the actions alluded to were indications not of pravity but of disease; and that the record of a life of exceptional purity and honor should not be overborne by the incidents of a period of physical disaster. This was the mature conclusion of the majority of the church. Having myself collected testimonies of medical experts and impartial observers—among others that of the venerated head of

Yale College, Dr. Woolsey—I came to the same conclusion; and, without reflecting in the slightest upon the excellent men who at the time judged differently, I feel constrained to record my deliberate judgment that the memory of Mr. Richards should be regarded as without a stain.

Since his dismission twenty-five years have passed. Two full years intervened before a successor was installed, and that successor was the present incumbent. Of him, of course, nothing is to be said. Of the period much might be written, did the occasion permit. Many recollections crowd upon me to which I dare not attempt to give utterance. A great company of faces come up before me whom I shall see no more on earth. I found here a congregation imposing in its appearance and interesting in its manifest intelligence and seriousness of purpose. I remember counting at one time over thirty liberally educated men among the stated attendants. Among them were many of the foremost citizens of the town. But they were largely of a generation that was beginning to pass away, and the fact that so many of those who welcomed me I have myself outlived casts a shadow over the retrospect of my ministry. Moreover, of the younger generation, which has succeeded, a surprisingly large proportion has found homes and opportunities of living elsewhere, and I think readily of a multitude of such as would naturally have filled the vacated places, scattered far and wide over many states, and even to the far west borders of the nation. None the less is there remaining here a goodly number of Christian men and women, young men and maidens, youth and children, easily keeping alive a pastor's hopes and sympathies, and most encouraging to his devout endeavors. Toward them one and all I cherish feelings which I cannot express and they cannot fathom. It is with undiminished affection for this ancient church that I have come to this anniversary. I rejoice that it has been so fitly celebrated. May other centuries be added to the honorable and fruitful history which we have commemorated—and the blessing of Almighty God rest upon it to the remotest generation!

HISTORIC SITES.

✢

1. SITE OF FIRST RESIDENCE. — Henry Summers. N. E. corner Park Ave. and Washington Ave.

2. SITE OF FIRST MEETING HOUSE. 1695. — Meeting House Hill, Park Ave.

3. SITE OF EARLY SCHOOL HOUSE. — West side of Park Ave. near North Ave.

4. SITE OF SECOND MEETING HOUSE. 1717. — N. W. corner Park Ave. and North Ave.

5. SITE OF FIRST ST. JOHN P. E. CHURCH. — N. W. corner North Ave. and Wood Ave.

6. SITE OF RESIDENCE OF REV. ROBERT ROSS. THIRD PASTOR STRATFIELD. — On "The Place," at the present N. E. corner of North Ave. and Laurel Ave.

7. THE STRATFIELD "TRAINING GROUND" AND ENTRANCE TO STRATFIELD BURIAL GROUND. — N. W. corner North Ave. and Clinton Ave.

8. NICHOLS TAVERN, OF THE TIME OF THE REVOLUTION, WHERE WASHINGTON WAS ENTERTAINED. — No. 910 North Ave.

9. FRANKLIN MILE STONE. 20 MILES TO N. H. — Opposite Nichols Tavern.

10. SITE OF RESIDENCE OF REV. CHARLES CHAUNCEY. FIRST PASTOR STRATFIELD. — Grove St. near Fairfield Ave.

11. SITE OF RESIDENCE OF REV. SAMUEL COOKE. SECOND PASTOR STRATFIELD. — Junction Grove St. and Laurel Ave.

12. SITE OF RESIDENCE OF MATTHEW SHERMAN, D. 1698, AND LAST RESIDENCE OF SAMUEL SHERMAN, SEN., D. APR. 5, 1700. — Park Ave., next lot north of the Second Meeting House.

13. SITE OF RESIDENCE OF DEACON DAVID SHERMAN. — Park Ave. extension—on the top of Toilsome Hill.

14. SITE OF RESIDENCE OF COLONEL JOHN BURR AND THE HISTORIC OAK. — 591 Fairfield Ave. (west of Hancock Ave.)

15. SITE OF RESIDENCE OF RICHARD HUBBELL, SEN. — S. E. corner Clinton Ave. and Maplewood Ave.

EXTRACTS FROM LETTERS.

[Hon. John Sherman, U. S. S.]

SENATE CHAMBER,
WASHINGTON, May 16, 1895.

MR. CHARLES SHERWOOD.

My Dear Sir:—I have received a very kind note from Rev. Dr. Charles Ray Palmer inviting me to join in your celebration of the two-hundredth anniversary of the organization of the Church of Christ in Stratfield. It would give me great pleasure to accept, but engagements have already been made which will prevent me from doing so. * * *

Very truly yours,
JOHN SHERMAN.

(A descendant of Samuel Sherman, Sr., who was the father of Deacon David, and of Matthew Sherman.)

[Hon. Chauncey M. Depew, LL.D.]

NEW YORK CENTRAL & HUDSON RIVER RAILROAD CO.
Grand Central Depot.
NEW YORK, May 21, 1895.

Dear Dr. Palmer:—I am in receipt of your very kind letter of May 14th. I am connected with the Chauncey family, and therefore the more regret that it will be impossible for me to be with you on the 13th of June.

Very truly yours,
CHAUNCEY M. DEPEW.

(A descendant of Rev. Charles Chauncey, through his mother's family.)

[Hon. John W. Sterling, LL.D.]

44 Wall St., NEW YORK, May 28, 1895.

Dear Sir:—Yours of the 27th instant is at hand.

I thank you very much for the invitation you have extended to me to respond for my family to some commemorative mention upon the occasion of the two-hundredth anniversary of the organization of the Church of Christ in Stratfield, on the 12th and 13th of June next; but regret that I shall not be able to attend on that memorable occasion.

Hoping that everything may pass off as successfully as you could wish, I am
Yours truly,
JOHN W. STERLING.

Rev. Charles Ray Palmer, Bridgeport, Conn.

(A descendant of Jacob Sterling.)

[Rev. J. Hardy Towne, D.D.]

ANDOVER, MASS., May 27th, 1895.

REV. C. R. PALMER, D.D.

My Dear Brother.—The cordial and very generous invitation which you and friends in Bridgeport extend to me and my daughter, to be present with you at the bi-centennial, deeply affects me. Nothing would be more gratifying to my feelings than to comply with your request. I can never forget Bridgeport, and the dear old North. I can never forget the happy years of my pastorate there. They remain, and ever will remain, a verdant and fragrant memory in the landscape of the past. But circumstances over which I have no control compel me to forgo the pleasure to which you welcome me. I am now an old man, a very old man. This very day is my ninetieth birthday! My hand in writing trembles with the infirmity of age. I have hardly crossed my door-step for several months. The journey would be too much for me; and even if I could reach Bridgeport, the excitement of the occasion, and the tender reminiscences that would be ever in my thoughts, would be a strain which, in my present feeble state, it would be imprudent for me to venture. I shall often think of you, and wish I could be with you. That you may have a rich blessing from the great Head of the Church, and that the union of two sister churches in the religious festivities to which you are looking forward with common interest, may knit you together in still closer fellowship and love, is the prayer of one who must ever rejoice in your prosperity.

I shall look for the report of your meetings with peculiar interest.

May our good Lord, my dear brother, spare your useful life many years.

Affectionately,

JOSEPH H. TOWNE.

[Rev. George L. Walker, D.D.]

46 PROSPECT STREET.
HARTFORD, CONN., June 8, 1895.

MY DEAR DR. PALMER.

I am very sorry that an unavoidable engagement at Andover prevents my attendance on the interesting exercises which are promised at your Church anniversary. You have a most interesting theme: your church has had a distinguished ministry, and the opportunity of telling its story is one which I have no doubt you rejoice in and will magnify.

I wish I could hear your address and the others which will be spoken, and only deny myself this privilege under sheer necessity.

Very truly yours,

GEO. LEON WALKER.

[Prof. Henry A. Rowland, LL.D., Johns Hopkins University.]

915 CATHEDRAL STREET,
BALTIMORE, June 2, 1895.

REV. CHARLES RAY PALMER.

Dear Sir:—I thank you most cordially for the kind invitation to be present at the two-hundredth anniversary of the First Church of Bridgeport.

My engagements, however, will prevent me from accepting it, although nothing would give me greater pleasure than to do so.

I would especially like to meet my relative, Rowland B. Lacey, Esq., to whom I wish to be remembered.

Yours sincerely,

HENRY A. ROWLAND.

(A descendant of Deacon Henry Rowland.)

[Rev. Horace C. Hovey, D.D.]

NEWBURYPORT, MASS., June 5, 1895.

MESSRS. DR. C. R. PALMER, CHAS. SHERWOOD, AND OTHERS, COMMITTEE OF INVITATION, BRIDGEPORT, CONN.

Dear Brethren :—On returning from Pittsburgh, last week, I was greatly pleased to find your invitation to attend the two-hundredth anniversary of the First Church and Society of Bridgeport.

I have delayed answering, hoping to be able to answer affirmatively; but my circumstances will not permit me to do so.

I trust you and your church, and the churches co-operating, may have a delightful occasion; and that the signal blessings of the past may be prophetic of larger blessings yet to come.

May grace, mercy, and peace abide with you. Amen.

Fraternally yours,

HORACE C. HOVEY.

[Rev. Charles H. Peck.]

N. BENNINGTON, VT., May 24, 1895.

MY DEAR MR. SHERWOOD.

I am pleased to be remembered by the invitation to the coming celebration in North Church.

I regret it will be quite impossible to attend.

May the occasion be a most happy one to all concerned.

Very truly yours,

CHARLES H. PECK.

[Rev. Alfred T. Waterman.]

BALDWIN, MICH., May 24, 1895.

MR. CHARLES SHERWOOD, BRIDGEPORT, CONN.

My Dear Sir :—Your kind invitation to attend the two-hundredth anniversary of the organization of the Church of Christ in Stratfield, is duly at hand and greatly appreciated.

I regret to say that it does not appear practicable to allow myself the pleasure of being present on that occasion.

Cordially yours,

A. T. WATERMAN.

(A grandson of Rev. Elijah Waterman.)

[Mr. David Sherman Lacey.]

CORONADO BEACH, CALIF., May 22, 1895.

GENTLEMEN OF THE COMMITTEE.

Dear Sirs :—Your cordial invitation to be present at celebration is at hand.

It gives me great pleasure and satisfaction to receive it, and it is with deep regret that I must say, that circumstances will not allow me to be with you on the occasion.

The fac-simile of tankard and cups from the old communion service, which heads your invitation, is wonderfully familiar to my eyes, they being among the earliest recollections of my boyhood.

The old North Church is still very dear to me—and I trust and pray that it may have a wonderful blessing in the future.

Very sincerely yours,

DAVID SHERMAN LACEY.

(A descendant of Dea. David Sherman, and also of Matthew Sherman.)

[Miss Julia E. Hunter.]

No. 62 WEST 93D STREET.
NEW YORK, June 7, 1895.

R. B. LACEY, ESQ., BRIDGEPORT, CONN.

Dear Sir :—Please accept my thanks for the cordial invitation from the committee and yourself to attend the two-hundredth anniversary of the First Church and Society in Bridgeport, and my regrets that I cannot be present.

My mother, now eighty-four years old, desires to send greetings.

Yours very truly,

JULIA E. HUNTER.

(Daughter of Rev. John H. Hunter.)

[Rev. J. J. Wooley.]

PAWTUCKET, R. I., June 3, 1895.

MY DEAR MR. LACEY.

I regret that an engagement here, or in Providence, will prevent my coming to Bridgeport to attend the "two-hundred anniversary" of the church organized in Stratfield, June 13, 1695. It will be an event of unusual interest, and I am sorry to be so situated as to be denied the privilege of attending the celebration. With many thanks for your invitation and kind regards, I am

Very truly yours,

J. J. WOOLEY.

(Descendant of Stephen Burroughs.)

[Mrs. Mary D. Wilcox.]

DICKINSON HOUSE, LAWRENCEVILLE SCHOOL,
LAWRENCEVILLE, N. J., May 20, 1895.

MR. ROWLAND B. LACEY.

Dear Friend :—The invitation to attend the two-hundredth anniversary of the First Church of Bridgeport came to me to-day.

I wish to thank you for so kindly remembering us.

As a descendant of one of the first deacons, it would give me much pleasure to be present at the exercises, but I fear that at that time it will not be possible for me to leave home. * * *

I remain yours very sincerely,

MARY DUDLEY WILLCOX.

(Descendant of Dea. David Sherman, and Dea. Henry Rowland.)

[Mr. Joseph D. Bartley.]

BRADFORD, MASS., June 10, 1895.

MY DEAR DR. PALMER.

We thank you for the invitation to be present at the celebration of the "two-hundredth anniversary" of your church. It is pleasant to be remembered, though our names no longer stand on your roll, and I need not say it would give us the greatest pleasure, if it were possible, to join in the exercises of the occasion.

The ten years of our connection with the dear old church are fraught with precious and tender memories. * * *

You know we loved the church service, the Sabbath School, the Christian Endeavor Society, and the "mid-week meeting" in that upper room of hallowed associations ; and that our tender experiences connected with your own dear family bring loving and sympathetic tears as I write. May the record of the noble church and people be an inspiration to still greater results in the future, to the kingdom of our dear common Lord.

Though absent in body, we shall be with you in thought and spirit, on next Wednesday and Thursday.

In behalf of my family and myself,

I am yours most cordially,

JOSEPH DANA BARTLEY.

[Rev. Albert F. Pierce.]

DANBURY, CONN., June 11, 1895.

DEAR DR. PALMER.

I would greatly enjoy being present at the exercises to-morrow and Thursday commemorating the two-hundredth anniversary of the First Church, but absence from the state prevents. I hereby send most cordial greeting to the church, congratulating it upon its history of fruitfulness and good works, and praying for it an even more glorious future. Please accept for yourself my personal felicitations, together with the wish that you may long be spared to your church, and to your hosts of friends in all parts of the state.

With sincere and hearty congratulations and best wishes, I remain

Most truly yours,

ALBERT F. PIERCE.

[Prof. Arthur M. Wheeler.]

NEW HAVEN, June 11, 1895.

CHARLES SHERWOOD, ESQ., BRIDGEPORT, CONN.

My Dear Sir:—Please accept for yourself and your committee my cordial thanks for you kind invitation. Until to-day I thought it might be possible for me to come; but I find now that I cannot get away.

Sincerely yours,
A. M. WHEELER.

[Mr. Walter Hubbell.]

NEW YORK, June 11, 1895.

PASTOR OF THE FIRST CONGREGATIONAL CHURCH, BRIDGEPORT, CONN.

Dear Sir:—* * It is with regret that I must say I cannot be present on June 12th and 13th at your two-hundredth anniversary.

* * * I am descended from Richard Hubbell, Sr., and his son Richard Hubbell, Jr., both of whose names are among those of the nine original members, the founders.

Hoping the anniversary will be a grand celebration, worthy of so eventful an occasion, I am

Yours sincerely,
WALTER HUBBELL.

[Rev. Henry Blodgett, D.D.]

PLAINFIELD, N. J., June 11, 1895.

MY DEAR DR. PALMER.

I regret exceedingly that I cannot on the morrow and the day following sit with you and my good friends in Bridgeport under the shadow of two centuries that are past, and commemorate the good hand of our Lord upon us, and the lives of his faithful servants. May the church continue and flourish while Bridgeport remains, and until the Lord comes! You must rejoice in your lengthened pastorate, which covers more than one-tenth of the whole existence of the church. My best wishes are with you all.

We leave for Clifton Springs to-morrow to attend the convention of missionaries at that place.

Yours most sincerely,
H. BLODGET.

[Rev. Gerald H. Beard, Ph.D.]

SOUTH NORWALK, June 12, 1895.

MY DEAR MR. PALMER.

As I wrote to Mr. Sherwood, I intended to be present at the anniversary exercises of your church to-day. But I find that after all, I cannot have that pleasure.

Please extend, instead, my congratulations to your church; and accept my sincere regard and good wishes for yourself.

May God continue to bless and prosper you in the noble work you are doing. I trust these anniversary days may be full of satisfaction and blessed memories for you, and a benefit to all.

Fraternally yours,
GERALD H. BEARD.

RECORD OF MEMBERSHIP OF THE FIRST CHURCH OF BRIDGEPORT, CONN.

1695 to 1806.

The following list has been practically compiled from the scanty material found in the ancient volumes of the Church and Society records and is necessarily imperfect. The invaluable account kept by the Rev. Charles Chauncey, first minister of the church, 1695 to 1714, was not continued by his successors. The partial list of baptisms, marriages and deaths given, the mortuary record kept by Abijah Sterling, Esq., from 1767 to 1802, and the transcript of inscriptions on stones in the old Stratfield burying-ground, copied by the late William R. Bunnell, Esq., also Mr. Bunnell's list of family records, all found in the first of the church volumes, have been drawn upon liberally, and by comparison of dates and relationships an approximately correct account has been obtained. In addition to the membership of 1695, of ten males and fifteen females, Rev. Samuel Cooke has left a record for 1731 (which is printed elsewhere, verbatim), showing at that time forty-five male and sixty-eight female members in full communion; and a list was prepared by Rev. Elijah Waterman, at the beginning of his ministry, in 1806. The last includes seventeen male and thirty female members, forty-seven in all, in full communion; in addition to which were thirty-six men and thirty-three women, a total of sixty-nine, who had owned the covenant and brought their children to baptism.

LIST OF MEMBERS, 1695 TO 1806.

ABBREVIATIONS.

L. Admitted by Letter. P. Admitted upon Profession of Faith. R.C. Renewed Covenant. F.C. Admitted to Full Communion, D. Dismissed. *æ.* Age. *bap.* Baptized. *m.* Married. *d.* Died. *dau.* Daughter. *s.* Son. *w.* Wife. *wid.* Widow.

Name.	Admitted.	Removed.	Remarks.
Austin, Maj. and Dea. (1807) John P.	L. 1806, fr. N. Haven	d. after 1809	
Austin, Susannah	before 1806.		w. of John P.
Allen, Nehemiah		d. 1810, æ. 81	
Bennett, Lt. James, Sr.	June 13, 1695, fr. Stratford	d. 1707	Freeman of Fairfield, 1669.
Beardsley, Capt. Samuel, b. 1638	L. June 13, 1695, fr. Stratford		
Bennett, Mary	L. July 10, 1695, fr. Stratford	d. after 1731	w. of James, Sr.
Beardsley, Abigail	L. July 10, 1695, fr. Stratford		w. of Samuel.
Bingham, Abel	F.C. May 10, 1696.	d. June 22, 1707	m. 1694, Elizabeth Odell.
Bingham, Elizabeth	F.C. May 10, 1696.		
Beardsley, Daniel	R.C. Feb. 8, 1697.	d. after 1731	
Beardsley, Capt. John, Sr.	R.C. Feb. 8, 1697.	d. 1730?	m. 2d, 1711, Deborah Hull.
Beardsley, Mary (L. July 26, 1702)	R.C. Feb. 8, 1697, fr. Fairfield	d. Jan. 7, 1711	w. of John.
Beardsley, William	R.C. Feb. 8, 1697.	d. after 1718	
Beardsley, Ebenezer	R.C. Feb. 8, 1697.	d. after 1700	
Beardsley, Benjamin	R.C. Feb. 8, 1697.	d. after 1736	
Bennett, Joseph	R.C. Feb. 8, 1697.	d. after 1716	
Beardsley, Rebecca	R.C. Feb. 8, 1697.		
Bennett, Justice James, Jr.	F.C. Nov. 7, 1697.	d. after 1736	
Bennett, Sarah	F.C. Nov. 7, 1697.	d. after 1714	w. of James, Jr.
Bennett, Isaac	R.C. May 1, 1698.	d. after 1731	
Burr, Col. John, Recorder	R.C. Aug. 28, 1698.	d. June 13, 1750	æ. 79.
Burr, Deborah (Harlow)	R.C. Aug. 28, 1698.	d. 1726	w. of John, æ. 52.
Beardsley, William, Jr.	1700.		
Beardsley, Elizabeth	F.C. Apl. 22, 1705.		w. of William.
Beardsley, Anne	F.C. Feb. 13, 1709.	d. after 1731	w. of Daniel.
Booth, Rachel	F.C. Mch. 27, 1709.		w. of Jonathan.
Burritt, Sarah	F.C. Dec. 1709.		w. of Peleg.
Beecher, Elizabeth	F.C. Jan. 1, 1710.		dau. of Sarah.
Booth, Sergt. Dea. Joseph	F.C. Jan. 1712.	d. 1763	Deacon 1733; æ. 75.
Booth, Sarah	F.C. Jan. 1712.	d. 1784	w. of Joseph, æ. 76.
Bennett, Martha	F.C. Mch. 9, 1712.		w. of Isaac.
Beardsley, Nathan	1706 R.C. Mch. 30, 1712.	d. Aug. 6, 1750	m. Jan. 7, 1713, Eliz. Hubbell.
Bennett, James	R.C. Oct. 26, 1712.	d. after 1733	s. of James, Jr.
Bennett, ——	R.C. Oct. 26, 1712.	d. after 1731	w. of James.
Bradley, Abigail	R.C. Oct. 26, 1712.		m. 1717, Ephraim Hubbell.
Bennett, Abigail	R.C. Oct. 26, 1712.		m. Jan. 26, 1714?, Zach. Hubbell; (dau. of James, Jr.)
Bronson, Moses	R.C. Dec. 27, 1713.		
Bronson, Jane	F.C. Mch. 7, 1714.		w. of Richard.
Booth, Esther		D. Apl. 8, 1716	w. of Jonathan; to New-town.
Burritt, Charles	R.C. Feb. 2, 1718.	d. after 1750	
Burritt, Mary	R.C. Feb. 2, 1718.	d. after 1733	w. of Charles.
Beardsley, Anne or (Lake), bap. 1705	R.C. Aug. 8, 1731.		dau. of Daniel.
Beardsley, Obadiah, bap. 1706	R.C. Oct. 31, 1731.	D. before 1770	s. of John.
Beardsley, Mercy	R.C. Oct. 31, 1731.		w. of Obadiah.
Burr, ——	before 1731.		w. of Sergt. Burr.
Beardsley, Deborah (Hull)	1720	d. after 1731	w. of John, Sr. ; m. 1711.
Burrows, Stephen	1731.	d. after 1735	[1724.
Burrows, Abigail (French)	1731.	d. after 1733	w. of Stephen; m. Oct. 8,
Bennett, Stephen, bap. 1702	1732.	d. after 1736	s. of James; m. 1724.
Beardsley, Martha	Apl. 16, 1732.		
Bennett, Lieut. Dea. (1754) William	R.C. Apl. 16, 1732.	D. 1756, d. 1788,	m. Hannah Seeley, 1731, m. æ. 79. Cath. Hawley, 1739; s. of Joseph.
Bennett, Eunice?	R.C. Apl. 16, 1732.	d. 1796?	w. of William.
Beardsley, Ruth, bap. 1713	R.C. Mch. 17, 1734.		dau. of Nathan.
Beardsley, Rebecca, bap. 1716	R.C. Mch. 17, 1734.		m. 1735, James; dau. Nathan.
Beardsley, Samuel, bap. 1712	R.C. Mch. 31, 1734.	d. 1782	s. of John.
Beardsley, Andrew, bap. 1713	R.C. Mch. 31, 1734.	d. after 1781	s. of John.
Burrows, Patience	R.C. Apl. 7, 1734.		[Beardsley, 1735.
Beardsley, James	R.C. 1735.	d. after 1736	m. Rebecca, dau. of Nathan
Beardsley, John, Jr., bap. 1704	F.C. Feb. 18, 1736.	d. after 1742	

Name.	Admitted.	Removed.	Remarks.
Bennett, Martha, *bap.* 1717	R.C. Apl. 4, 1736.	....	*dau.* of Isaac.
Beardsley, Deborah	R.C. Nov. 28, 1736.	....	*dau.* of John.
Beardsley, Abigail	R.C. Nov. 28, 1736.	....	*dau.* of John.
Brinsmade, Joseph	R.C. Oct. 14, 1749.	*d.* after 1750	
Brinsmade, Ruth (Winton)	R.C. Oct. 14, 1749.	*d.* 1784, æ. 53	*w.* of Joseph.
Booth, John	R.C. Nov. 25, 1749.	....	
Booth, Lydia	R.C. Nov. 25, 1749.	....	
Burr, Capt. ? John, Jr., *bap.* 1698	R.C. Apl. 15, 1750.	*d.* 1771	
Burr, Eunice (Booth)	R.C. Apl. 15, 1750.	*d.* after 1770	wife of John; *m.* 1750.
Barlow, John	R.C. Jan. 6, 1750.	*d.* after 1754	*m.* 1749.
Barlow, Beulah (Bennett), *bap.* 1731	R.C. Jan. 6, 1750.	....	*dau.* of Isaac; *w.* of John;
Burritt, Josiah	R.C. Sept. 9, 1750.		
Burr, William, *bap.* 1712	before 1762.	*d.* 1769, æ. 58	*s.* of Maj. John Burr; *m.* 1774, Mrs. Charity (Wells) Strong.
Brothwell, Joseph .... 1710?	before 1762.	*d.* after 1770	
Blatchford, Rev. Samuel 1767	I. Nov. 22, 1797.	D. Mch. 20, 1804 *d.* Mch. 17, 1828	*m.* 1788, Alicia Windeatt.
Beach, Dr. and Dea. (1806) James Eaton 1778	before 1806.	*d.* 1838	
Backus, Joseph 1799	before 1806.	D. Jan. 24, 1830	*m.* Huldah Burroughs.
Burroughs, Griswold (Grizzell)	before 1806.	*d.* 1812, æ. 78	*wid.* of Edw. who *d.* 1776,
Beach, Huldah	before 1806.	....	*w.* of James Eaton. (æ. 42
Burr, Jemima	before 1806.	*d.* 1821, æ. 60	*w.* of Samuel.
Burr, Samuel	R.C. before 1806, R.C. Mch. 5, 1808.	*d.* 1825, æ. 65	
Brothwell, Thomas, Sr. 1797	before 1806.	*d.* 1842, æ. 76	*s.* of Joseph.
Brothwell, Hannah	R.C. before 1806.	*d.* 1829, æ. 63	*w.* of Thomas
Burr, Deborah	R.C. before 1806. F.C. 1807.	*d.* 1817, æ. 57	*w.* of Elijah.
Burroughs, Edward	R.C. before 1806. F.C. 1815.	D. Jan. 24, 1830	
Burroughs, Elizabeth	R.C. before 1806. F.C. 1815.	....	
Burroughs, Polly	R.C. before 1806. F.C. 1815.	....	
Burr, Elijah 1792	R.C. before 1806. F.C. 1807.	D. Jan. 24, 1830	
Chauncey, Rev. Charles	June 13, 1695.	*d.* 1714, æ. 48	
Chauncey, Sarah (Burr)	F.C. Dec. 20, 1696.	*d.* 1697	*w.* of Rev. Charles.
Crane, Elijah	R.C. Feb. 8, 1697.	*d.* after 1732	
Crane, Mary	F.C. Oct. 22, 1699.	....	
Castle, William	R.C. Mch. 9, 1712.	*d.* after 1718	
Castle, Rebecca	R.C. Mch. 9, 1712.	....	*w.* of William; *m.* 1711.
Chauncey, Israel, *b.* 1633	R.C. Nov. 23, 1712.	*d.* after 1731	*m.* 1721, Martha Wakeman, *dau.* of Capt. John.
Chauncey, Robert, *bap.* 1701	1712.	*d.* after 1742	*m.* 1722, Hannah Wheeler.
Crawford Quintin ?	R.C. Sept. 27, 1713.	*d.* after 1719	
Cooke, Rev. Samuel	I. July —, 1715.	*d.* 1747, æ. 60 or 61	[1708.
Cooke, Anne (Trowbridge)	F.C. Dec. 16, 1716.	*d.* 1721 æ. 33.	*w.* of Samuel; *m.* Nov. 30,
Cocke, Deliverance	F.C. Apl. 20, 1718.	....	sister of Rev. Samuel.
Crawford, Dorothy	R.C. Mch 24, 1717.	....	*w.* of Quintin.
Cooke, Elizabeth		*d.* May 16, 1732	
Cable, Samuel	R.C. Aug. 8, 1731.	*d.* after 1734	*m.* 1731, Anne Wheeler.
Cooke, John, *b.* 1715	1731.	*d.* 1813	*s.* of Rev. Samuel.
Crane, Elijah	R.C. July 29, 1733.	*d.* after 1734	
Crane, Elizabeth (Wakeley)	R.C. July 29, 1733.	....	*w.* of Elijah; *m.* 1732.
Curtis, Jared	1732.	*d.* after 1734	
Cole, Caleb	R.C. Aug. 8, 1731	*d.* after 1735	
Cole, Rebecca	R.C. Aug. 8, 1731	....	*w.* of Caleb.
Comstock, David	R.C. May 6, 1731	....	
Cooke, Samuel, Jr.	R.C. Dec. —, 1731	....	*m.* 1731, Abigail Moss; *s.* of
Comstock, Sarah *Aug.* 1751	R.C. Dec. —, 1731	....	*d.* of Daniel. [Rev. Sam'l.
Comstock, Daniel, Jr.	R.C. Dec. 29, 1734.	*d.* after 1735	
Comstock, Elizabeth	R.C. Dec. 29, 1734.	....	*w.* of Daniel, Jr.
Comstock, Mary	F.C. Dec. 12, 1736.	....	*w.* of Daniel.
Camp, Dea. Abraham	before 1775.	....	
Cable, Jerusha	before 1806.	*d.* 1810, æ. 64	*w.* of Samuel.
Dego, James	F.C. June —, 1717.	....	
Dickinson, Daniel	R.C. Aug. —, —	....	
Dibble, Dea. John	before 1806.	D. Jan. 24, 1830	
DeForest, Capt. and Dea. William	F.C. Dec. —, 1806.	*d.* æ. about 80.	

Name.	Admitted.	Removed.	Remarks.
Dudley, Hannah	.... before 1806.	....	w. of Azel.
Dudley, Azel	R.C. before 1806.	....	
DeForest, Sally	.... 1807.	D. Jan. 24, 1830	w. of William.
Edwards, Capt. John, Sr.	.... before 1731.	d. 1744, æ. 82	
Edwards, Mary	.... before 1731.	d. 1749, æ. 82	w. of John, Sr.
Edwards, Joseph	.... 1731.	d. after 1736	m. 1731, Prudence Wakeley
Edwards, Thomas	.... 1731.	d. after 1736	
Edwards, John, Jr.	.... 1733.	d. after 1735	
Fairchild, Alexander	R.C. Feb. 8, 1697.	d. after 1732	m. 1721, Mary Mallory.
French, Abigail	R.C. Feb. 8, 1697.	....	dau. of Samuel Sherman; w.
French, Samuel	F.C. Mch. 8, 1697.	d. after 1709	[of Samuel.
Fairchild, Hannah	L. Sept. 10, 1699, fr. Stratford		
Ferris, Zachariah, Sr.	L. Sept. 19, 1705.	D. Nov. 18, 1716	To New Milford.
Fairchild, Deborah, bap. 1706	.... 1706?	....	dau. of Alexander.
Ferris, Zachariah, Jr.	F.C. May 23, 1708.	d. after 1709	
Ferris, Mary	R.C. Apr. 17, 1709.	....	
Ferris, Martha	R.C. Oct. 21, 1711.	....	w. of Samuel. [Sherwood.
Fayerweather, Benjamin 1704	F.C. April 5, 1712.	d. 1725, æ. 55	m. 1693, Sarah, dau.of Matt.
Frost, Joseph	R.C. Oct. 26, 1712.	....	[Francis Hall.
Frost, Abner	R.C. Oct. 26, 1712.	....	m. 1723, Rebecca, dau. of
Fairchild, Caleb	R.C. Oct. 26, 1712.	d. after 1717	
French, Sergt. Samuel.....1704	R.C. Nov. 2, 1712.	d. Dec. 23, 1732	
French, ----	.... before 1731.	d. after 1734	w. of Samuel.
Fairchild, Mary (Mallory)	.... before 1731.	....	w. of Alexander.
Fayerweather, Joseph, bap. 1707	R.C. Dec. 5, 1731.	d. Sept. 3, 1732	s. of Benjamin.
Fayerweather, Sarah (Sherwood)	.... before 1731.	d. 1743, æ. 67	w. of Benjamin.
Fairchild, James	.... before 1731.	d. after 1734	
Fairchild, ----	.... before 1731.	....	w. of James.
Fayerweather, Widow	.... before 1731.	....	
French, ----	.... before 1731.	d. after 1732	w. of Samuel, Jr.
Fayerweather, John, bap. 1704	.... 1732.	d. after 1762 ?	s. of Benjamin.
Fayerweather, Anne	R.C. Dec. 30, 1733.	d. 1773, æ. 61	w. of John.
Fayerweather, Abigail	.... Mch. 10, 1734.	....	wid. of ?
French, Samuel, Jr.	F.C. April 8, 1736.	d. 1773	
Fayerweather, Lt. Benj., bap. 1717.	....	d. 1791, æ. 74	m. 1742, Elizabeth Beach.
Fayerweather, John, bap. 1736	....	d. after 1762 ?	s. of John.
Fayerweather, Daniel 1795	R.C. before 1806. F.C. 1809.	d. 1849	
Fayerweather, Betsey	R.C. 1806.	d. 1858	w. of Daniel.
Freeman, Primus	R.C. before 1806.	....	
Freeman, Chloe Colored	R.C. before 1806.	....	w. of Primus.
Freeman, Thomas	R.C. before 1806.	d. after 1815	
Freeman, Chloe	R.C. before 1806.	....	w. of Thomas.
Gregory, Sergt. Samuel, Sr.	.... June 13, 1695, fr. Fairfield	d. after 1717	
Gregory, Rebecca	L. July 10, 1695, fr. Fairfield	....	[Beardsley.
Gregory, Abigail	R.C. Feb. 8, 1697.	....	w.of Benjamin; dau.of Jno.
Gruman, Samuel	R.C. Nov. 2, 1712.	....	
Gregory, Joanna	R.C. Dec. 7, 1712.	....	
Gregory, Mary	F.C. July 13, 1718.	....	w. of Sergt. Samuel.
Gregory, Esther	.... before 1731.	d. 1790, æ. 83	w. of Enoch.
Gregory, Thaddeus, bap. 1701	.... before 1731.	d. 1777	s. of Samuel, Jr.
Gregory, Hulda	.... before 1731.	....	w. of Thaddeus.
Gregory, Abigail (Wakeley)	.... before 1731.	d. after 1731	w. of Ensign Samuel.
Gregory, Sergt. Ebenezer	.... 1734.	d. Mch. 8, 1750	s. of Samuel, Sr.
Gregory, Benjamin	F.C. Sept. 22, 1734.	....	
Gregory, Ensign ? Samuel 1734	R.C. Dec. 17, 1749.	d. 1766	
Gregory, Naomi, bap. 1733	R.C. Dec. 17, 1749.	....	dau. of Ebenezer.
Gregory, Ezra	R.C. before 1806. F.C. Jan. 1, 1815.	d. after 1835 ?	
Gregory, Sarah	R.C. before 1806. F.C. Jan. 3, 1808.	d. 1816, æ. 58	w. of Ezra.
Gouge, Thomas 1792	R.C. before 1806. R.C. Mch. 4, 1827.	d. 1848	
Gouge, Ruth	R.C. before 1806. F.C. 1815.	d. 1826, æ. 56	w. of Thomas.
Gregory, James	R.C. before 1806. F.C. 1807.	....	
Gregory, Philena 1792	R.C. Mch. 1, 1807. F.C. 1807.	....	w. of James.
Hubbell, Serg't Richard, Sr.	.... June 13, 1695, fr. Stratford	d. 1699	Freeman Fairfield, 1669.
Hubbell, Lieut. Richard, Jr.	.... June 13, 1695, fr. Stratford	d. after 1731	

—167—

Name.	Admitted.	Removed.	Remarks.
Hall, Susannah	F.C. Jan. 5, 1695.	....	....
Hubbell, Abigail	L. July 10, 1695, fr. Stratford	d. after 1715	w. of Richard, Sr.
Hubbell, Temperance	L. July 10, 1695, fr. Stratford	....	w. of Richard, Jr.
Hubbell, Sarah	R.C. Feb. 8, 1697.	....	....
Hawley, Dea. Thomas	L. 1699, fr. Stratford	d. 1729, æ. 44	....
Hall, Jane	F.C. April 7, 1700.	....	....
Hollinsworth, Ruth	F.C. Apl. 15, 1711.	....	....
Hubbell, Peter	R.C. Apl. 13, 1712.	....	....
Hubbell, Katharine	R.C. Apl. 13, 1712.	....	w. of Peter; m. 1710.
Hubbell, Ebenezer ...1703	R.C. Oct. 26, 1712.	d. after 1720	s. of Ebenezer.
Hubbell, Zachariah, b. 1694	R.C. Oct. 26, 1712. / F.C. April 8, 1736.	....	s. of Richard, Jr.
Hall, David	R.C. Oct. 26, 1712.	....	[Bradley.
Hubbell, Lt. Ephraim	R.C. Oct. 26, 1712.	d. after 1755	m. Oct. 17, 1717, Abigail
Hubbell, Jonathan	R.C. Oct. 26, 1712.	....	m. 1713, Peacable Silliman.
Hubbell, John	R.C. Oct. 26, 1712.	d. 1774, æ. 85	....
Hubbell, Anne (Wells)	R.C. Oct. 26, 1712.	....	....
Hubbell, Elizabeth	R.C. Oct. 26, 1712.	d. after 1733	m. Nathan Beardsley.
Hall, Samuel ...1700	R.C. Nov. 2, 1712.	d. after 1731	m. Sarah Silliman; s. of Isaac.
Hubbell, Samuel, Sr.	F.C. Nov.16, 1712.	d. Sept. 18, 1713, æ. 57.	m. E. Wilson, 1687; m. T. Preston, 1688.
Hubbell, Capt. Daniel	R.C. Nov.23, 1712.	d. after 1731	m. 1716, Esther Beach.
Hawley, Gideon	F.C. Jan. 18, 1713.	d. 1730, æ. 43	....
Hawley, Anna (Bennett)	F.C. Jan. 18, 1713.	d. 1727, æ. 36	w. of Gideon; m. 1711.
Hubbell, Dea. Richard, Jr.	R.C. Feb. 7, 1714. / F.C. Feb. 27, 1732.	d. 1787, æ. 91	1750, 1774. [Squire, 1721.
Hubbell, Stephen	R.C. Feb. 7, 1714.	d. 1792, æ. 98	s. of Samuel; m. Abigail
Hubbell, Hannah, bap. 1698	R.C. Feb. 7, 1714.	....	dau. of Richard.
Hall, John	F.C. Feb. 17, 1717.	d. 1749, æ. 71	s. of Isaac, Sr.
Hall, Abigail, bap. 1700?	F.C. Feb. 17, 1717.	....	w. of John.
Hall, Mary	R.C. Mch. 3, 1717.	....	w. of Jonathan.
Hall, Martha	F.C. May 5, 1717.	....	....
Hall, Margaret (Stiles)	R.C. Oct. 6, 1717.	d. after 1731	w. of Francis, Sr.
Hall, Samuel	R.C. Oct. 6, 1717.	d. after 1734	....
Hall, Hannah	R.C. Oct. 6, 1717.	....	w. of Samuel.
Hall, Sergt. Francis, Sr.	 1717	d. after 1733	m. Dec. 8, 1702, Mary Stiles.
Hubbell, Hannah	.... Jan. 12, 1718.	....	w. of Lieut. Richard.
Hubbell, Anna	F.C. July 13, 1718.	d. after 1731	w. of John.
Hall, Mother of Samuel	....	d. after 1731	....
Hubbell, Esther (Beach)	.... before 1731.	....	w. of Daniel.
Hall, Francis, Jr., bap. 1705	.... before 1731.	d. Feb. 26, 1735	....
Hodgdon, Mrs.	.... before 1731.	....	....
Hubbell, Sergt. James ...1703	.... before 1731.	....	....
Hubbell, Widow,	.... before 1731.	....	....
Hall, Widow Sarah	.... before 1731.	d. 1770	....
Hubbell, Capt. David, bap. 1698	R.C. Aug. 8, 1731.	d. 1735	s. of Samuel, Sr.
Hall, Mary, bap. 1700	F.C. Aug. 8, 1731.	....	dau. of Isaac, Sr. ?
Hawley, Ebenezer, bap. 1703	R.C. Aug. 8, 1731.	....	s. of Thomas.
Hall, Richard, bap. 1713	R.C. Feb. 27, 1732.	d. after 1750 ? may be 1773	s. of Francis, Sr.
Hall, Hannah (Booth)	R.C. Feb. 27, 1732.	d. 1775	w. of Richard; m. 1731.
Hubbell, Penelope	F.C. Feb. 27, 1732.	d. 1791, æ. 87	w. of Richard, Jr.
Hubbell, Andrew, bap. 1706	.... before 1732.	d. after 1734	s. of James.
Huan, Nathaniel	Mch. 8, 1733.	....	....
Hall, Elnathan, bap. 1711	R.C. Sept.23, 1733.	d. after 1749	s. of John.
Hall, Abigail, bap. 1700	R.C. April 7, 1734.	d. 1746, æ. 26	dau. of John. [Richard.
Hubbell, Abigail, bap. 1709	F.C. Apl. 14, 1734.	....	w. of Zach.; dau. of Sergt.
Hawley, Sergt. James, bap. 1713	R.C. Apl. 28, 1734.	d. 1746, æ. 34	s. of Gideon.
Hawley, Eunice (Jackson)	R.C. Apl. 28, 1734.	d. 1796, æ. 82	w. of James; m. 1733.
Hall, Abigail	F.C. Sept.29, 1734.	....	w. of Burgess, bap. 1701, s. [of Isaac.
Hurd, Nathan, bap. 1706	F.C. Apl. 20, 1735.	d. after 1736	w. of Nathan.
Hurd, ———	F.C. Apl. 20, 1735.	....	dau. of Capt. Richard ?
Hubbell, Mary, bap. 1709	R.C. Jan. 25, 1736.	d. 1741, æ. 26	w. of Elnathan ; m. 1732.
Hall, Hannah (Hawley)	F.C. Feb. 18, 1736.	d. 1747, æ. 31	dau. of Samuel.
Hall, Martha, bap. 1717	F.C. Feb. 18, 1736.	d. 1775	s. of Gideon.
Hawley, Zachariah, bap. 1717	R.C. June 13, 1736.	d. 1778 ?	m. 1746, Zachariah Sanford.
Hall, Widow Anne	F.C. April 3, 1736.	d. 1778	w. of Joseph.
Hubbell, Keziah	F.C. July 11, 1736.	....	....
Hawley, Capt. Ezra, bap. 1711	F.C. Oct. 17, 1736.	d. 1771, æ. 62	s. of Thomas.
Hawley, Abigail	F.C. Oct. 17, 1736.	d. 1782, æ. 71	w. of Ezra; m. 1735.
Hall, Rev. Lyman	Ord. Sept.27, 1749.	D. June 18, 1751	d. 1770.
Hubbell, Abel	R.C. Nov. 5, 1749.	d. 1812, æ. 103	....
Hubbell, Martha	R.C. Nov. 5, 1749.	d. 1747	w. of Abel.
Hodgdon, Mary	L. Sept.21, 1750.	....	w. of Timothy.
Hubbell, Daniel	R.C. Sept 23, 1750.	d. 1801, æ. 77	....

Name.	Admitted.	Removed.	Remarks.
Hubbell, Sarah (Gregory)	R.C. Sept. 23, 1750.	d. 1801, æ. 73	w. of Daniel; m. 1749.
Hodgdon, David	R.C. Feb. 3, 1751.	d. 1795	[m. 1750.
Hodgdon, Sarah (Lacey)	R.C. Feb. 3, 1751.	....	dau. of John; w. of David;
Hubbell, Jabez	R.C. Mch. 17, 1751.	d. 1770	s. of Stephen. [1750.
Hubbell, Mary	R.C. Mch. 17, 1751.	d. after 1770	w. of Jabez; m. June 28,
Holberton, John	....	d. June 21, 1750	....
Hubbell, Richard, Jr., b. 1742	.... before 1763.	d. 1829, æ. 87	....
Hubbell, Ensign Hezekiah	.... before 1773.	d. 1784, æ. 36	s. of Dea. Richard, Jr.
Hawley, Dea. Elijah	.... before 1776, resigned 1790	d. 1825, æ. 81	m. 1770, Mary Bennett, d.
Hubbell, Anne	.... before 1806.	....	wid. of ——. [1841, æ. 90.
Hubbell, Ellen	.... before 1806.	....	wid. of ——.
Hubbell, Anne	.... before 1806.	d. 1818, æ. 86	wid. of ——.
Hawley, Ellen	.... before 1806.	d. 1823, æ. 84	wid. of Wolcot.
Hubbell, Mary (Middlebrook)	.... before 1806.	d. 1813, æ. 92	wid. of Benjamin.
Hull, Irena	.... before 1806, fr. Greenfield	....	w. of William B.
Hawley, Samuel, Jr.	.... before 1806.	d. 1826, æ. 66	....
Hawley, Lucy	R.C. before 1806. F.C 1807.	....	w. of Samuel.
Hawley, Capt. Abijah	R.C. before 1806. F.C. Feb. 4, 1810.	d. 1818, æ. 50	....
Hawley, Polly ... 1802	R.C. before 1806. F.C. Feb. 4, 1810.	D. Jan. 24, 1830	w. of Abijah.
Hawley, Capt. David ... 1781	R.C. before 1806.	d. 1807	....
Hawley, Aaron, Jr. ... 1798	R.C. before 1806. F.C. Jan. 18, 1810.	....	....
Hawley, Griswold,	R.C. before 1806. F.C. Jan. 18, 1810.	D. Jan. 24, 1830	w. of Aaron.
Hawley, Capt. Wilson ... 1803	R.C. before 1806. F.C. Feb. 24, 1810.	D. Jan. 24, 1830	....
Hawley, Charity	R.C. before 1806. F.C. Feb. 24, 1810.	D. Jan. 24, 1830	....
Hawley, Gurdon ... 1804	R.C. before 1806.	d. 1855	....
Hawley, Anne	R.C. before 1806. F.C. July 5, 1812.	d. 1855	w. of Gurdon.
Hawley, Ruth (Morehouse)	R.C. before 1806. F.C. Aug. 2, 1812.	d. 1829, æ. 75	wid. of Ezra.
Hawley, Capt. Ebenezer	R.C. before 1806.	d. 1822, æ. 58	....
Hawley, Zalmon ... 1791	R.C. before 1806.	....	....
Hawley, Anne	R.C. before 1806.	d. 1810, æ. 70	w. of Zalmon.
Hubbell, Salmon ... 1790	R.C. before 1806.	d. after 1821	....
Hubbell, Sarah	R.C. before 1806.	d. 1827, æ. 69	w. of Salmon.
Hubbell, Capt. Ezekiel ... 1799	R.C. before 1806.	d. 1834	....
Hubbell, Catharine	R.C. before 1806.	d. 1830	w. of Ezekiel.
Hubbell, Aaron	R.C. before 1806.	d. 1848, æ. 87	....
Hubbell, Sally	R.C. before 1806.	d. 1851, æ. 84	w. of Aaron.
Hubbell, David ... 1802	R C. before 1806.	d. after 1819	....
Hubbell, Anne	R.C. before 1806.	....	w. of David.
Hull, Stephen	R.C. before 1806. F.C. Mch. 5, 1808.	d. after 1814	....
Hull, Abigail	R.C. before 1806.	....	w. of Stephen.
Hubbell, Miriam	.... May 3, 1807.	....	wid. of ——.
Jackson, Elizabeth	R.C. Feb. 8, 1697.	....	....
Jackson, Mary	L. Dec. 20, 1697, fr. Norwalk	....	m. 1709, John Sturdevant.
Jackson, Joseph	R.C. Oct. 20, 1700.	d. after 1712	....
Jackson, Hannah, bap. 1701	F.C. Sept. 3, 1704.	....	dau. of Samuel; m. 1709.
Jackson, Henry, bap. 1701	F C. Apl. 25, 1708.	d. Dec. 17, 1717	s. of Samuel.
Jackson, Mary	F.C. Apl. 25, 1708.	d. after 1731	w. of Henry; m. 1704.
Jackson, Robert	R.C. July 20, 1707.	d. after 1718	m. 1706, Sarah Hutton.
Judson, Joseph	R.C. April 3, 1709.	....	....
Judson, Hannah	R.C. April 3, 1709.	....	....
Jackson, Mary	R.C. Aug. 20, 1710.	d. Aug. 7, 1734	w. of Daniel.
Jackson, Sarah	R.C Oct. 17, 1714.	....	w. of John.
Joacocks, Thomas	F.C. Mch. 31, 1717.	....	w. of Thomas.
Joacocks, Abigail ... 1706	F.C. Mch. 31, 1717.	d. Jan. 3, 1734	w. of Moses, Jr.
Jackson, ——	.... before 1731.	d. after 1735	....
Jackson, Corp. John	.... before 1731.	....	....
Jackson, David, Sr.	.... before 1731.	d. after 1736	s. of Samuel.
Jackson, Gabriel, bap. 1709	.... before 1732.	d. 1734	....
Jackson, Moses ... 1708	.... before 1733.	....	....
Jones, Rebecca	F.C. Nov. 17, 1734.	....	w. of John.
Jackson, Samuel	R.C. Jan. 21, 1750.	d. after 1756	....
Jackson, Penninah	R.C. Jan. 21, 1750.	....	w. of Samuel.
Jackson, Moses, Sr., bap. 1698	....	d. after 1699	....

Name.	Admitted.	Removed.	Remarks.
Knapp, Nathaniel	R.C. Feb. 8, 1697.	d. after 1710	m. May 28, 1712.
Knapp, ——	before 1731.	....	w. of Daniel.
Knapp, Capt. Joseph	before 1806.	d. 1814, æ. 83	....
Kellogg, Bela	before 1814.	....	....
Lacey, Abigail	F.C. Jan. 1, 1710.	....	w. of Edward, Jr.
Lacey, Edward 1703	F.C. Nov. 16, 1712.	d. after 1732	....
Lacey, Elizabeth	R.C. Oct. 26, 1712.	....	....
Lacey, John 1702	R.C. Nov. 2, 1712.	d. after 1723	....
Luff, John	R.C. Aug. 8, 1731.	....	w. of Zachariah.
Lawrence ——	before 1731.	....	....
Lacey, Mother of Edward	....	d. after 1731	....
Lacey, ——	before 1731.	d. after 1750	w. of Edward.
Little, Doct. William	....	d. 1781	m. Ruth (Winton), wid. of Joseph Brinsmade; she d. 1784, æ. 53.
Lockwood, Lambert	1795.	d. 1825, æ. 68	....
Lacey, Capt. Josiah 1774	1798.	d. 1812, æ. 66	....
Lacey, Mary	before 1806.	d. 1810, æ. 91	wid. of John.
Lockwood, Elizabeth	before 1806.	D. Nov. 5, 1826.	w. of Lambert.
Lacey, Anne	before 1806.	d. 1812, æ. 45	w. of Josiah
Lewis, Ichabod	R.C. before 1806.	....	....
Lewis, ——	before 1806.	....	w. of Ichabod.
Lacey, Capt. Daniel	before 1806.	d. 1828, æ. 85	....
Lovejoy, Capt. Phinehas	before 1807.	....	....
Mallett, John, Sr.	R.C. Apr. 29, 1705.	d. 1764, æ. 101	....
Morehouse, Jonathan	R.C. Mch. 14, 1708.	d. after 1731	....
Morehouse, Noah	R.C. May 7, 1710.	d. Feb. 13, 1750	m. 1708.
Morehouse, Martha	R.C. May 7, 1710.	....	w. of Nathan
Morehouse, Samuel, Jr. 1697	R.C. Oct. 26, 1712.	d. Nov. 25, 1732	[Henry Lacey.
Morehouse, Hannah, bap. 1702	R.C. Nov. 23, 1716.	....	dau. of Samuel; m. 1716,
Morehouse, Daniel	R.C. Dec. 14, 1712.	....	....
Morehouse, Rebecca (Hall)	F.C. July 13, 1718.	....	w. of Jonathan.
Miles, Mrs. Elizabeth	....	D. 1716 or '26	To New Haven.
Mann, John	before 1730.	d. after 1751	m. 1715, Rebecca Nichols.
Mead, Zachariah	before 1731.	d. after 1753	....
Mead, ——	before 1731.	d. after 1734	w. of Zachariah.
Middlebrook, John	before 1731.	....	....
Middlebrook	before 1731.	....	w. of John.
Mallet, David, bap. 1705	R.C. Mch. 5, 1732.	d. after 1735	s. of John, Sr.
MacHard Matthew	R.C. Dec. 2, 1733.	d. 1736, æ. 28	....
MacHard, Sarah (Fayerweather)	R.C. Dec. 2, 1733.	....	w. of Matthew; m. 1732.
Morehouse, Katharine	R.C. Dec. 30, 1733.	....	....
Mallett, John, Jr.	before 1733.	d. after 1735	....
Morehouse, Keziah, bap. 1710	R.C. Dec. 18, 1734.	....	dau. of Noah.
Morehouse, Sarah, bap. 1717	R.C. April 4, 1736.	....	dau. of Noah.
Morehouse, Jemima	R.C. April 4, 1736.	....	dau. of Noah. [John.
Morriss, Daniel	F.C. Feb. 25, 1749.	d. after 1772	m. Sarah Summers, dau. of
Mallet, Lewis	1800.	d. 1825, æ. 69	....
Mallett, Anne 1795	before 1806.	D. Jan. 24, 1840	w. of Lewis.
Morehouse, Abijah	R.C. before 1806.	d. 1819, æ. 40	....
Morehouse, Rachel	R.C. before 1806.	d. 1817, æ. 34	w. of Abijah.
Morehouse, Rachel	F.C. May 1, 1808.		
Meeker, Anne	K.C. before 1806.	d. 1861, æ. 96	wid. of ——.
	F.C. Sept. 5, 1813.		
Meeker, David	R.C. before 1806.	d. 1828, æ. 73	....
	F.C. Jan. 1, 1815.		
Meeker, Esther	R.C. before 1806.	d. 1812, æ. 48	w. of David.
Morgan, Drew	R.C. before 1806.	....	....
Morgan, ——	R.C. before 1806.	....	w. of Drew.
Nichols, Rebecca	F.C. Jan. 31, 1714.	....	wid. of Benjamin; m. 1716,
Nichols, Sarah	R.C. Feb. 7, 1714.	....	[John Mason.
Nichols, John	1708.	d. after 1815	Baptist.
Odell, Sergt. John, Jr.	June 13, 1693, fr. Fairfield	d. 1743, æ. 77	....
Odell, Mary	L. July 10, 1704, fr. Fairfield	d. after 1731	w. of John, Sr.
Odell, Sarah	L. July 2, 1705, fr. Fairfield	d. 1741, æ. 72	w. of John, Jr.
Odell, Capt. Samuel, Sr.	R.C. Feb. 8, 1697, fr. Fairfield	d. after 1714	....
Odell, Hannah	R.C. Feb. 8, 1697.	....	dau. of John, Sr.
Odell, John, Sr.	F.C. Feb. 20, 1698.	d. after 1709	Freeman of Fairfield, 1669.
Odell, Mary Jr. (sic)	F.C. May 22, 1698.	d. after 1731	w. of John, Jr.
Odell, Anne	F.C. Nov. 2, 1712.	....	m. Betiah Bacon, 1713.
Odell, Deborah	R.C. Dec. 7, 1712	....	m. John Downs, 1713.

Name.	Admitted.	Removed.	Remarks.
Odell, Lt. Hezekiah, *bap.* 1700	F.C. Apl. 18, 1725.	....	d. after 1752	s. of John ; m. Deborah.
Odell, Deborah	F.C. Apl. 18, 1725.	....	d. 1756, æ. 55	w. of Hezekiah.
Odell, Samuel, *bap.* 1705	R.C. Jan. 11, 1736.	....	d. 1755, æ. 69	m. 1712, Judith Ann Wheeler, m. Johannah Peck.
Odell, William, *b.* 1697	F.C. Apl. 8, 1736.	....	d. 1772, æ. 75	s. of John ; m. 1718, Abigail
Odell, Gershom	R.C. Nov. 28, 1736.	....	d. after 1756	s. of Hezekiah. [Smith.
Odell, Anne	R.C. Nov. 28, 1736.	....	....	....
Odell, Azariah	R.C. Apl. 10, 1750-1.	....	d. after 1750	....
Odell, Mary (Brinsmade)	R.C. Apl. 10, 1750-1.	....	d. after 1754	w. of Azariah ; m. 1749.
Odell, Beulah	F.C. July 1. 1750.	....	d. 1756, æ. 27	dau. Hezekiah and Deborah
Preston, Edward	F.C. Mch. 27, 1696.	....	....	....
Porter, Nathaniel	R.C. Feb. 8, 1697.	....	d. after 1719	....
Parrott, John	R.C. Dec. 8, 1706.	....	d. after 1716	....
Parrott, Hannah	R.C. Dec. 8, 1706.	....	....	w. of John.
Packer, John	R.C. Aug. 8, 1731.	....	....	....
Patchin, Margaret	R.C. Oct. 24, 1731.	....	....	w. of Samuel.
Phippeny, Benjamin	.... before 1733.	....	....	....
Porter, John, *bap.* 1700	.... before 1733.	....	d. after 1736	m. Hannah ; s. of Nathaniel
Penny, Samuel	.... before 1806.	....	....	....
Penny, Jemima	.... before 1806.	....	....	w. of Samuel.
Parish, Huldah	.... before 1806.	....	....	w. of Joel.
Parrot, Abraham, Jr	R.C. before 1806. / F.C. May 21, 1815.	....	d. 1805, æ. 42 or 48?	....
Parrot, Lucy (Wells)	R.C. before 1806. / F.C. May 21, 1815.	....	d. 1856, æ. 80	w. of Abraham, Jr.
Parrot, Abraham, Sr	R.C. before 1806.	....	d. 1817, æ. 64	....
Parrot, —— Esther?	R.C. before 1806.	....	d. Sept. 1852?	w. of Abraham, Sr.
Rowell, Valentine	R.C. July 20, 1707.	....	d. after 1709	....
Rowell, Mary	R.C. July 20, 1707.	....	....	w. of Valentine.
Rowland, Dea. and Sergt. Henry, *bap.* 1712.	.... about 1723.	....	d. June 14, 1775	s. of Henry ; m. Tamar Sherman, 1718, dau. of David,
Rossel, Mercy	R.C. Aug. 8, 1731.	....	....	....
Rossel, Sarah	R.C. Aug. 8, 1731.	....	....	....
Risden, Nathaniel	F.C. Apl. 8, 1736.	....	....	....
Risden, ——	F.C. Apl. 8, 1736.	....	....	w. of Nathaniel.
Rowland, Mary	L. Feb. 25, 1750.	....	....	w. of Henry.
Rowland, Edward	R.C. Dec. 10, 1749.	....	....	....
Rowland, ——	R.C. Dec. 10, 1749.	....	....	w. of Edward.
Ross, Rev. Robert	L. Nov. 28, 1753, resigned 1756	d. Aug. 29, 1799, æ. 75.	....
Risley, William	R.C. before 1807.	....	d. after 1810	....
Risley, Lavinia	R.C. before 1807. / F.C. Jan. 5, 1817.	....	d. Jan. 1857	w. of William.
Sherman, Matthew	.... June 13, 1695, fr. Stratford	d. after 1713	m. 1710.
Sherman, Dea. and Capt. David	L. June 13, 1695, fr. Stratford	d. Jan. 1, 1753, æ. 88.	s. of Samuel, Jr.; m. Mary Judson.
Sherwood, Mary	L. July 10, 1695, fr. Fairfield	d. 1730, æ. 87	w. of Capt. Matthew.
Sherwood, Elizabeth	L. July 10, 1695, fr. Fairfield	....	m. 1710, Rev. Chas. Chauncey, and 1716, Lt. Richard Miles.
Sherman, Mercy	L. July 10, 1695, fr. Stratford	d. after 1731	w. of David, Sr.
Seeley, Joseph	F.C. Dec. 8, 1695.	....	d. after 1735	....
Seeley, Sarah	F.C. Dec. 8, 1695.	....	....	w. of Joseph.
Sherman, Hannah	R.C. Jan. 5, 1696.	....	....	....
Sherwood, Matthew, Jr	R.C. Feb. 8, 1697.	....	d. after 1706	....
Summers, Serg't Samuel	R.C. Feb. 8, 1697.	....	d. after 1723	before 1732.
Summers, Abigail	R.C. Feb. 8, 1697.	....	d. after 1731	w. of Samuel.
Smedley, Samuel, *m.* 1700	R.C. Feb. 8, 1697.	....	d. after 1734	m. 1721, Martha Treadwell, *bap.* 1702, d. 1734?
Seeley, Rebecca	R.C. Feb. 8, 1697.	....	....	w. of John.
Sherwood, Joanna	F.C. Sept. 21, 1696.	....	....	....
Sherwood, Capt. Matthew	L. 1697, fr. Fairfield	d. 1715, æ. 72	Freeman of Fairfield, 1669.
Summers, Henry	R.C. Aug. 29, 1703.	....	d. after 1731	m. Sarab, dau. of John [Beardsley.
Seeley, Lieut. James	F.C. Apl. 2, 1704.	....	d. af. 1761, æ. 93	....
Seeley, Sarah (Gregory)	F.C. Apl. 2, 1704.	....	....	w. of James ; m. 1702.
Smith, William, Sr	.... 1704.	....	....	....
Smedley, Abigail (Dimon)	F.C. Apl. 22, 1705.	....	d. about 1718	m. 1700.
Sherwood, Capt. Samuel	R.C. Nov. 4, 1705.	....	d. Nov. 10, 1732, æ. 52.	m. 1704, Rebecca Burr.
Sherwood Rebecca (Burr)	R.C. Nov. 4, 1705.	....	d. May 16, 1721, æ. 40.	w. of Samuel ; m. 1704.
Summers, Sarah (Beardsley)	F.C. May 4, 1707.	....	d. after 1731	dau. of John Heardsley ; w. [of Henry Summers.
Sherman, Wilmot	R.C. Apl. 3, 1709.	....	....	....

Name.	Admitted.	Removed.	Remarks.
Sherwood, Dr. ? Thomas	R.C. Nov. 6, 1709.	....	d. after 1727
Summers, John	R.C. May 11, 1712.	d. after 1731	m. 1710, Mary ——.
Sherman, Capt. David, Jr.	1712.	d. 1752, æ. 65	[penv; m. A. Silliman.
Sherwood, Dea, Lemuel	R.C. July 6, 1712.	d. Sept. 2, 1732	m. E. Wheeler; m. J. Phip-
Sherwood, Experience (Wheeler)	R.C. July 6, 1712.	d. Aug. 27, 1721	w. of Deac. Lemuel.
Sherwood, ——	F.C. Aug. 31, 1712.	....	w. of Thomas.
Seeley, Ebenezer	R.C. Oct. 26, 1712.	d. 1717	s. of Nathaniel.
Sherman, Sarah	R.C. Oct. 26, 1712.	....	w. of Benajah Strong.
Sherman, Jerusha	R.C. Oct. 26, 1712.	....	....
Summers, Abigail, bap. 1705 or 1700	R.C. Oct. 26, 1712.	....	dau. of Serg't Samuel.
Sherman, Tamar	R.C. Oct. 26, 1712.	d. 1735, æ. 42	m. Henry Rowland 1718.
Silliman, Peacable	R.C. Oct. 26, 1712.	....	m. Jonathan Hubbell, 1713.
Sherman, Abiah	R.C. Feb. 7, 1714.	d. 1717, æ. 19	dau. of Dea. David & Mercy
Sherman, Sarah	R.C. Nov. 21, 1714.	....	w. of John.
Seeley, Jerusha	F.C. Mch. 10, 1717.	d. after 1731?	w. of Ebenezer.
Squire, Abigail	F.C. June 3, 1716.	d. 1777, æ. 84	m. Stephen Hubbell.
Sherman, Jabez	F.C. Jan. 14, 1729.	....	s. of Matthew.
Sherman, ——	F.C. Jan. 14, 1729.	....	w. of Jabez.
Summers, Samuel, Jr., bap. 1700	F.C. Jan. 14, 1729.	....	s. of Serg't Samuel.
Summers, ——	F.C. Jan. 14, 1729.	....	w. of Samuel, Jr.
Sherman, Dinah (Rice)	before 1731.	d. 1732, æ. 37	w. of Capt. David, Jr.
Sherwood, Mary	before 1731.	d. 1743, æ. 61	2d w. of Capt. Samuel.
Summers, Mary ?	before 1731.	....	w. of John. [1728.
Silliman, Ann	....	d. after 1731	m. Dea. L. Sherwood, 3d w.,
Silliman, Nathaniel 1724	before 1731.	d. after 1735	....
Silliman, Hannah	before 1731.	....	w. of Nathaniel.
Sterling, Jacob	before 1731.	d. 1765, æ. 88	[Seeley.
Silliman, Hannah (Odell)	before 1731.	d. 1756, æ. 77	w. of Jacob; wid. of Nath'l
Sherwood, Capt. John, bap. 1705	1731	d. 1774, æ. 74	m. M. Walker, 1733; s. of Samuel.
Sherman, Enos	before 1731.	d. after 1736	dau. of Capt. David; m. R. Denison, 1733.
Sherman, Prudence, bap. 1706	R.C. Aug. 8, 1731.	....	dau. of Samuel; m. D. Fitch,
Sherwood, Sarah, bap. 1709	R.C. Aug. 8, 1731.	d. after 1732	s. of Samuel. [1732.
Summers, David, bap. 1702	R.C. Aug. 8, 1731.	d. 1751? æ. 54	w. of Nathan.
Summers, Martha	R.C. Aug. 8, 1731.	....	w. of Joseph.
Seeley, Hannah	Nov. 7, 1731.	d. after 1734	From Fairfield.
Sandford, Widow	1732.	d. 1781, æ. 79	w. of Nathaniel.
Seeley, Elizabeth	Apl. 16, 1732.	d. 1772, æ. 70	s. of Samuel.
Summers, Nathan, bap. 1703	R.C. Aug. 8, 1731.	d. 1784, æ. 78	s. ofSamuel; m. MercySher-
Sherwood, Dea. Nathaniel, bap. 1707	R.C. May 28, 1732.	d. 1767, æ. 58?	man, dau. of Dea. David.
Sherwood, Mary	R.C. Mch. 11, 1733.	d. 1757, æ. 63?	w. of Capt. John ?
Sandford, Thomas, Jr. ?	Sept. 3, 1732.	d. 1753, æ. 73	w. of Thomas, Jr.
Sandford, Hannah ?	Sept. 3, 1732.	d. 1774	m. 1733, Sarah Treadwell.
Sanford, Ezekiel 1706	R.C. June 2, 1734.	....	....
Stanley, James	F.C. Apl. 8, 1736.	....	w. of James.
Stanley, ——	F.C. Apl. 8, 1736.	....	w. of Peter.
Sherman, Martha	R.C. May 16, 1736.	d. 1778, æ. 75	w. of Nathaniel of Stratford,
Sherwood, Mercy (Sherman)	R.C. Aug. 8, 1736.	d. 1807, æ. 85?	dau. of Dea. David.
Summers, Abiah	R.C. May 16, 1736.	....	w. of Jabez.
Speer, Abigail	R.C. Apl. 29, 1750.	d. 1779	w. of Ebenezer.
Sherman, Elnathan, bap. 1709?	R.C. Feb. 3, 1751.	d. 1793	s. of David Sherman, Jr.
Sherman, Eunice (Gregory)	R.C. Feb. 3, 1751.	....	w. of Elnathan; m. 1750.
Sherwood, Elizabeth	F.C. Sept. 2, 1750.	d. 1787	w. of Matthew
Sanford, Zachariah,	before 1762?	d. 1773, æ. 52	Householder 1722; m. 1736,
Silliman, Daniel,	before 1762.	d. 1777	m. Sarah. [Ann Hall.
Seeley, Lt. Nathan	before 1762.	d. 1797, æ. 62	w. of Dea. Seth.
Seeley, Joanna	....	d. 1810, æ. 84	m. Mercy, who d. 1819, æ. 98.
Seeley, Dea. Abel	before 1776.	....	....
Smith, Joseph	before 1769.	d. 1817, æ. 79?	s. of Joseph.
Seeley, Dea. Seth, bap. 1733	before 1782.	d. 1807, æ. 53	Dea, 1799; s. of Elnathan.
Sherman, Dea. Seth	....	d. 1805	s. of Elnathan.
Sherman, Dea. Silas	before 1790.	d. after 1806	m. Mary, dau. of Joseph and
Sturges, Lewis	1797	d. after 1806	[Anna (Knowles) Porter.
Smith, Justin	1800	d. 1807, æ. 80	Prof. Mathematics, Yale
Strong, Prof. Nehemiah	before 1805.	d. 1811, æ. 68	m. Mary ——. [College.
Summers, Capt. Stephen, Sr.	R.C. before 1806. F.C. Dec. 1806.	....	....
Sherman, Mary	before 1806.	d. 1810, æ. 73	w. of Dea. Silas [Sherman.
Sherwood, Eunice	before 1806.	d. 1808, æ. 88	d. of Nathaniel and Mercy
Sterling, Eunice (Summers)	before 1806.	d. 1811, æ. 98	dau. of John; wid. of
Seeley, Mercy	before 1806.	d. 1841	wid. of Dea Abel. [Stephen.
Sherman, Charity	before 1806.	....	w. of Ebenezer.

Name.	Admitted.	Removed.	Remarks.
Sherman, Rebecca (French)	before 1806.	d. 1825, æ. 70	w. of Capt. David (lost at sea.)
Summers, Betsey	before 1806.	d. 1825, æ. 47	w. of Capt. Stephen, Jr.
Sturges, Mary	before 1806.		w. of Lewis.
Smith, ——	before 1806.	d. after 1830	w. of Justin.
Seelye, Miss Anna	before 1806.	d. 1815, æ. 52	d. of Dea. Seth and Joanna.
Strong, Joseph	R.C. before 1806.	d. 1816, æ. 75	s. of Joseph and Charity Wells, m. Comfort Nichols.
Sherman, Silas	R.C. before 1806. F.C. Mch. 5, 1808.	d. 1825, æ. 66	
Sherman, Abbe	R.C. before 1806. F.C. Mch. 5, 1808.		w. of Silas.
Summers, Aaron		d. 1806, æ. 81	
Summers, Stephen, Jr.	R.C. before 1806.	d. 1810	(Sherwood.
Sterling, David	R.C. before 1806.	d. 1843, æ. 72	s. of Abijah and Eunice
Sterling, Deborah	R.C. before 1806. F.C. Nov. 6, 1808.	d. 1849, æ. 74	dau. Joseph and Comfort (Nichols) Strong; w. of David.
Sterling, Sarah	R.C. before 1806.		wid. of ——.
Sterling, Philip	R.C. before 1806. F.C. Mch. 7, 1819.	Trumbull 1822.	
Sterling, Ruth	R.C. before 1806. F.C. May 4, 1817.		w. of Philip.
Smith, Betsey	R.C. before 1806.		w. of Brace.
Sherwood, Zachariah	R.C. before 1806.		
Sherwood, Anne	R.C. before 1806.	d. 1811, æ. 65	w. of Zachariah.
Summers, Mary	Jan. 7, 1807.	d. 1824, æ.	w. of Stephen.
Summers, Mary		d. 1811, æ. 65	wid. of Samuel
Sterling, Sherwood	Oct. 7, 1821.	D. Jan. 24, 1830	s. of David and Deborah.
Seeley, Ruth		d. 1815, æ. 29	w. of Joseph.
Seeley, Rhoda		d. 1819, æ. 80	wid. of Seth.
Treadwell, Ruth	L. July 10, 1695, fr. Fairfield		
Treadwell, Edward	R.C. Dec. 23, 1695.	d. after 1734	both F.C. May 10, 1713.
Treadwell, ——	R.C. Dec. 23, 1695.	d. after 1731	w. of Edward.
Treadwell, John	R.C. Feb. 8, 1697.	d. after 1712	d. before 1716.
Treadwell, Samuel, Sr.	F.C. Feb. 20, 1698.	d. after 1705	
Treadwell, Samuel, Jr.	R.C. Apr. 23, 1698.	d. after 1713	
Treadwell, Martha	R.C. Apr. 23, 1698.		w. of Samuel.
Treadwell, Ephraim	R.C. Mch.19, 1704.	d. after 1708	
Treadwell, Abigail	L. Nov.24, 1704,fr. Woodbury		
Treadwell, Timothy	R.C. Feb. 17, 1705.	d. 1720, æ. 37	m. March 24, 1714, Deborah Burr, dau. of Joha and Sarah Fitch.
Treadwell, Sarah	R.C. Feb. 17, 1705.		m. 1733, Ezekiel Santord.
Treadwell, Deborah	1705.	d. after 1749	wid. of Timothy.
Trowbridge, Joseph	R.C. June 5, 1709.	d. 1716	
Trowbridge, Anne	R.C. June 5, 1709.	d. after 1734	w. of Joseph.
Trowbridge, Samuel, Sr.	1699 F.C. July 23, 1710.	d. after 1732	
Trowbridge, Sarah (Lacey)	R.C. Feb. 14, 1714.	d. after 1731	w. of Samuel, m. 1697.
Treadwell, Lt. Hezekiah, bap. 1707	R.C. Feb. 27, 1732.	d. 1776	s. of John.
Treadwell, Mehitable	R.C. Feb. 27, 1732.		w. of Hezekiah.
Treadwell, Zachariah 1700	R.C. Aug. 8, 1731.	d. 1786	
Treadwell, John, bap. 1705	R.C. Aug. 8, 1731.		s. of John.
Trowbridge, John, bap. 1705	R.C. Aug. 8, 1731.		s. of Samuel.
Treadwell, Elizabeth, bap. 1700	R.C. Aug. 8, 1731.		dau. of Edward.
Treadwell, Samuel, bap. 1704	before 1731.	d. 1787	s. of Ephraim.
Trowbridge, Samuel, Jr., bap. 1709.	before 1731.	d. after 1736	m. 1722.
Trowbridge, Sarah (Seeley)	before 1731.		w. of Samuel, Jr., m. 1722.
Treadwell, Jacob, bap. 1706	R.C. Feb. 27, 1732.	d. after 1736	s. of Ephraim.
Treadwell, ——	R.C. Feb. 27, 1732.		w. of Jacob.
Turney, Robert	R.C. July 9, 1732.	d. after 1735	
Turney, ——	R.C. July 9, 1732.		w. of Robert, dau. Joseph.
Trowbridge, Anne, bap. 1713	R.C. Mch.11, 1733.		m. 1735, Jacob Wakeley.
Trowbridge, Sarah, bap. 1716.	R.C. Jan. 22, 1734.		dau. of Samuel, Sr.
Treadwell, Benjamin, bap. 1700	1733.	d. after 1735	s. of Edward.
Turney, Jonah	1735.		
Turney, John	R.C. Mch.16, 1735.	d. after 1735	
Turney, Hannah (Porter)	R.C. Mch 16, 1735.		w. of John, m. 1734.
Treadwell, Hezekiah	before 1806.	d. 1806	
Treadwell, Robert	before 1806.		
Treadwell, Mary	before 1806.		wid. of ——.
Wheeler, Dea. Isaac, Sr.	June 13, 1695.	d. before 1732?	
Wheeler, Anne	L. July 10, 1695, fr. Fairfield		
Wheeler, Mercy	L. July 10, 1695, fr. Fairfield		

—173—

Name.	Admitted.	Removed.	Remarks.
Wells, Abigail	L. July 10, 1695, fr. Fairfield	....	m. Thomas Turney, 1709?
Wakeley, Abigail	L. July 10, 1695, fr. Stratford	....	dau. of Henry, m. Samuel Gregory, Jr.
Wheeler, Sarah	R.C. Jan. 31, 1696.	....	w. of Ephraim.
Wheeler, Rebecca	F.C. Oct. 25, 1696.	d. about 1719	
Wells, Sergt. Samuel, Sr.	R.C. Feb. 8, 1697.	d. before 1731	[3d w, m. Oct. 25, 1711, Abigail —.
Wheeler, Sergt. Samuel	R.C. Feb. 8, 1697.	d. after 1703	
Wakeley, Jonathan, Sr.	R.C. Feb. 8, 1697.	d. after 1732	
Walker, Joanna	R.C. Feb. 8, 1697.	....	
Wheeler, Ruth	R.C. Feb. 8, 1697.	....	
Wakeley, Ruth	R.C. Feb. 8, 1697.	....	
Wheeler, Joseph	L. 1695, fr. Concord	....	m. before 1697.
Wheeler, —	L. 1695, fr. Concord	....	w. of Joseph.
Wheeler, Rebecca	F.C. Aug. 28, 1698.	....	wid. of Isaac.
Whitacus, Sarah	L. June 17, 1705, fr. Concord	....	
Wakeley, Rachel, bap. 1707	....	....	w. of Henry.
Wakeley, Henry	R.C. Feb. 29, 1708.	d. 1743, æ. 60	m. 1710, Sarah Frost.
Wheeler, Dr. John	R.C. Mch. 5, 1710.	d. after 1731	
Wakeley, Sarah (Frost)	R.C. Oct. 28, 1710.	d. after 1731	w. of Henry, m. 1709.
Wakeley, Joseph	R.C. Mch. 11, 1711.	d. after 1732	
Wakeley, Israel	R.C. July 22, 1711.	d. after 1731	[Turney.
Wheeler, Timothy, Sr.	R.C. Oct. 26, 1712.	d. 1730, æ. 70	m. Apr. 11, 1683, Rebecca
Wheeler, Isaac	R.C. Oct. 26, 1712.	d. Nov. 17, 1733	
Wakeley, Anne	R.C. Oct. 26, 1712.	....	w. of Timothy Wheeler, Jr.
Wells, Samuel, Jr.	R.C. Dec. 21, 1712.	d. Apr. 16, 1751	
Wells, Sarah	R.C. Dec. 21, 1712.	....	w. of Samuel.
Wakeley, Nathaniel	R.C. Oct. 26, 1712.	d. after 1721	
Wakeley, Rebecca	F.C. Mch. 9, 1712.	....	w. of Nathaniel.
Wheeler, Ebenezer	R.C. Feb. 7, 1714.	d. after 1733	s. of Isaac.
Wheeler, Abiah	R.C. Feb. 7, 1714.	....	dau. of Ephraim.
Wells, Elizabeth	R.C. Feb. 7, 1714.	....	dau. of Samuel, Sr., m. 1718, John Chuckstone. [ley.
Wakeman, Anne	R.C. Feb. 7, 1714.	....	
Whitney, Richard	1716.	d. after 1732	m. 1750, Experience Beards-
Wheeler, Hannah	F.C. Feb. 16, 1718.	d. after 1731	w. of Dr. John.
Wells, Abigail	F.C. June 22, 1718.	d. after 1731	Third w. of Samuel, Sr.
Wakeley, Mary	F.C. Sept. 7, 1718.	d. after 1731	w. of Jonathan, Sr.
Werden, Dr. Nathaniel	F.C. Dec. 21, 1718.	....	
Werden, ——	F.C. Dec. 21, 1718.	....	w. of Dr. Nathaniel.
Wakeley, ——	before 1731.	....	w. of Israel.
Worden, Jemima	R.C. Aug. 8, 1731.	....	w. of Thomas.
Wheeler, Andrew, bap. 1693	before 1731.	....	s. of Ephraim.
Wheeler, ——	before 1731.	....	w. of Andrew.
Wheeler, Samuel, bap. 1701	Apr. 16, 1732.	....	s. of Samuel.
Wheeler, ——	Apr. 16, 1732.	....	w. of Samuel.
Wakeley, Rebecca	Mch. 10, 1734.	....	w. of Jonathan, Jr.
Wheeler, Timothy, Jr., b. 1691	F.C. Feb. 18, 1736.	d. 1752, æ. 63	m. 1712.
Wheeler, Anne (Wakeley)	F.C. Feb. 18, 1736.	d. 1764, æ. 72	w. of Timothy, Jr., m. 1713.
Wheeler, Benjamin	R.C. Mch. 25, 1750.	d. 1798, æ. 74	
Wheeler, Mary	R.C. Mch. 25, 1750.	d. 1738, æ. 71	w. of Benjamin.
Wheeler, David, bap. 1713	R.C. July 29, 1750.	d. after 1753	s. of Dr. John.
Wheeler, Lois (Chauncey)	R.C. July 29, 1750.	....	w. of David.
Wells, David, bap. 1718	R.C. Mch. 30, 1751.	d. 1793	s. of Samuel, Jr.
Wells, Ruth (Burrows)	R.C. Mch. 30, 1751.	d. 1766, æ. 35	m. 1750, w. of David.
Wheeler, Timothy, bap. 1750	before 1806.	d. 1815, æ. 65	s. of Benjamin.
Worden, Capt. William, Sr. ...1768	before 1806.	d. 1868, æ. 73	
Worden, William, Jr. 1788	before 1806.	d. 1811, æ. 54	
Wheeler, Griswold (Grissell)	before 1806.	d. 1816, æ. 62	w. of Timothy.
Worden, Nancy	before 1806.	d. 1846	w. of Samuel. [m. 1893.
Waterman, Rev. Elijah	L. Jan. 1, 1806.	d. 1825, æ. 56	2d w., Mrs. Lucy Talcott,
Waterman, Lucy (Abbe)	1806	d. 1822, æ. 44	w. of Rev. Elijah.
Worden, Dorcas (Cooke), b. 1763	before 1806.	d. 1854	w. of William, Jr.
Wade, Nathaniel 1793	R.C. before 1806.	d. after 1834	
Wade, Ruth	{ R.C. before 1806. F.C. Apr. 8 1810. }	1856	d. 1856	w. of Nathaniel.
Worden, Samuel 1795	{ R.C. before 1806. F.C. 1807. }		d. after 1835	

CHURCH MEMBERS IN 1731

As recorded by Rev. Samuel Cooke in book No. 1, page 38.

The present members of this Church in full Communion this 28th day of July, 1731; at diverse times admitted are Nathan Beardsles[1] wife, John Hubbel & his wife, the Widdow Odel[2], Alexander Fairchilds wife, Henry Summers his wife, *Mrs. Smedly, Dr. Wheeler & his [3]wife, Justice Bennitt & his wife, *Deacon Sherwood & his wife, Serj[t] Burr[4] & his [5]wife, Henry Rowland[6] & his wife, Widow Wells, *Cap[t] Sherwood & his wife, Nathaniel Wakely his wife, *Andrew Wheeler & his wife*, M[rs] Hodgdon[7], Widow Hubbel[8], Widow Fayerweather, Major Burr & his wife, Lieu[t] Richard Hubbel, *Moses Jacksons wife, Widow Jackson[9], John Jackson, Lieu[t] Daniel Hubbel & his wife, Edward Lacy[11] & his wife & mother, Stephen[12] Hubbel his[13] wife, Samuel Cooke & *his wife, David[14] Sherman & *his wife, Hez.[15] Odel & his[16] wife, Zech Meads[17] wife, Ens[o] Gregory's wife[18], Enoch Gregory's wife[19], Jonathan Wakely's wife[20], Henry Wakely & his wife, John Beardsle[21] & his [22]wife, John Hall & his [23]wife, Widow[24] Seelye, Edward Tredwell[25] & his wife, Widow Tredwell[26], Francis Hall[27] & his wife, Zechariah Lawrence his wife, David Jackson, Samuel Trowbridge & his wife, Serj[t] Odel & his wife, Samuel[28] Hall & his [29]wife & mother, Cap[t] Sherman[30] & his wife, Samuel Trowbridge Jun[r] & his wife, Mr. Edwards & his wife, Thomas Edwards & his wife, John Edwards & his wife, Joseph Edwards, Israel Wakely & his wife, John Middlebrook & his wife, John Summers & his wife, James Hubbel, Ebenezer Wheelers wife, James Fairchild & his wife, Thaddeus[31] Gregory & his wife[32], Charles Burritts wife[33], Widow Summers[34], Jacob[35] Starling & his wife, Serj[t] Joseph[37] Booth & his[38] wife, Widow [39]Hawley, *Serj[t] French & his [40]wife, Samuel French Jun[r] his wife, Daniel Beardsles wife, Stephen Burrows[41] & his [42]wife, Nathaniel[43] Silliman & his [44]wife, Daniel Knaps wife, Jonathan Morehouse & his wife, all in good standing; besides whom there is the Widow Sarah Hall but lying at present under a publick Censure of Admonition.

REV. ELIJAH WATERMAN'S LISTS,

In book No. 1, pages 66–69, Church Record for 1806.

1806.	Names of Communicants.
Males.	Rev. Elijah Waterman, Pastor.
	Deacon Seth Seelye.
	Deacon Seth Sherman.
	John Cooke (aged 91, son of Rev. Mr. Cooke).
	Abel Seelye.
	Joseph Knap.
	Nehemiah Strong (quondam Professor at College).
	Timothy Wheeler.
	William Warden, Sen.
1798.	Josiah Lacy.
	Deacon James E. Beach—chosen Deacon Oct. 1806.
1795.	Lambert Lockwood.
	Samuel Penny.
1800.	Lewis Mallet.
1797.	Lewis Sturges.
	William Warden, Jun.
1800.	Justin Smith.
1798.	John Nichols.
	Hezekiah Treadwell. Total, 19.
Dec. 1806.	Stephen Summers (Senior).
	William DeForrest.
	Joseph Backus.
	Robert Treadwell.
May 3, 1807.	Talcot Hawley.
Sept. 20.	Samuel Darling—and
	Nancy Darling, his wife.
Females.	Mary Sherman, wife of Deacon S. Sherman.
	Widow Mary Lacy.
	Widow Eunice Sterling.
	Widow Eunice Sterling, 2d.
	Mary Seelye, wife of Abel Seelye.
	Widow Anne Hubbell.
	Widow Ellen Hubbell.
	Widow Anne Hubbell.
	Widow Ellen Hawley.
	Widow Griswold Burroughs.
	Widow Mary Hubbell.
	Widow Mary Treadwell.
	Huldah Beach, wife of Dr. J. E. Beach.
	Griswold Wheeler, wife of Timothy Wheeler.

1806.	Names of Communicants.
Females.	Huldah Parish, wife of Joel Parish.
	Charity Sherman, wife of Ebenezer Sherman.
	Nancy Warden, wife of Samuel Warden.
	Rebecca Sherman, wife of David Sherman.
	Elizabeth Lockwood, wife of Lamt. Lockwood.
	Lucy Waterman, wife of Rev. E. Waterman.
	Jemima Penny, wife of Samuel Penny.
	Betsey Summers, wife of Stephen Summers, Jun.
	Jemima Burr, wife of Samuel Burr.
	Hannah Dudley, wife of Azel Dudley.
	Jerusha Cable, wife of Samuel Cable.
	Anne Lacy, wife of Josiah Lacy.
	Mary Sturges, wife of Lewis Sturges.
	Irena Hull, wife of William B. Hull.
	——— Smith, wife of Justin Smith.
	Anne Mallet, wife of Lewis Mallet.
	Dorcas Warden, wife of William Warden, Jun.
	Miss Anna Seelye. Total, 32.
Jan. 1807.	Mary Summers, wife of Stephen Summers.
	Sally Deforrest, wife of William Deforrest.
	Huldah Backus, wife of Joseph Backus.
	Sophia Treadwell, wife of Robert Treadwell.
March 1, 1807.	Philena Gregory, wife of James Gregory.
May 3.	Widow Miriam Hubbell.

NAMES OF THE CHURCH MEMBERS

Who have come with their children to the Ordinance of Baptism.

1806.	Samuel Hawley and Lucy his wife.
	Abijah Hawley and Polly his wife.
	David Hawley.
	Aaron Hawley and Griswold his wife.
	Wilson Hawley and Charity his wife.
	Gurdon Hawley and Anne his wife.
	Widow Ruth Hawley.
	Ebenezer Hawley.
	Zalmon Hawley and Anne his wife.
	Salmon Hubbell and Sarah his wife.
	Ezekiel Hubbell and Catharine his wife.
	Aaron Hubbell and Sally his wife.
	David Hubbell and Anne his wife.
	Joseph Strong.
	Silas Sherman and Abbe his wife.
	Abijah Morehouse and Rachel his wife.
	Stephen Summers, Jun., and Betsey his wife.
	Samuel Burr.
	Ezra Gregory and Sarah his wife.
	Stephen Hull and Abigail his wife.
	Thomas Gouge and Ruth his wife.
	David Sterling and Deborah his wife.
	Nathaniel Wade and Ruth his wife.
	William Deforrest and Sally his wife.
	Daniel Fayerweather and Betsey his wife.
	Samuel Warden.
	Ichabod Lewis.
	Thomas Brothwell and ——— his wife.
	Widow Ann Meaker.
	Elijah Burr and Deborah his wife.
	David Meaker and Esther his wife.
	Widow Sarah Sterling.
	Drew Morgan and his wife.
	Polly Burroughs.
	Capt. Stephen Summers and Mary his wife.
	James Gregory and Philena his wife.
	Philip Sterling and Ruth his wife.
	Azel Dudley. Total, 71.
July 31, 1806.	Primus Freeman and Chloe his wife. } Negroes.
	Thomas Freeman and Chloe his wife. }
	Betty Smith, wife of Brace Smith.
	Zechariah Sherwood and Anna his wife.
July 5, 1807.	William Risley and Lavina Risley his wife.

NAMES OF PERSONS

Connected with the parish, mentioned in the church record, many of whom may have been church or covenant members, but who are not so designated in the records, 1695 to 1830.

Name.	Year of Mention.	Death.	Remarks.
Adams, Freegrace	1704	....	Stratford Church, 1701.
Allen, Ebenezer	1792	1830, æ. 77	
Allen, Edna (Wheeler)	....	1809, æ. 74	dau. of wid. Hannah, w. of Nehemiah.
Allen, Nehemiah	....	1810, æ. 81	
Allen, Samuel B.	....	1818, æ. 35	
Andrews, ——	....	1821, æ. 22	w. of ———.
Allen, ——	....	1824	w. of James, 3d.
Allen, Capt. James, 3d	....	1826, æ. 40	
Allen, ——	....	1828	w. of Ethan.
Allen, Hannah	....	1828, æ. 68	w. of Ebenezer.
Burr, Sarah....m. June 29,	1692	before 1698	dau. of Col. John, w. of Rev. Charles
Burr, Rebecca	1704	....	m. Capt. Sam. Sherwood. [Chauncey.
Barly, ——	1706	....	wid. of ———.
Burroughs, John....1706,	1711	....	
Bostwick, Joseph	1709	....	
Bulkley, Peter	....	....	m. 1709, Hannah ———.
Booth, Jonathan 1709,	1710	....	
Beardsley, Nathaniel	1710	....	
Beardsley, ——	1710	....	w. of Nathaniel.
Beecher, Sarah	1710	....	
Bennett, Isaac, Jr., bap.1711,	1736	....	
Bacon, Beriah	1713	....	m. Anne Odell.
Bronson, Richard	1714	....	
Bennett, Jeremiah	1716	1773	
Beach, Esther	1716	....	m. Capt. Daniel Hubbell.
Burroughs, Hannah	1720	....	
Bassett, Jonadab	....	....	m. 1719, Mary Phippany.
Burroughs, Eunice	1720	....	
Burr, Thaddeus	1732	....	
Barnham, Abner	....	....	m. 1732, Rachel Wakeley.
Burr, Nathaniel	....	....	m. 1732, Mary Turney.
Burrows, Patience	....	....	m. 1736, David Sanford.
Brown, Ann...........b.	1742	....	m. Wolcott Chauncey.
Burr, Mary	....	1742, æ. 33	w. of William.
Beach, Elizabeth	1742	....	m. Lt. Benjamin Fayerweather.
Bennett, Hannah	....	1743, æ. 31	w. of Dea. William.
Burton, Ruth	....	1748, æ. 30	w. of Solomon.
Beardsley, Robert....1750,	1754	....	
Burritt, Charles, Jr.	1750	1799, æ. 61?	
Beardsley, Johannah	....	....	m. 1750, Hezekiah Seeley.
Benedict, Joseph	....	....	m. 1750, Elizabeth Hall.
Beardsley, Experience	....	1780	m. 1750, Richard Whitney.
Burr, Capt. John	....	1752, æ. 55	
Burr, Catharine	....	1753, æ. 53	w. of John.
Burr, Joseph	1754	....	

Name.	Year of Mention.	Death.	Remarks.
Burr, Charity (Wells)	....	1769, æ. 48	dau. of John Wells, wid. of William
Burrit, Elihu	1758	1793	[Burr, m. Joseph Strong.
Bennett, Mary	1770	....	dau. of Dea. Wm. and Eunice; m.
Burr, John	....	1771, æ. 44	[Dea. Elijah Hawley.
Bangs, ——	....	1771	w. of Lemuel.
Bennett, ——	....	1772	w. of Jeremiah.
Burton, ——	....	1772	w. of Richard.
Burton, Richard	....	1773	
Burr, Daniel	1773	....	
Burr, Margaret	1773	....	w. of Daniel.
Burroughs, Lieut. Edward	....	1776, æ. 42?	
Burrit, Comfort	....	1777	w. of ——.
Bennett, Joseph Wilson	1778	1813, æ. 62?	
Burritt, Isaac	....	1782, æ. 24	s. of Elihu and Eunice.
Bennett, Sarah	1785	....	
Burritt, Lucy	....	1788	w. of Charles.
Booth, Jerusha	1789	....	w. of Samuel.
Beardsley, ——	....	1790	w. of Squire.
Burroughs, ——	....	1791	wid. of ——.
Bennett, ——	....	1792	w. of Joseph W.
Burr, Capt. Gershom	1793	....	
Burr, Charity	....	1794, æ. 27	dau. of Ozias.
Burr, Rebecca	....	1794, æ. 27	dau. of Ozias.
Baker, ——	....	1795	w. of Scotts.
Burroughs, David	....	1795	
Beach, ——	....	1795	w. of Lazarus.
Beach, Lazarus	1796	....	
Burritt, ——	1796	....	wid. of Sherman.
Burr, Susannah	....	1796, æ. 24	dau. of Daniel and Margaret.
Burr, ——	....	1797	w. of Ozias, Jr.
Bradley, ——	....	1797	wid. of ——.
Burroughs, Ephraim	....	1798	
Bennett, ——	....	1798	w. of Philip.
Beardsley, Truman	....	1798	
Benedict, Thaddeus	....	1800	s. of Thaddeus.
Broadfoot, —— ——	....	1801	w. of ——.
Baker, ——	....	1801	w. of Capt. Jonathan.
Burritt, Charles?	....	1801, æ. 80	
Burritt, Lucy	....	1801, æ. 80	w. of Charles.
Bennett, Elizabeth	....	1802	
Burroughs, Hulda	....	1803, æ. 66	dau. of Peter and Mary, w. Stephen.
Beardsley, Wheeler	....	1804	
Burritt, Sarah	....	1805, æ. 63	w. of Elijah.
Burtington, N ——	....	1805	
Bennett, Philip	....	1807, æ. 80	
Beardsley, Abijah	....	1807, æ. 23	
Brinsmade, Samuel	....	1808, æ. 57	
Benedict, ——	....	1808, æ. 53	w. of Jesse.
Blakeman, Capt. Curtis	1810	....	
Backus, Rev. Simon	1805	1823, æ. 85	
Benedict, Esther	....	1810, æ. 35	w. of Jesse.
Burr, Hephzibah (Nichols)	....	1810, æ. 77	wid. of Justus.
Burroughs, Mary	....	1811, æ. 41	w. of Capt. Stephen.
Burr, Jesse	....	1813	
Burr, Aaron	....	1814, æ. 57	
Burritt, Abigail	....	1814, æ. 81	
Burritt, Sarah	....	1815	w. of Elijah.

Name.	Year of Mention.	Death.	Remarks.
Brothwell, Mehitable		1815, æ. 75	wid. of Joseph.
Bennett, Abijah		1815, æ. 22	
Burroughs, Elizabeth Ann.		1815, æ. 41	w. of Edward.
Brinsmade, ——		1817	sister of Elijah Burritt, wid. of ——.
Burrit, Comfort		1818	
Brothwell, Capt. William		1818, æ. 25	s. of Thomas.
Bradley, Charity		1818, æ. 27	sister of Sturges.
Beardsley, Amos		1818, æ. 74	
Botsford, Moses K.	1819		
Beers, Mary		1819, æ. 52	
Benedict, William		1819, æ. 41	
Boughton, John	1819		
Burr, Sarah		1820, æ. 81	w. of Ozias.
Booth, Ebenezer		1820, æ. 47	
Baldwin, Phebe		1821, æ. 34	w. of Eliada.
Birch, David	1822		
Brown, Ebenezer	1822		
Bradley, ——		1822, æ. 82	wid. of Hezekiah.
Boughton, Chauncey		1825, æ. 25	
Benedict, Deborah		1825, æ. 69	wid. of Thaddeus, Esq.
Benedict, Comfort		1825, æ. 62	w. of ——.
Boughton, Daniel		1826, æ. 59	
Blackman, Frederick		1826, æ. 19	
Bulkley, ——		1826	w. of Morehouse.
Banks, Laura		1826, æ. 33	
Beardsley, Lucy		1828	w. of ——.
Brothwell, William		1828, æ. 73	
Benedict, Thaddeus		1838	
Booth, Comphy		1843, æ. 66	wid. of Ebenezer. [David Sherman.
Beardsley, Drusilla		1839, æ. 87	wid. of Ensign Abijah, dau. of Dea.
Chauncey, John	b. 1695		s. of Rev. Charles.
Chauncey, Ich. Wolcot	b. 1703		s. of Rev. Charles.
Clark, Ephraim	1704		
Corbit, John			m. 1712, Mary Peat.
Cole, Samuel	1716, 1717		
Chuckstone, John	1718		m. Elizabeth Wells.
Chauncey, Wolcot	b. 1732	1805	s. of Robert, m. Ann Brown.
Cooke, Sarah			m. 1734, James Sherman.
Chapman, Hope	1744, 1755		
Chauncey, Lois			m. 1749, David Wheeler.
Cable, Andrew		before 1771	
Clifford, Dr. Daniel	1773	1781	
Cope, John		1776	
Cook, ——		1777	w. of Thomas.
Cable, Wheeler		1782	s. of Samuel ?
Cole, Mary		1782	
Crofut James	1785	1810	
Clark, Bensom	1792		
Cable, Samuel	1765, 1782, 1793	1806	
Cable, Mary		1793, æ. 54	w. of Samuel.
Cooke, ——		1799	w. of John
Clifford, Daniel	1801, 1825		
Cable, William	1803	1822, æ. 55	
Cooley, Benjamin		1803	
Cadwell, Deborah		1806	
Clark, David	1812		

Name.	Year of Mention.	Death.	Remarks.
Clark, Caty	1812	....	w. of David.
Cooke, Thomas	....	1814, æ. 64	
Canfield, Ransom E.	1815, 1829	....	
Curtis, Polly	....	1813, æ. 33	w. of Matthew.
Coleman, Lemuel	1821, 1838	....	
Clarke, Sarah	....	1822, æ. 37	w. of Joseph.
Curtis, Selina	....	Oct. 7, 1823, æ. 28	w. of Epenetus.
Curtis, Epenetus	....	Dec. 5, 1823, æ. 37	
Chatfield, Mary	....	1824, æ. 99	wid. of ——.
Clifford, Mary	....	1825, æ. 24	w. of Daniel.
Clifford, Emily	....	1825, æ. 24	w. of James.
Cannon, John S.	....	1828, æ. 74	
Cable, ——	....	1829	w. of Thomas.
Curtis, Blakeman	....	1838	
Curtis, David	....	1838	
Dunning, John	1703, 1713	....	
Dunning, Benjamin	1707, 1713	....	
Downs, John	1713	....	M. Deborah Odell.
Davis, Mary	....	....	m. 1718, Samuel Lyon.
Dennie, John	1732	....	
Davison, James	1732	....	
Dibble, Abigail	....	....	m. 1731, Samuel Starr.
Dibble, Ezra	....	....	m. 1733, Elizabeth Wheeler.
Denison, Robert	....	....	m. 1733, Prudence Sherman.
Dumond, ——	....	1782	w. of William.
Daskam, ——	....	1803	w. of James.
Dickinson, Amelia	....	1819, æ. 28	
DeForest, Philo	....	1826, æ. 46	
Downs, ——	....	1827	
Edwards, ——	1733	....	w. of Thomas.
Edwards, Samuel	1796	....	
Edwards, Shelton	....	1796	
Ells, Hannah	1798	....	w. of Nathaniel.
Edwards, Zachariah	....	1809, æ. 35	
Edgerton, Patience	1811	....	w. of Eleazar.
Evitts, Daniel	....	1815, æ. 54	
Edwards, Prime	....	1822	
Edmonds, George	....	1823, æ. 62	
Ellis, Elisha	....	1825, æ. 44	
Everett, Benjamin	....	1825, æ. 24	
Everts, ——	....	1827	w. of ——.
Emery, Thomas	....	1828, æ. 27	
Eaton, Polly (Sherman)	....	1830, æ. 51	dau. of Elnathan, w. of William.
French, Deborah, bap. 1696	....	....	
Fairchild, Spidon?	1704	....	
Fairchild, ——	1704	....	wid. of ?
Frost, Sarah	....	....	m. 1710, Henry Wakeley.
Ferris, Samuel	1711	....	
Fairchild, David	1713	....	
Fairchild, Daniel	1713	....	
Frost, Eleanor	....	....	m. 1718, Jacob Weed.
Fitch, Daniel	....	....	m. 1732, Sarah Sherwood.
French, Martha	....	....	m. 1734, Peter Sherman.
French, Gamaliel, Sr.	....	1738, æ. 32	

Name.	Year of Mention.	Death.	Remarks.
French, Hannah		1745, æ. 33	w. of Gamaliel, Sr.
French, Line			m. 1750, Jedediah Wells.
French, Sarah	1754		w. of Gamaliel.
French, Ichabod		1776	
Frost, Benjamin		1776	
French, Hannah		1777	
Fayerweather, Nathaniel		1779	
French, ———		1785	w. of James.
French, Wheeler		1790	
Fowler, Nehemiah	1791		
Fairchild, Gershom		1792	
Fayerweather, James	1798	1820, æ. 46	
French, Capt. Samuel	1802	1803	
French, Mary		1803, æ. 45	w. of James.
French, Mehitable		1811, æ. 71	w. of James.
French, Mary		1814, æ. 72	w. of Benjamin.
French, John	1818		
French, Gamaliel, Jr.		1828, æ. 72	
French, ———		1830	w. of Joseph B.
French, Ann		1841, æ. 70	w. of James R.
Gregory, Samuel, Jr.	1701		
Gregory, Miriam			m. 1732, Ebenezer Hartshorn.
Gold, John	1732		
Garner, Edward	1736		
Gregory, Ruth		1772, æ. 36	w. of Seth.
Gregory, ———		1786	wid. of Thaddeus, Sr.
Gregory, ———		1786	w. of Samuel.
Gregory, ———		1787	w. of James.
Gregory, Ebenezer		1811	
Goodsell, William	1819		
Green, Jane		1821, æ. 27	w. of Thomas.
Gregory, Robert		1825, æ. 40	
Gouge, Frederick C.		1825, æ. 18	
Gibbs, Augusta		1829, æ. 20	
Hubbell, Capt. David ...b. 1690		1735	
Hall, Rebecca, bap. 1703	1723		dau. of Francis; m. Abner Frost.
Henrie, Samuel 1705,	1712		
Hall, Burgess, bap. 1701	1734		s. of Isaac.
Hawley, Joseph	1705		
Huttun, Sarah	1706		m. Robert Jackson.
Hollinsworth, Richard	1711		
Hull, Deborah	1711		m. John Beardsley, Sr.
Hall, Sarah		1729, æ. 26	w. of John.
Handford, ———	1732		w. of ———.
Hartshorn, Ebenezer	1732		m. Miriam Gregory.
Hawley, Catharine	1739		m. Lt. William Bennett.
Hall, Francis		1739, æ. 39	
Hubbell, Elnathan	1743		
Hubbell, Sarah (Seeley)		1744, æ. 22	w. of Jabez.
Hawley, Ephraim	1747		
Hawley, Sarah	1747		w. of Ephraim.
Hawley, Sarah	1748		w. of Samuel.
Hall, Ichabod	1749	1800	
Hubbell, Ebenezer	1750		
Hodgdon, Mehitable			m. 1750, Nehemiah Mead.

Name.	Year of Mention.	Death.	Remarks.
Hall, Elizabeth	....	....	m. 1750, Joseph Benedict.
Hill, Mary	....	....	m. 1750, Elnathan Parrott.
Hubbell, Onesimus	....	1754, æ. 23	
Hubbell, Rebecca	....	1754, æ. 19	dau. of Samuel and Rebecca.
Hawley, Molly	....	1765, æ. 17	dau. of Samuel and Sarah.
Hunt, Grissel	1770	....	w. of Isaac.
Hall, Stephen (Hull?)	1770	....	
Hall, Sarah	1770	....	w. of Stephen.
Hubbell, Roxana	1770	1805, æ. 60	w. of Richard, Jr.
Hubbell, Ann	....	1770, æ. 23	dau. of Benjamin.
Hall, James	1770	....	
Hall, Abigail	1770	....	w. of James.
Hall, Benjamin	1770	1774	
Hawley, Abigail	1772	1786, æ. 71	w. of Ezra.
Hubbell, Esther	....	1772	wid. of ———.
Hall, Huldah	....	1773, æ. 20	dau. of Richard and Hannah.
Hall, Mary Stiles	....	1773	
Hubbell, Joseph	1774	1777	
Hubbell, Katharine	....	1776, æ. 23	w. of Capt. Amos.
Hawley, Elizabeth	....	1776, æ. 35	dau. of Capt. Ezra; 1st w. of Aaron.
Hall, Nathan	....	1776	
Hawley, Ephraim, Jr.	....	1777, æ. 30	
Holberton, Ruth	1777	....	w. of Capt. Thomas.
Hubbell, Joseph, Jr.	1777	....	
Hubbell, William	1777	1805	
Hubbell, Walter	1777	....	
Hubbell, Ruth	1777	....	w. of Walter.
Hubbell, Daniel, Jr.	....	1778, æ. 28	
Hawley, Ann	....	1778	dau. of Ephraim.
Hubbell, Capt. Isaac	1778	1787	
Hall, ———	....	1778	w. of Ebenezer.
Hawley, Sarah	....	1781	w. of David.
Hoyt, Elizabeth	....	1781	
Haws, W.	....	1781	
Hall, Island	1782	....	
Hinman, ———	....	1782	wid. of ——.
Hawley, William	....	1784	
Hubbell, ———	....	1785	w. of Gideon.
Hawley, Ephraim	1786	before 1795	
Hubbell, ———	....	1786	w. of Capt. Isaac. [Aaron.
Hawley, Sarah (Comstock)	....	1786, æ. 39	dau. of Jonathan; 2d w. of Maj.
Hoyt, Capt. James	....	1787, æ. 54	
Hubbell, Benjamin, Jr.	....	1788	
Halberton, William	1790	1797	
Hillard, William	1792	....	
Hubbell, Hezekiah	....	1792	
Hawley, Isaac	....	1792	
Hawley, Isabel	....	1793	
Hinman, Isaac	1794	1817, æ. 54	
Hubbell, Eunice	....	1794, æ. 38	wid. of Abraham.
Hodgson, Hannah	....	1794	
Hubbell, Isaac	....	1795	
Hall, Gershom	....	1795, æ. 28	
Hall, John B.	1795	....	
Hall, Lucy	....	1796	dau. of Stephen.
Hubbell, Rebecca	....	1796	
Hawley, David, Jr.	....	1797	

Name.	Year of Mention.	Death.	Remarks.
Hawley, Samuel	1797	....	....
Hall, ——	....	1797	w. of Drew.
Hubbell, Capt. Wilson	1798	1799, æ. 26	....
Hubbell, ——	....	1798	w. of Wilson.
Hubbell, Rebecca	....	1798, æ. 39	dau. of Daniel.
Hubbell, Philo	....	1798	s. of Richard.
Hubbell, Sarah	....	1798, æ. 19	....
Hawley, Capt. Daniel	....	1799	....
Hubbell, ——	....	1799	w. of Abel.
Hoyt, George	1800	....	....
Hoyt, Deborah	1800	....	....
Hall, Philena	....	1801	dau. of Stephen.
Hubbell, Mary Alice	1801	....	w. of Capt. Ezekiel.
Hall, ——	....	1801	w. of Stephen.
Hollinsworth, Ruth	....	1802	....
Hall, Martha	....	1802	wid. of ——.
Hubbell, Esther	....	1802, æ. 36	dau. of Daniel.
Hodgden, William	....	1803	....
Hubbell, ——	....	1804	w. of Ezra.
Hoyt, James	....	1804, æ. 44	....
Hubbell, Elinor	1805	....	w. of Salmon.
Hubbell, Capt. Ezra	....	1805	....
Hall, Ebenezer	....	1805	....
Hall, Mabel	....	1807, æ. 91	wid. of ——.
Hoyt, Sarah	....	1807, æ 72	wid. of Capt. James?
Hubbell, ——	....	1807, æ. 40	wid. of Timothy.
Hubbell, John	....	1808, æ. 63	s. of Benjamin.
Hopkins, John	....	1808, æ. 51	....
Hinman, Charity	....	1808	w. of Isaac.
Hall, Lucy	....	1809, æ. 22	....
Hawley, Capt. Aaron	....	1810. æ. 40	....
Hultz, ——	....	1810	....
Hubbell, Betsey	....	1811, æ. 23	w. of David, Jr.
Hawley, Salmon	1811	....	....
Hubbell, Henry	....	1814, æ. 22	s. of Salmon.
Hull, Samuel	....	1814, æ. 27	s. of Stephen.
Hawley, Elijah	....	1815, æ. 77	....
Hubbell, Abigail	....	1816, æ. 66	wid. of ——.
Hull, Wakeman. 1817, 1850,	1861	....	....
Hultz, Polly	....	1819	wid. of ——.
Hall, Richard	....	1819	....
Hubbell, Anson	....	1819, æ. 32	....
Hubbell, Charles Raymond	....	1819, æ. 34	....
Holberton, Capt. Thomas	....	1822, æ. 84	....
Hodges, ——	1823	....	....
Hopkins, Mehitable	....	1824, æ. 51	....
Holberton, Bathsheba	....	1824	w. of Capt. Thomas.
Hawley, John	....	1823, æ. 18	s. of Abijah, Sr.
Hubbell, Onesimus	....	1824, æ. 69	s. of Daniel.
Hopkins, ——	....	1824	wid. of ——.
Hawley, Betsey	....	1825, æ. 26	w. of Capt. Abijah.
Hinman, Capt. Munson	1825	....	....
Hoyt, George, Cashier	....	1825, æ. 56	....
Hopkins, Catharine	....	1825, æ. 22	....
Holman, Dr. Thomas	....	1826, æ. 32	....
Hawley, Samuel, Jr.	....	1826, æ. 27	....
Hawley, Frederick	....	1827	....

Name.	Year of Mention.	Death.	Remarks.
Hubbell, George		1828	
Hubbell, Alfred		1828	
Hall, Ebenezer		1828	
Hall, ———		1828	w. of Elias.
Hawley, Isaac		1828, æ. 35	s. of Samuel, Dec'd.
Hawley, John		1829	
Hubbell, Anson Ezekiel		1830, æ. 23	s. of Capt. Ezekiel.
Hubbell, George William		1831, æ. 35	s. of Capt. Ezekiel.
Hubbell, Eunice		1838, æ. 68	
Hubbell, Catharine		1838	
Hoyt, Mercy Nichols		1839, æ. 80	
Hubbell, Elizabeth		1840, æ. 90	dau. of Benjamin.
Hubbell, Sarah		1842, æ. 81	w. of Abel.
Hubbell, Thaddeus		1849, æ. 85	
Hubbell, Penelope		1864, æ. 92	dau. of Richard, Jr., and Roxana.
Jackson, Esther, bap. 1696.			w. of Moses, Sr.
Jackson, Joshua	1698		
Jennings, Eunice			m. 1731, Elnathan Lyon.
Jennings, John	1732		
Jones, John	1734		
Jackson, Rachel	1739		w. of Isaac.
Jackson, David	1750		
Jackson, Amos	1754		
Jennings, Sally		1803	
Jackson, Aaron		1823	
Jones, Dr.	1825		
Jones, Ira		1836, æ. 65	
Jennings, Sarah (Ross)		1839, æ. 83	dau. of Rev. Robert, w. of Eliphalet.
Jones, Charity		1845, æ. 73	dau. of Jos. Strong, Esq., w. of Ira.
Knapp, Daniel	1731		
Knapp, Mary			m. 1733, Phinehas Price.
Kimberly, Prudence			m. 1735, Josiah Smith.
Knapp, Freelove		1771, æ. 31	w. of Capt. Joseph.
Knapp, ———		1782	w. of James.
Knapp, ———		1784	w. of Capt. Joseph.
Knapp, ———		1786	w. of James.
Kirtland, Zebulon	1788	1803, æ. 58	m. Betsey Cook.
Kirtland, Olive		1790, æ. 14	dau. of Ezra.
Knapp, Abijah	1790		
Knapp, John		1795, æ. 82	
Knapp, Hannah		1796, æ. 76	w. of John.
Kirtland, Ezra, Jr.		1799, æ. 47	
Kirtland, Olive (Wakeley)		1803, æ. 69	dau. of Zebulon, wid. of Ezra.
Kirtland, Elijah		1810	
Keith, John		1811	
Knapp, Lyman P.		1813, æ. 50	
Keeler, Anne		1815, æ. 63	1st w. of Patrick.
Knapp, Mary		1825, æ. 18	dau. of Ephraim.
Keeler, Patrick		1829, æ. 76	
Knapp, Robert		1834, æ. 52	
Lacey, Ebenezer, bap. 1704.	1735		s. of Edward.
Lake, Thomas	1706		
Leavenworth, Thomas	1708		
Lyon, Hannah	1709, 1714		w. of Nathaniel.

Name.	Year of Mention.	Death.	Remarks.
Lyon, Nathaniel	1711, 1714	....	....
Lacey, Henry,	1716, 1717	....	....
Lacey, Hannah	1717	....	w. of Henry.
Lyon, Samuel	....	....	m. 1718, Mary Davis.
Lawrence, Zachariah	1731	....	....
Lyon, Elnathan	....	....	m. 1732, Eunice Jennings.
Lacey, Ephraim	1749, 1754	....	s. of John.
Loveland, Asa	1770	....	....
Lacey, ———	....	1780	w. of Capt. Josiah.
Lemon, George	....	1781	[William.
Little, Ruth (Winton)	....	1784, æ. 53	wid. of Joseph Brinsmade, w. of Dr.
Lake, ———	....	1785	w. of Thomas.
Little, Otis	....	1788	....
Lacey, Ruth	....	1788, æ. 27	w. of Capt. Josiah.
Lacey, Margaret	....	1792, æ. 52	wid. of Benjamin.
Lacey, Molly	....	1793, æ. 32	w. of Capt. Josiah.
Lacey, John	....	1793, æ. 84	....
Lake, Reuben	....	1811, æ. 73	....
Lake, ———	....	1812	wid. of Reuben.
Linus, Nathaniel	....	1813, æ. 24	....
Lacey, Tabitha	....	1814, æ. 64	w. of Capt. Daniel.
Linus, Polly	....	1816, æ. 34	....
Lacey, Josiah	....	1818, æ. 22	....
Lyman, Eunice	....	1819, æ. 65	wid. of George.
Lacey, Squire	....	1819, æ. 30	....
Lacey, Betsey	....	1822, æ. 38	....
Linus, Mary	....	1824, æ. 71	w. of Nathaniel.
Lewis, Hazard	....	1825, æ. 71	....
Lewis, Clark	1825	....	....
Lewis, Everit	1825	....	....
Layfield, ———	....	1827	w. of ———.
Layfield, Mary	....	1827, æ. 18	....
Lewis, Truman	....	1830, æ. 61	....
Lewis, Chary	....	1831, æ. 64	....
Lacey, Michael	....	1835, æ. 51	....
Lacey, Sarah	....	1838, æ. 65	....
Leavens, Eleanor	....	1835, æ. 55	....
Mallery, Peter	1709	....	....
Morehouse, ———	1709	....	w. of Noah.
Morehouse, Nathan	1710	....	....
Miles, Lt. Richard	....	....	m. 1716, Mrs. Elizabeth Chauncey.
Mallory, Mary	1721	....	m. Alexander Fairchild.
Meeker, Ebenezer	1732	....	....
Moss, Abigail	....	....	m. 1733, Samuel Cooke.
Moss, Mrs. Mary	....	....	m. 1736, Rev. Ebenezer White.
Morris, George	1738, 1744	....	....
Merritt, George	1748, 1753	....	....
MacKane, ———	1750	....	....
Mead, Nehemiah	....	before 1773	m. 1750, Sarah Hodgdon.
Machard, Matthew, Jr.	....	1757, æ. 21	s. of Matthew and Sarah.
Morehouse, Ruth	1770	....	w. of Seth.
Morehouse, David	1770	1801	....
Mead, Sarah	....	1773	wid. of Nehemiah.
Meeker, William	....	1777	....
Mann, Hannah	....	1777	wid. of ———.
Mekinzy, Gilbert	1777	....	....

Name.	Year of Mention.	Death.	Remarks.
Meeker, ————	....	1777	wid. of ———.
Meeker, John	1778	1810, æ. 76	
Mackain, ————	....	1784	wid. of ———.
Morehouse, ————	....	1786	w. of David.
MacDimon, ————	....	1787	w. of ———.
Meeker, Peter	1791	....	
Morehouse, Martha	....	1792	
Morehouse, Isaac	....	1796	
Meeker, Lyman	1800	....	
Minot, ————	....	1800	wid. of ———.
Morehouse, Eunice	....	1801, æ. 27	w. of Lyman.
Mackenzie, John	....	1802	
Mackenzie, James	....	1802	
Meeker, Clark	....	1812	
Middlebrook, Samuel	....	1815	
Meeker, Polly	....	1817, æ. 26	w. of Seeley.
Middlebrook, Jerusha	....	1819	w. of Bradley.
Mallet, Avis	....	1819 or 1829	
Mallory, Jonathan	....	1821, æ. 77	
Mallory, Sarah	....	1829? 1822? æ. 74	wid. of Jonathan.
Morehouse, Anne	....	1823, æ. 37	
Morse, Samuel C.	1824, 1826	....	
Mason, ————	....	1825, æ. 22	w. of Isaac.
Miller, George	....	1826, æ. 42	
Morehouse, Abijah	....	1826, æ. 44	
Minot, Sarah	....	1826, æ. 64	w. of ———.
Mills, Jonathan	....	1826, æ. 56	
Mitchell, Patience	....	1826, æ. 56	w. of Joel.
Mills, ————	....	1826	w. of Jonathan.
Moore, Mark	1827	....	
Morgan, Elizabeth	....	1828	wid. of ———.
May, ————	....	1828, æ. 40	w. of Joseph.
Morehouse, ————	....	1837, æ. 82	
Morehouse, Lorinthia	....	1841, æ. 30	dau. of Anson and Anna.
Nichols, Abram	1703	....	
Nichols, Benjamin..before	1714	....	
Nichols, Esther	....		m. 1717, Daniel Wheeler.
Nichols, Mehitable	....	1735, æ. 32	w. of John.
Nichols, Rebecca	....	1749, æ. 36	w. of John.
Nichols, Sarah	....	1753, æ. 19	
Nichols, Hulda	....	1759, æ. 40	w. of John.
Nickerson, ————	....	1781	w. of Nathaniel.
Nichols, ————	....	1785	w. of John.
Nichols, ————	....	1786	wid. of ———.
Nichols, Reuben	....	1797	
Nichols, Philip	....	1807, æ. 80	
Nichols, Mary	....	1811, æ. 77	wid. of Philip.
Nichols, Nancy	....	1812, æ. 27	w. of George.
Nichols, Samuel	....	1814, æ. 22	
Nichols, Catharine	....	1815, æ. 47	w. of Richard P.
Nash, Grace	....	1815, æ. 44	wid. of ———.
Northrop, Norman	1825	....	
Nichols, Phebe	....	1835, æ. 82	wid. of John, Jr.
Niles, Samuel	....	1838	
Nichols, Hannah	....	1855, æ. 69	

—188—

Name.	Year of Mention.	Death.	Remarks.
Odell, Sarah	....	....	m. 1713, Dan. Comstock, of Norwalk.
Odell, Ebenezer	....	1743, æ. 19	s. of William and Sarah.
Odell, Johannah (Peck)	....	1776, æ. 37	w. of Samuel.
Odell, Phinehas	....	1776	
Odell, Hannah	....	....	m. Nath. Seeley, m. Stephen Sterling.
Odell, Walker	1789	....	
Odell, Temperance	....	1794, æ. 27	
Odell, Isaac	....	1801	s. of Isaac.
Odell, Isaac	....	1826, æ. 68	
Pigsly, William	1703	....	
Paterson, Andrew	1703	....	
Peat, Mary	....	....	m. 1712, John Corbit.
Phippany, Mary	....	....	m. 1719, Jonadab Bassett.
Phippany, Johannah	....	1727	m. 1722, Dea. Lem. Sherwood.
Prime, Capt. Joseph	1732	....	
Price, Phinehas	....	....	m. 1733, Mary Knapp.
Prince, Samuel	1750	....	m. 1733, Abigail Wells.
Parrott, Elnathan	....	....	m. 1750, Mary Hill.
Porter, Hannah	....	1763, æ. 61	w. of John.
Parish, Joel	1770, 1806	....	m. Abigail Hawley.
Plant, Joel	....	1774	
Parish, Abigail (Hawley)	1770	1777, æ. 37	sister of Maj. Aaron Hawley, w. of [Joel.
Price, Mary	....	1780	wid. of Phinehas.
Patchin, Ann	....	1780	wid. of ——.
Pratt, ——	....	1785	wid. of ——.
Patchin, ——	....	1789	w. of James.
Patchin, Abijah	....	1789	
Patchen, Wolcott	1794	1799	
Patchin, Serjt. Isaac, 1777?	1794	1832, æ. 85	
Patchen, ——	....	1794	w. of Isaac.
Patchin, Salmon	1795	1807, æ. 40	m. Mabe ——.
Porter, Samuel	....	1795, æ. 78	m. Anna ——.
Peck, ——	....	1799	w. of John B.
Parrott, ——	....	1799	w. of Ebenezer.
Porter, Lucy	1800	....	w. of John.
Pixley, Anna	....	1800, æ. 69	wid. of William.
Porter, Anna	....	1801, æ. 76	wid. of Abiah.
Porter, Abiah (Hubbell)	....	1805	w. of Samuel.
Porter, Sarah	....	1805, æ. 25	w. of Samuel, Jr.
Patchin, Ruah	....	1808, æ. 63	w. of Elijah.
Porter, Lucy	....	1812, æ. 31	w. of Ezra.
Porter, John	....	1813	
Patchin, Victory	....	1815, æ. 22	
Page, Harvey	....	1815, æ. 32	
Peet, Anson	....	1816, æ. 21	
Parrott, Isaac	1816	....	
Parsons, Mercy	....	1818, æ. 30	w. of Titus.
Pendleton, Eunice	....	1820, æ. 59	wid. of ——.
Piercy, Nathaniel	....	1822	
Perry, Polly	....	1824	w. of Burr.
Peet, ——	....	1825, æ. 78	mother of Samuel, wid. of ——.
Pixley, ——	....	1825, æ. 62	w. of Peter.
Peet, Henry	1825	....	
Penfield, Hannah	....	1826, æ. 84	wid. of ——.
Perry, Tolman	....	1826, æ. 34	
Perry, Burr	....	1826, æ. 32	

Name.	Year of Mention.	Death.	Remarks.
Parrott, William	....	1826	....
Pool, ———	....	1829	w. of John B.
Plumb, John	1829	....	....
Parrott, Sally	....	1839, æ. 49	w. of Thomas.
Peet, Anna	....	1843, æ. 76	....
Parrott, Thomas	....	1851, æ. 58	....
Rugier, Anthony	1732	....	....
Rowlandson, Elizabeth	1733	....	[Robert.
Ross, Sarah (Edwards)	....	1772	wid. of Samuel Hawley, w. of Rev.
Rowland, Charity	....	1773	....
Ross, John	....	1777	....
Ross, Eulilia (Bartram)	....	1785, æ. 49	w. of Rev. Robert.
Raymond, Miss Betsey	....	1792, æ. 17	....
Risley, Ruth	....	1794, æ. 36	dau. of David Wells, wid. of Timothy.
Ross, Sarah (Merrick)	....	1799, æ. 52	w. of Rev. Robert, m. 1786.
Ross, James Merrick	....	1799	s. of Rev. Robert.
Robertson, ———	1800	....	....
Rose, Peter	....	1801	....
Royce, Rev. Stephen	....	1802, æ. 47	....
Rose, William	....	1812, æ. 90	....
Rose, ———	1813	....	wid. of ———.
Rockwell, Eliada	....	1822, æ. 24	....
Roberts, Mary	....	1826	w. of ———.
Robins, Capt.	1827, 1829	....	....
Robinson, ———	....	1837	w. of ———.
Sherwood, Sarah	1693	....	m. Benjamin Fayerweather.
Seeley, Nathaniel	1696, 1736	....	m. Hannah Odell.
Swillaway, Mary, bap. Nov. 8, 1696		....	....
Stiles, Mary 1702? 1706, 1717		....	....
Sherman, Benjamin 1703, 1707		....	....
Seeley, Hannah, bap. 1703	1731	....	m. Lt. Wm. Bennett; dau. of John.
Sherman, Mercy, bap. 1704	....	....	dau. of Dea. David; m. M. Sherwood.
Seeley, Sarah, bap. 1704	....	....	m. 1713, J. Sherwood; dau. of James.
Sherman, Nathaniel	1705	....	m. Jemima ———.
Sherman, James, bap. 1707	....	....	s. of Benj.; m. 1734, Sarah Cooke.
Sherman, Bezaliel	1708	....	....
Sturdevant, John	1709	....	m. Mary Jackson.
Squire, Jonathan	....	....	m. 1711, Bashia ———.
Strong, Benaiah	1713	....	m. Sarah Sherman.
Sherman, John	1714	....	....
Silliman, Sarah	1714	....	m. Samuel Hall.
Smith, Abigail	1718	....	m. William Odell.
Starr, Samuel	....	....	m. 1731, Abigail Dibble.
Silliman, Robert, Jr.	1732, 1735	....	....
Silliman, Robert, Sr.	1732, 1735	....	m. Ruth ———.
Sturges, Jonathan	1732	....	....
Stanley, Mary	....	....	m. 1733, Peter Walker.
Seeley, ———	1733	....	w. of R———.
Sanford, Daniel	1734	....	....
Smith, Josiah	....	1786	m. 1735, Prudence Kimberly.
Sanford, David	....	....	m. 1736, Patience Burrows.
Sherman, Peter	1736	....	m. 1734, Martha French.
Starr, Elizabeth	....	....	m. 1736, Joseph Webb.
Sterling, Mary	....	1737, æ. 23	dau. of Jacob and Hannah.

Name.	Year of Mention.	Death.	Remarks.
Seeley, Eunice	....	1745, æ. 28	w. of Nathan.
Sherwood, Andrew	1749	1767, æ. 47	s. of Capt. John?
Silliman, Sarah	....	....	m. 1750, Noah Wilson.
Summers, Mary	....	1751, æ. 50	1st w. of Nathan.
Seeley, Betsey	....	1756, æ. 85	w. of James.
Silliman, Ruth	....	1756, æ. 58	w. of Robert, Sr.?
Sterling, Mary	....	1757, æ. 23	dau. of Jacob.
Summers, Comfort	....	1765 or 1772, æ. 63	2d w. of Nathan.
Sherman, Amos	....	1760, æ. 36	
Seeley, Nathan	....	1766, æ. 52	
Somers, Mary	1770	....	w. of Samuel.
Silliman, John	1771	....	
Silliman, Katharine	1771	....	
Sherwood, Gurdon	....	1772, æ. 33	s. of John.
Silliman, Sarah	....	1773, æ. 48	w. of Daniel.
Sherman, Jonathan	....	1775	
Stevens, Isaac	....	1776	
Sherman, Isaac	....	1777	
Seeley, Nehemiah	....	1781, æ. 79	
Sherman, Eunice, bap. 1751?	....	1781	dau. of Elnathan?
Seeley, Michael	1784	1798	
Shaylor, Capt. Timothy	....	1786	
Seeley, Lieut. Nathaniel	....	1787, æ. 44	m. Deborah ——.
Seeley, Denton	1786, 1803	....	
Smith, John	....	1790	
Summers, ——	....	1793	w. of Elnathan.
Sherwood, Abigail	....	1793	wid. of ——.
Silliman, Seth	....	1794, æ. 21	s. of Capt. Seth and Lois.
Smith, Josiah	....	1794, æ. 37	m. Beulah ——.
Summers, Ann	....	1794	dau. of Elnathan.
Smith, Prudence (Kimberly)?	....	....	
Seeley, Sarah	....	1797	dau. of Michael.
Sherwood, Prudence	....	1797	
Seeley, Hephzibah	....	1797	dau. of Michael.
Strong, Anne	....	1798, æ. 19	dau. of Joseph.
Summers, Elijah	....	1798, æ. 30	
Seeley, Truman	....	1798	
Sherwood, William	....	1798	s. of David.
Seeley, Peninnah	....	1800	
Seeley, Abigail	....	1800, æ. 31	w. of Seth, Jr.
Seeley, ——	....	1800	wid. of Michael.
Seeley, ——	....	1801	w. of Isaac.
Strong, Comfort	....	1801, æ. 20	dau. of Joseph.
Seeley, Isaac	....	1801	
Sturges, Anna (Knowles)	....	1801, æ. 80	w. of Joseph.
Seamon, ——	1802	....	dau. of William.
Sterling, Sherwood	....	1802	s. of Abijah, Esq.
Strong, Sarah	....	1804, æ. 33	dau. of Joseph.
Strong, Comfort (Nichols)	....	1804, æ. 65	w. of Joseph.
Sherman, Sterling	1805	....	s. of Capt. David.
Summers, Rebecca	....	1805	wid. of ——.
Sherman, Anna (Kirtland)	1805	....	w. of Sterling.
Stephenson, I.	1805	....	
Summers, Aaron	....	1806, æ. 81	m. Huldah Wakeley.
Sherman, Jemima	....	1806	wid. of Nathaniel?
Summers, Mary	....	1806, æ. 25	w. of Abel.
Strong, ——	....	1807, æ. 76	w. of Nehemiah.

Name.	Year of Mention.	Death.	Remarks.
Silliman, Lois		1807, æ. 67	w. of Capt. Seth.
Silliman, Capt. Seth		1808, æ. 67	
Sherman, Capt. David, Jr.		Dec. 1809, æ. 24, at sea.	s. of David 4th.
Summers, William		1810, æ. 34	
Smith, Beulah		1810, æ. 70	wid. of George; wid. of Wm. Peet.
Sherwood, Capt. David		1811, æ. 49	
Seeley, Deborah		1811, æ. 68	wid. of Lt. Nathaniel.
Smith, ——		1811	wid. of ——.
Scofield, ——	1812, 1818		
Standish, John	1813, 1816	1825, æ. 35	
Seeley, Odell	1814		
Smith, Mary		1815	wid. of ——.
Sherwood, Zachariah	1815		
Sherwood, Charles	1818, 1840		
Smith, J. Stebbins	1819, 1825		
Squire, Samuel		1819, æ. 74	
Staples, Martha		1820, æ. 61	wid. of ——.
Sterling, Sherman		1820, æ. 34	
Seeley, Mary		1822, æ. 81	w. of Ezra.
Seeley, Catharine		1823, æ. 18	dau. of James.
Summers, Rhoda		1823, æ. 36	
Sherman, Rebecca (French)		1825, æ. 70	wid. of Capt. David, 4th.
Seeley, Michael		1826, æ. 70	
Sherman, Jane		1826, æ. 20	w. of Isaac, Jr.
Summers, ——		1826, æ. 74	w. of Elnathan.
Sherwood, Ephraim	1826		
Sherwood, Ethan		1826, æ. 51	
Sherwood, Sally		1826, æ. 44	w. of Ephraim.
Sheppard, Doct. William		1827	
Seeley, ——		1828	w. of Munson.
Summers, ——		1828, æ. 45	w. of David.
Sherman, ——		1829	wid. of Wheeler.
Strong, Joshua	1829		
Strong, Tryphena (Whetmore)		1829, æ. 56	wid. of John.
Sherwood, Lucetta		1831, æ. 35	
Seeley, Mary		1835, æ. 24	dau. of Ruth and Joseph.
Sherman, C. H.		1838	
Sterling, Anson		1835, æ. 44	
Summers, Anson		1836, æ. 39	
Sherwood, Stephen		1837, æ. 89	
Strong, Comfort		1841, æ. 77	2d w. of Joseph.
Seeley, Jennette		1850, æ. 35	w. of George B.
Sterling, David B.		1849	s. of David and Deborah.
Seeley, George B.		1850	
Summers, Ubana		1849, æ. 68	dau. of Elnathan. [Deborah.
Sterling, Ann		1859	w. of Moore; dau. of David and
Sterling, Hannah		1861	
Sterling, Feed Abijah		1862, æ. 73	s. of Abijah and Eunice.
Sterling, Sally		1866	w. of F. Abijah.
Sterling, Capt. John		1866	s. of David and Deborah.
Turney, Thomas			m. 1709, Abigail Wells.
Treadwell, Martha, bap. 1702		1731	dau. of Samuel; m. 1721, Samuel
Tucker, Nehemiah		1717, æ. 23	[Smedley.
Turney, Mary			m. 1732, Nathaniel Burr
Treadwell, Stephen		1755, æ. 44	m. 1751, Sarah Wakeley.
Treadwell, Sarah	1753		wid. of ——.

Name.	Year of Mention.	Death.	Remarks.
Treadwell, Sarah	1770	1776	w. of Hezekiah.
Treadwell, ————	....	1776	w. of Samuel.
Treadwell, Josiah	1776	1798	
Treadwell, ————	....	1782	w. of Samuel.
Treadwell, David	1783	....	
Treadwell,	....	1788	w. of Josiah.
Treadwell, Jerusha	....	1793	wid. of Samuel.
Treadwell, Samuel	....	1801	
Thompson, ————	....	1808, æ. 47	w. of ————.
Treadwell, Elijah	1815	....	
Turney, Silas	1819	....	
Tisdale, Dr. N.	1823, 1825	....	
Tisdale, Betsey	....	1824, æ. 42	w. of Dr. N.
Treat, Madison A.	....	1831, æ. 24	
Thompson, Joseph	....	1839	
Wolcott, Sarah	....	1703	m. 1698, Rev. Charles Chauncey.
Whitacus, Jonathan	1700	....	[Chauncey.
Wheeler, Hannah, bap. 1703	....	....	dau. of Samuel ; m. 1722, Robert
Wheeler, Hannah	1708	....	wid. of ————.
Wakeman, Capt. John	1712	....	
Wheeler, David	....	....	m. 1717, Esther Nichols.
Weed, Jacob	....	....	m. 1718, Eleanor Frost.
Wells, Mercy	....	1731, æ. 23	
Wheeler, Anne	1731	....	m. Samuel Cable.
Wakeley, Prudence	1731	....	m. Joseph Edwards.
Wakeley, Jacob	1732, 1736	....	m. 1735, Anne Trowbridge.
Wilson, Daniel	1732	....	
Wilson, Nathaniel	1732	....	
Wurden, Thomas	1732, 1733	....	
Wheeler, Judith Ann	....	....	m. 1732, Samuel Odell.
Wheeler, Jonathan	1732	....	
Walker, Peter	....	....	m. 1733, Mary Stanley.
Wheeler, Elizabeth	....	....	m. 1733, Ezra Dibble.
Walker, Mary	....	....	m. 1733, Serj't John Sherwood.
Wells, Abigail	....	....	m. 1733, Samuel Prince.
Wheeler, Lieut.	1734	....	
Wakeley Zebulon	1734	1767, æ. 55	
Webb, Joseph	....	....	m. 1736, Elizabeth Starr.
White, Rev. Ebenezer	....	....	m. 1736, Mrs. Mary Moss.
Wheeler, David	....	....	m. 1749, Lois Chauncey.
Wilson, Noah	....	....	m. 1750, Sarah Silliman.
Wells, Jedidiah	....	....	m. 1750, Line French.
Wells, David	1751	1777	m. Ruth Burrows.
Wakeley, Sarah	....	....	m. 1751, Stephen Treadwell.
Wilson, Elizabeth	....	....	m. 1751, Thaddeus Bennett.
Wheeler, Jabez	1751	....	
Wilson, Sarah ?	....	1771, æ. 26	w. of James.
Wheeler, Sarah	1772, 1776	....	dau. of Benjamin ; m. Ezra Kirtland, [Jr.
Wheeler, Ephraim	....	1774	
Wheeler, Ann	....	1775	dau. of John.
Wilson, John, Jr.	....	1776, æ. 29	s. of Robert and Catharine.
Wheeler, Timothy	....	1776	
Wakeley, Sarah	....	1781	w. of Lieut. Samuel.
Wakeley, Clark	....	1788	
Wells, ————	....	1788	w. of David.
Wheeler, Zachariah	....	1789	

Name.	Year of Mention.	Death.	Remarks.
Wakeley, Jonathan		1790, æ. 47	
Wakeley, Abel		1793	
Wilson, Eleanor (Lacey)		1795, æ. 27	dau. of Benjamin ; w. of Amos.
Wheeler, Abigail ?		1795	w. of Hezekiah.
Wing, Charles	1796		
Wing, ———		1796	w. of Charles.
Whitmore, Robert W.	1796		
Wheeler, Abigail (Odell ?)		1798, æ. 40	wid. of William ?
Wakeley, Isaac		1798	
Wakeley, Tabitha		1800	wid. of ———.
Wheeler, Dorothy (Sherman)		1800, æ. 87	wid. of John; dau. of Dea. David.
Waistcoat, Tiba		1800	
Wheeler, Eunice		1804	
Wells, Frederick		1804	
Worden, Anna (Odell)		1805	dau. of Samuel ; w. of Capt. Wm.
Walker, Joseph	1805		
Wakeley, Mary		1809, æ. 78	
Woolsey, Maj. Benj. M.		1813, æ. 55	
Wilson, Robert		1813, æ. 57	
Wakeley, Sally		1813	
Wells, Mehitable		1814, æ. 90	
Wheeler, Samuel		1819, æ. 58	
Wheeler, Tuttle		1820	
Whiting, William		1821, æ. 57	
Whiting, John		1822, æ. 73	
Wagner, George		1822	
Wakeley, Walker		1823	
Whiting, Mary		1823, æ. 74	wid. of John.
Whiting, ———		1824	w. of Samuel.
Wilson, Eleanor		1824	
Worden, William	1824	1831, æ. 48	
Worden, Elmer		1824, æ. 28	
Wells, Stephen		1825, æ. 70	m, Mary ———.
Wilson, Rhoda		1825, æ. 57	
Woolsey, Hannah		1825, æ. 64	wid. of ———.
Wilson, Summers		1826, æ. 22	
Wakeley, Grace		1826, æ. 74	
Wells, Jedidiah		1827, æ. 75	
Wells, Mary		1827, æ. 69	wid. of Stephen.
Wade, Stephen		1827, æ. 25	
Wakeley, Charles		1827, æ. 35	
Wilson, Silliman		1833, æ. 68	
Wells, Hannah		1838, æ. 84	dau. of Jedidiah.
Young, Joseph		1785	
Young, Mary		1786	wid. of ———.
Young, Daniel	1797	1800	
Young, Jesse		1798	
Young, Daniel, Jr.	1800	1803	

NAMES OF MEMBERS OF THE PARISH,

Pew-holders and others not known to be Church Members, mentioned in the records of the First Society of Bridgeport, Conn., 1695 to 1895.

"Undoubtedly besides these members in full communion, the other heads of families in the settlement were most or all of them associated with the church under 'the half-way covenant,' conformably to the practice of the churches of the colony generally, at that time — a practice continued in this church until within the present century."— *Palmer's Hist. First Church.*

Names.	Year of Mention.
Angevine, Zachariah	1754
(janitor 1736), salary £3. 10s. 4d., d. 1779.	
Abell, Elijah	1788
Allen, James, 2d	1811, 1814
Adams, A. H.	1820
Allen, Justus, d. 1863, æ. 63.	
Atwater, Merritt	1846
Andrews, E.	1846
Ames, Dyer	1856, 1857
Ainsley, J.	1868
Allen, Frank C.	1879, 1882
Anderson, John Joseph	1890
Burr, Nathaniel, Sr.	1698
Bennett, Samuel	1706
Beardsley, Sarah	1710
Bennett, John	1712
bap. 1704, *s.* of James and Sarah.	
Burton, John	1748
Bennett, Nehemiah	1754
Beers, Nathaniel	1754
Burr, James	1754
Burton, Solomon	1748, 1754
Bennett, Capt. Thaddeus	1754
d. after 1777, *m.* Elizabeth Wilson 1751.	
Burr, Justus	1765
m. Hephzibah Nichols ; *d.* 1766, æ. 32, *s.* of Col. John.	
Beardsley, Andrew	1767
Burr, Ozias	1770
d. 1836 æ. 98, *s.* of Col. John.	
Bangs, Lemuel	1770, 1786
Burroughs, Edward	1771, 1797
bap. 1732, *s.* of Stephen.	
Burroughs, Capt. Stephen	1772
b. 1729, *d.* 1817, æ. 88?	
Burritt, Elijah, *d.* 1841, æ. 98	1776
Booth, Samuel	1778, 1789
Beardsley, Ensign Abijah, *bap.* 1750, *d.* 1789, æ. 40, *m.* Drusilla, *dau.* of David Sherman, she *d.* 1839, æ. 87; *s.* of Robert.	

Names.	Year of Mention.
Brothwell, Benjamin, *s.* of Joseph	1788
Benedict, Thaddeus, *d.* 1799, æ. 51	1796
Botsford, Francis?	1797, 1800
Benedict, William	1803
Burroughs, Edmund (Edward?)	1803
Barker, Esq.	1804
Benedict, Jesse, *d.* 1815	1804
Backus, Simon	1808
Burroughs, Capt. Stephen, Jr.	1797, 1824
Benjamin, Barzillai	1808
Beardsley, Anson	1808
Beach, Caleb	1809
Baldwin, Simeon	1809
Beach, Barnum	1810, 1817
Brooks, Joseph	1810
Blackman, Nathan	1810
Burr, Henry, *d.* 1822, æ. 32	1814
Benjamin, Meigs	1814
Beard, Daniel	1815
Bouton, Chauncey	1818, 1824
Baldwin, Capt. Eliadia	1815, 1821
Beardsley, Abijah	1820, 1850
Booth, Roswell	1822
Baldwin, Brinsmade	1823
Benedict, E. B.	1823
Bradley, Enos	1824
Black, Alexander	1826, 1835
Bassett, Freeman C.	1827, 1856
Bassett, James	1828
Bartram, Capt. Thomas	1834, 1837
Betts, Coley E.	1834
Brooks, Cornelius	1834
Bunnell, William	1834
Botsford, Cyrus	1835
Bartlett, Louisa	1835
Bray, Judson	1835
Beach, Sheldon	1840
Burr, Henry	1840
Beers, Widow	1840, 1844
Beach, Mary (Widow)	1841, 1850
Barnum, Philo F.	1844, 1856
Blake, Edgar	1844
Burr, Horace	1850
Billings, John L.	1856, 1869

Names.	Year of Mention.
Beardsley, Henry N.	1856, 1875
Blunt, W.	1856
Birdseye, E. 2d.	1856
Benham, J. H.	1856, 1857
Blank, A. Edward	1856, 1861
Baker, Dr. E.	1857, 1863
Botsford, H. H.	1857, 1861
Birdseye, N. D.	1857
Beach, George E.	1861, 1869
Bartlett, T.	1861
Barker, R. R.	1863
Brooks, Mrs. Eunice	1863
Blakeman, B.	1863
Brooks, W. E.	1874
Beach, John M.	1874
Banks, Edwin	1874
Burton, Silas	1874
Bullock, J. M.	1874, 1875
Blush W. C., *janitor*	1884, 1886
Birdseye, Frank	1886
Burr, Ebenezer	1886
Barri, John A.	1886
Bullard, W. H.	1886, 1889
Brooks, Mrs. E. E.	1889
Briggs, Warren R.	1890
Banks, John W.	1894

Curtis, Joseph	1706
Cooper, Robert	1706
Chambers, Thomas	1716, 1719
Crawford, Quintin	1713, 1719
Cooke, Esther	1724
Cooke, John, *b.* 1715, *d.* 1813, *s.* of Rev. Samuel	
Cable, Widow Rebecca, *d.* 1799, *æ.* 80, *wid.* of Andrew.	1771
Chapman, Joshua	1801
Couch, Nash	1809
Cooke, Joseph P.	1809
Clark, Joseph	1810, 1825
Curtiss, Matthew	1811
Curtiss, Eli	1811
Crocker, John A.	1814
Clark, Eliza	1815
Cable, Richard	1819
Curtiss, Andrew	1824
Cooke, Horace	1834
Crane, Ambrose	1844, 1846
Chesney, Samuel M.	1850, 1856
Clark, Elijah	1856, 1857
Chapin, Walter E.	1861
Childs, C. M.	1868
Cogswell, Henry C.	1853
Canfield, Charles Stewart	1879
Corbusier, A. B.	1886
Chittenden, E. D.	1886

Dickinson, Nathaniel	1754
DeForest, Charles	1824
Davis, S. A.	1850

Names	Year of Mention.
Dunlap, J. J.	1856, 1868
DeMartin, J.	1856
Davenport, Daniel	1884
DeForest, Marcus	1875
Edwards, Isaac	1788
Eaton, William	1795, 1844
Ells, Nathaniel	1798
Edmonds, William	1809
Edgerton, Eleazar	1811, 1835
Eells, Waterman	1815
Edwards, Benjamin	1840, 1849 ?
Ellis, M. N.	1868
Elliott, A.	1868, 1874
Edmonds, George B.	1886
Fairchild, Zachary	1698, 1701
Fairchild, Hannah, Jr.	1697, 1706
Fairchild, Ebenezer	1710
French, Ebenezer	1732, 1754
bap. 1699, *s.* of Samuel.	
Fairchild, Stephen	1755
Fairchild, Ephraim	1756
French, Benoni	1782
s. of Samuel, *d.* 1823, *æ.* 85.	
French, Gamaliel	1754, 1758
bap. 1706 ? *d.* 1783.	
French, Gamaliel, Jr., *d.* 1828, *æ.* 72..1788 ?	
French, Samuel	1801
bap. 1734, *s.* of Ebenezer ?	
French, Capt. Joseph	1809, 1838
Farnam, Samuel	1810
French, William	1818, 1845, 1857
French, James R., *d.* 1835, *æ.* 83..1803, 1821	
French, Simeon	1828
French, Wheeler, Jr., *d.* 1879.	
Fayerweather, William	1843
Ferrin, Sidney	1847
Fowler, Anderson	1850
Fayerweather, G. M.	1856
Fayerweather, Betsey	1857
Fuller, John E.	1868
Fairchild, Daniel	1886
Gregory, Enoch	1733, 1753
bap. 1707, *d.* 1776, *s.* of Samuel.	
Gregory, Seth	1760, 1772
Gregory, Thaddeus, Jr.	1767, 1798
Grey, Ruel	1785, 1788
Gibbs, David	1811
Gill, Charles	1825
Griffith, Theodore	1842
Gray, James W.	1856, 1857
Glenn, M.	1868
Gilbert, ——	1874
Griswold, George W.	1893
Hawley, Samuel	17.0, 1.2.
Hendricks, Samuel	
Hendricks, Phebe	

—196—

Names.	Year of Mention.
Hall, Isaac, Sr.	1695, 1706, 1712?
Hawley, Thomas, Jr.	1706
Hall, Jonathan	1706, 1717
Hull, Hannah	1706
Hubbell, Joseph	1706, 1732
bap. 1702, *d.* bef. 1778.	
Hinman, Edward	1704, 1716
Hall, James	1710
Hall, Isaac, Jr.	1695, 1711
Hubbell, Samuel, Jr.	1713, 1719
Hutchinson, Aaron	1747
Hawley, Samuel, *d.* 1749, *æ.* 31	1748
Hall, Ebenezer, *d.* after 1778	1749, 1759
Holberton, Widow Mary, *d.* 1788	1752
Hubbell, Capt. Gershom	1754, 1758
Hubbell, Nehemiah	1750, 1759
Hubbell, Benjamin	1761
bap. 1717, *d.* 1793, *æ.* 76, *s.* of John?	
or Dea. Richard, Jr.	
Hubbell, Gideon,	1762, 1785
bap. 1731, *d.* 1806, *æ.* 76, *s.* of	
Capt. Daniel.	
Hawley, Maj. Aaron	1764, 1796
d. 1803, *æ.* 63.	
Hunt, Isaac, *d.* 1770	1764
Hall, John	1764
bap. 1717? *d.* 1791, *s.* of John?	
Hawley, Woolcot	1765, 1795
d. 1799, *æ.* 62, wife *d.* 1799.	
Hawley, Ezra, *d.* 1796, *æ.* 50	1769
Hawley, Thomas	1776
bap. 1735? *d.* 1797, *æ.* 59, *s.* of	
Ezra?	
Hubbell, Abraham, *d.* 1783	1779
Hubbell, Capt. Amos	1775
First Warden of the Borough, *d.*	
July 2, 1801, *æ.* 55, *s.* of Richard,	
Jr.	
Hubbell, Capt. Asa	1788
d. July 5, 1801, *æ.* 55.	
Hubbell, James	1791
d. 1827, *æ.* 70? *s.* of Aaron?	
Hubbell, Capt. Salmon	1791
Hubbell, Amos, Jr., *d.* 1798, *æ.* 18	1797
Hawley, Amos	1797
Hubbell, John, *d.* 1808, *æ.* 63	1799
Hawley, Joseph	1800
Hubbell, Ezra, *d.* 1801.	
Hubbell, Thaddeus	1794, 1802
Hawley, Ebenezer	1776, 1803
Hawley, Capt. Samuel	1792, 1805
bap. 1751, *d.* 1821, *s.* of Ezra.	
Hull, W. L. (W. B.?)	1806, 1808
Hubbell, Onesimus	1809
bap. 1732? 1755? *s.* of Joseph or	
Daniel.	
Hubbell, Charles Benj., 1810, 1825, 1834, 1869	
s. of Amos.	
Hubbell, Nathaniel I.	1811
Hubbell, Benjamin	1811
Hubbell, Lemuel	1818
Hatch, Capt. Daniel	1821
Hubbell, David, Jr., *d.* 1830, *æ.* 65..1811,	1821
Hubbell, Solomon	1823
Hawley, Munson	1824
Hubbell, Alfred	1826, 1827
Hamlin, Alanson	1827, 1834
Hubbell, Alexander	1835
Humiston, Nathaniel	1835
Higgins, Polly	1837
Hathaway, Capt.	1838, 1841
Hawley, Gurdon	1839, 1845
Hutchins, Thomas	1830, 1840
Hubbell, Merritt	1839, 1840
Higgins, Amos	1844, 1861
Hubbell, Edward	1847
Hubbell, George A	1847
Hubbell, David	1850
Hopkins, L. M.	1850
Hall, C. B.	1850
Hall, Polly J.	1856, 1857
Hopkins, Alfred, *d.* 1894	1826
Hubbell, George W.	1857
Hubbell, Laura	1861, 1875
Hubbell, George H.	1868, 1869
House, Henry A.	1868
Hawley, Marcus C.	1868
Horr, William L.	1868
House, James A.	1868
Hill, W. B.	1874
Hunter, Samuel S.	1874
Hall, Mrs. S. B.	1874
Hall, F. S.	1875
Hyde, Miss Mary	1882
Hawley, Jane M.	1886
Hubbell, Mrs. George H.	1886, 1893
Hughes, Frank J.	1886
Hart, W. E.	1888
Havens, George O.	1889
Hopson, William R.	1893
Hawley, Alexander,	1893
Ives, Francis, *d.* Jan. 27, 1895, *æ.* 77	1850
Jackson, Daniel	1708, 1734
Jackson, Samuel	1695, 1709
Judson, John	1710
Jackson, Isaac	1746
bap. 1712, *d.* 1777? *s.* of Henry.	
Jennings, Elijah	1788
Jennings, Eliphalet	1795
d. 1839, *æ.* 85, *m.* Sarah, *dau.* of	
Rev. Robert Ross.	
Judson, Harry	1828
Jennings, Robert R., *s.* of Eliphalet	1828
Judson, Jeremiah	1837, 1846
Johnson, George	1840, 1841
Jameson,	1868
Judson, Mrs. F. J.	1874
Joy, Misses	1887

—197—

Names.	Year of Mention.
Kimberly, Eleazar	1699
Kind, Arthur	1700
Knapp, Mary, *d.* Nov. 23	1711
Kirtland, Ezra...........1759, 1772,	1790
m. Olive, *dau.* of Zabulon Wakeley, *d.* 1800, *æ.* 70.	
Knapp, James, *d.* 1798, *æ.* 74	1778
Kellogg, Jervis	1800
Kirtland, Wheeler	1803
King, William	1812
Knapp, Ephraim, *d.* 1831 1813,	1825
Knapp, Joseph 1828,	1847
Kimball, M.	1843
Kiefer, Jacob L. 1856,	1857
Kellogg, W. F.	1856
Keeler, Frank 1874,	1875
Kensett, Mrs. Sarah A.	1874
Keeler, Walter F.	1875
Knapp, Howard H.	1890
Leads, Cary	1708
Lane, Charles	1710
Lane, Johannah	1710
Loring, Nehemiah	1714
Lacey, David, *bap.* 1753, *d.* 1803, *s.* of John.	
Lacey, Edward, Jr...........1750,	1755
Lamson, Joseph 1745,	1755
d. 1773, Missionary Ch. of Eng.	
Lacey, Widow Hannah	1759
Lacey, Benjamin, *d.* 1784, *æ.* 45-1765,	1772
Lyons, Robert	1789
Lewis, Abel	1791
Lacey, Eleazar 1795,	1825
Lewis, Robert	1797
Lockwood, Samuel	1799
Lewis, Daniel, *m.* Hulda———	1814
Lewis, Roswell	1820
Linsley, Benjamin D.	1823
Lyon, Levi 1823, 1824,	1843
Lewis, Joseph C............1828,	1835
Lane, Joseph 1844,	1845
Lyon, William H.	1850
Lewis, William A. 1856,	1857
Lewis, E. A.	1856
LaMonte, Mrs.	1857
Lindley, N. H............1861,	1863
Livingston, A. P.	1864
Lewis, Miss	1864
Little, J.	1865
Lewis, W. W.	1874
Lewis, H. William, janitor	1882
Lyon, Miss Louise	1886
Lyon, F. C.	1886
Lockwood, Frederick J. 1886,	1894
Lyon, Mrs. E. H..........1886,	1893
Lewis, Mrs. C. B.	1889
Lyon, Willis S. 1892,	1893
Maclen, Jacob	1700
Morehouse, David	1707

Names.	Year of Mention.
Morehouse, Samuel, Sr..........1708,	1714
Mitchell, Widow	1759
Messer, Daniel	1798
Mosher, Daniel S.	1799
Morehouse, Edward	1805
Munn, Isaac, *d.* 1817, *æ.* 37	1806
May, Major Henry.......1808, 1814,	1829
Marvine, Matthew	1809
May, Joseph...........1810,	1828
May, Sylvester...........1822,	1826
Munson, Sherlock, *d.* 1825, *æ.* 27.	
Moore, Luther	1827
Matthews, or Martha, Titus C...1827,	1856
Milne, Robert 1834,	1845
Merhwal, Oliver	1835
Messerole, J. B............1840,	1842
Morris, Dwight...........1841,	1894
Moore, Edward..........1841, 1843,	1844
McGrath, William.........1846,	1850
Marsh, Edgar	1850
McGregor, Richard	1850
McNeil, John	1852
Morgan, George 1857,	1863
Murphy, N. L.	1863
Martin, Mrs.	1868
Morris, John	1875
Mason, Frederick A. 1886,	1891
Middlebrook, Mrs. Stiles M.	1886
Meeker, Edward F.	1893
Manchester, J. A., janitor	1893
McEwen, Mrs............1893,	1894
Nickleson, James	1702
Nichols, Richard...........1708,	1732
Nichols, Ezra	1762
Nichols, Silas	1762
Nichols, John, *d.* 1785	1780
Nichols, John, Jr., *d.* 1801, *æ.* 57	1783
Nichols, Elijah	1808
Nichols, Charles L...........1824,	1828
Norman, Peter, *d.* 1894 1843,	1857
Noyes, William	1850
Nickerson, Samuel	1863
Nichols, C. L.	1868
Near, John N.	1870
Nash, Andrew E............1870,	1880
Norton, Dr.	1874
Nash, Jesse S.	1870
Nichols, Walter	1886
Nettleton, W. A.	1886
Noble, George B.	1890
Odell, Nehemiah Smith	1765
bap. 1733, *d.* 1772, *s.* of William.	
Odell, John, *bap.* 1710? *s.* of Samuel?	1779
Oviatt, Daniel B.	1810
Olmstead, Ashbel, *d.* 1825, *æ.* 42 ..	1810
Oram, James D.	1839
Olmstead, George	1840
Orcutt, Rev. Samuel	1888

Names.	Year of Mention.
Phippeny, Joseph	1702, 1705
Patchen, Samuel, d. 1776	1731, 1755
Peet, Daniel	1762
Patterson, Andrew	1777, 1779
Peet, William	1788, 1811
Peet, Elijah	1796
d. 1841, æ. 81, m. Anna ——.	
Peabody, William H., d. 1832	1798
Porter, Samuel	1804, 1805, 1838
m. Abiah Hubbell.	
Peck, Ira	1809, 1818, 1846
Pilgrim, Benjamin	1826
Perry, Burr	1826
Pixley, Agur	1827
Porter, Edwin	1827, 1829
Platt, Moses	1838, 1863
Pearsall, Daniel	1839, 1840
Peck, Eliza	1838, 1840
Pearsall, Mrs.	1841
Place, Benajah	1842, 1843
Peck, David K., d. 1894	1843
Preston, James	1849
Platt, Miss	1850
Peet, Orville H.	1850
Prindle, I. H.	1850
Patterson, S. C.	1856
Peet, Charles H.	1856
Pettit, Isaac O.	1857, 1868
Patchin, William T.	1861, 1863
Perry, William H.	1861, 1863
Pitts, Philander, janitor	1858
Painter, William	1863
Parmlee, Eleazar	1874, 1875
Parrott, Frederick W., 2d	1880
Parker, Mrs. E. M.	1882, 1884
Plumb, Hanford C.	1886
Phillips, Dr. A. N.	1886
Parrott, Harry	1893
Rogers, William (schoolmaster)	1711
Rowland, Edmond	1759
Ripley, Hezekiah	1808, 1810
Roberts, William, Jr.	1810
Rowland, Sherman	1814
Raymond, Hawley S.	1837
Rood, Edwin	1840, 1844
Rowland, George M.	1868
Rand, C. F.	1872, 1874
Rogers, Noah	1875
Richardson, George W.	1886
Rockwell, William G.	1889
Silliman, David	1698
Sanford, Elnathan	1698
Squier, Samuel	1698
Seeley, John	1697, 1707
Sherman, Matthew, Jr.	1703
Summers, Thomas	1710
Sherman, Capt. David, Jr., s. of Capt. David, 3d. m. Mary Sterling, dau.	

Names.	Year of Mention.
of Stephen and Eunice (Summers,) d. 1771, æ. 35, she d. 1765, æ. 25.	
Summers, Daniel	1745, 1754
m. Eunice ——, d. 1789?	
Summers, Jabez, d. 1801. æ. 80,..1746,	1750
Sherwood, Thomas	1750, 1753
Sanford, Ebenezer	1757
Sterling, Sergt. Stephen	1754, 1758
s. of Jacob and Hannah Odell (Seeley), d. 1793, æ. 81, m. Eunice Summers.	
Sherman, Roger	1761
Sherwood, David	1762
bap. 1734, d. 1763, s. of Nathaniel.	
Seeley, Hezekiah	1763
m. 1750, Johannah Beardsley.	
Sherwood, Samuel, Jr.	1765
Sherwood, Samuel, 3d.	1766
Sanford, Ezekiel	1766
Seeley, Elnathan	1768, 1795
Seeley, Seth, Jr.	1769, 1772, 1800
Sterling, Capt. Abijah	1767, 1795
m. Esther dau. of Nathaniel Sherwood, s. of Stephen and Eunice (Summers,) d. 1802, æ. 56.	
Smith, Jonathan, d. 1810, æ. 72..1775,	1781
Seeley, Ezra	1775
m. Mary ——, d. 1827, æ. 81.	
Sayre, John, Missionary Ch. of Eng.	1775
Sherman, Thomas	1776
Sherwood, Capt. Samuel, 2d	1779
bap. 1732, d. 1802, æ. 71, s. of Nathaniel.	
Sterling, Stephen, Jr.	1782
bap. 1754, d. 1797, æ. 43.	
Sherman, Capt. David, 4th	1783
s. of Capt. D. 3d, d. August 22, 1810, æ. 55.	
Summers, Aaron, d. 1826, æ. 82?	1783
Summers, Samuel	1770, 1785
d. 1810, æ. 74. m. Mary ——.	
Summers, Abijah	1785, 1788
Sherman, Ebenezer	1789, 1806
s. of Elnathan, d. 1819, æ. 62.	
Sherwood, Philemon	1792, 1799
m. Hephzibah, dau. of Justus Burr, d. 1835, æ. 76.	
Stevenson, Tertullus, m. Sarah ——	1797
Sturgis, Levi	1799
Sterling, Sherman	1799
Sherwood, David, d. 1826, æ. 72..1798,	1799
Sterling, Sherwood	1799, 1866
s. of David and Deborah.	
Strong, John	1801, 1821
s. of Joseph, d. 1822, æ. 54.	
Scofield, Jesse	1802
Sherman, Capt. Stephen	1803
Summers, Elnathan	1793, 1803, 1826?
d. 1831, æ. 85.	

Names.	Year of Mention.
Seeley, Jesse, d. 1822, æ. 39	1806
Southward, Robert	1808
Sherman, Abijah	1808
d. 1831, æ. 65, s. of Elnathan.	
Silliman, Levi	1808
Sherman, Widow Mary	1808
Seeley, James	1811, 1823
Shepard, Charles	1815
Skinner, Nathaniel L.	1815, 1825
d. 1826, æ. 40.	
Symes, Robert	1818
Snow, John	1819
Sherman, Ira, s. of Silas	1820, 1836, 1868
Sturges, Peter	1824
Stillman, Benjamin	1834
Seeley, D. V.	1835
Sterling, David	1837, 1839
Summers, David	1837, 1838
Scott, Albert	1839
Stevenson, William G.	1841, 1880
Sterling, David, Jr.	1842
Stevens, John	1844
Sanford, Daniel	1845
Stowe, Jirah	1845, 1846
Solly, George	1847
Smith, Chauncey	1850, 1857
Stevens, Mrs. Henry	1850
Smith, Aaron B.	1850
Sterling, Daniel H.	1850, 1876
Sherwood, Mary	1856, 1863
Stillman, Mrs. W.	1856, 1861
Spooner, Clapp	1856, 1863
Sterling, Woolsey G.	1856, 1863
Sherman, Starr	1857
Squire, Henry W.	1861
Sharp, Jacob	1861
Sherwood, Charles P.	1861
Sanborn, Anson	1861
Sturdevant, Henry N.	1863
Stevens, J. G.	1868
Stillman, William M.	1868, 1875
b. 1820, d. 1891.	
St. John, G. A.	1868
Sherwood, William	1868
Sterling, Julian H.	1870
Sibley, John L. B.	1870, 1880
Sherwood, David W.	1873, 1875
Stevens, C. H.	1874
Sterling, John H.	1879, 1880
Sprague, Arthur J	1886
Shattuck, M. L. P.	1888
Smith, William E.	1890
Sawyer, Walter W.	1893
Stevens, Mrs. H. W.	1893
Taylor, Jonathan	1703
Treadwell, Joshua	1709, 1716
Treadwell, David	1724
bap. 1698, s. of Samuel.	
Taylor, Baruch, d. 1782	1776

Names.	Year of Mention.
Tweedy, Reuben	1793, 1795
Treadwell, Robert	1804
Tuttle, Johnson	1810, 1826
Tuite, John	1811
Thorp, Ephraim	1811
Thorp, Beers	1815
Thompson, Lewis	1819
Treat, Isaac	1825
Treadwell, David	1828
Taylor, O. P.	1845, 1850
Treat, Amos S., d. 1886	1861, 1880
Trubee, William E.	1863
Trulock, Mrs. Amanda	1868
Turney, Mrs. S. A.	1868
Thompson, William, janitor	1890
Ufford, David, d. 1820	1819
VanSycle, Lewis	1874, 1875
Wilcox, Jacob	1700
Whelply, Joseph	1704
Wakeman, John	1706
Wheeler, Ephraim	1697, 1707
Wheeler, John	1747, 1775
bap. 1710, d. 1800, æ. 87, m. Dorothy ——, who d. 1790; s. of Dr. John, the schoolmaster.	
Wakeley, Jonathan, Jr.	1732, 1749
bap. 1706, d. 1800?	
Wakeley, Capt. Samuel	1759
bap. 1711? d. 1782, s. of Joseph?	
Wheeler, Hezekiah	1766, 1795
bap. 1732, m. Abigail ——, d. 1809, æ. 86, s. of Timothy.	
Whittemore, Samuel	1798, 1815
Wetmore, Robert W.	1800
Woodward, Thomas	1808
Whiting, Samuel, d. 1824, æ. 42	1809
Wordin, Thomas Cook	1809, 1852
b. 1787, s. of William, Jr.	
Winton, Maj. James	1811, 1814?
Wheeler, Ira B.	1811, 1843
Wheeler, Tuttle	1815
Wheeler, Daniel O.	1818
Wetmore, Thomas	1819
Wheeler, Benjamin	1823, 1856
Wheeler, Ezra	1811, 1823
Wallis, Abijah	1823
Wood, Joseph	1826
Willard, ——	1826
Wickes, Capt. E.	1834
Wheeler, David	1835, 1857
Woodruff, T.	1837, 1856
Wordin, Samuel W.	1837
Wilson, Mrs.	1842, 1844
Wilmot, Alexander	1842
Wells, Edwin	1844
Weed, Joseph B.	1845, 1854
Wood, Sherman	1845, 1850

Names.	Year of Mention.	Names.	Year of Mention.
Weed, Granville	1850	White, E. P.	1868
Wales, Henry	1856, 1857	Wheaton, George E.	1868, 1876
Walling, T. C.	1856	Wood, E. S.	1868
Wheeler, Ezra	1856, 1857	Whitney, John D.	1870
Wheeler, Mrs. Ira B.	1856, 1857	Waldo, George C.	1874
Wakeley, Sidney L.'	1857	Wilmot, C. E.	1882, 1884
Wheeler, Hannah	1856	Wilson, Dr. F. M.	1886, 1893
Wheeler, Mrs. C. B.	1863	Whitney, F. Archibald	1889
Wales, Salem H.	1863		
Woodburn, ——	1863	Young, Isaac	1788
Wooster, ——	1867	Young, Isaac L.	1842

—201—

FULL LIST OF MEMBERS

Received since the beginning of Mr. Waterman's ministry.

L. Letter.   P. Profession.   R.C. Renewed Covenant.   dism. Dismissed.   rem. Removed.
exc. Excommunicated.   *m.* Married.   *w.* Wife.   *wid.* Widow.
s. Son.   *dau.* Daughter.   *æ.* Age.

Name.	Admission.		Dismission.	Death.	Remarks.
Adams, Hiram	1813	L.	exc. 1828	....	from Danbury.
Atwell, Richard	1823	....	....	1833, æ. 67	....
Atwell, Anna	1823	L.	....	....	*w.* of Richard ; fr. Huntington.
Allen, Daily	....	....	....	1826	*wid.* of ——.
Allen, Dr. Addis	1830	....	....	1833	....
Atwell, Charles	1831	....	1836	....	....
Atkinson, Sarah	1831	....	dism.	....	....
Atwell, Ruth Ann	1831	....	dism.	....	....
Armstrong, Clarissa	....	....	....	....	Missionary to Sandwich Is.
Andrus, Susan	1832	....	....	....	....
Aymar, Harriet	....	....	1840 ?	....	....
Adair, Margaret	....	....	....	1834	....
Andrew, Jane	1841	....	dism.	....	....
Ames, Mary E.	1855	P.	1866	....	*m.* D. B. Hatch, Jr.
Ames, Charlotte L.	1857	P.	1862	....	*m.* Charles Foote, Jr.
Allen, Stephen T.	1858	P.	....	1872, æ. 42	....
Anderson, Joseph	....	....	....	....	....
Allen, Virginia H.	1858	P.	....	1878	*wid.* of Stephen T.
Anderson, Emily W. (Dyer)	1858	P.	....	....	*wid.* of John J.
Ayres, Sarah C.	1860	P.	....	....	*w.* of Cornelius H.
Ayres, Cornelius H.	....	....	....	....	....
Adams, Miss Mary L.	1861	....	1865	....	*m.* Cornelius C. Bulkley.
Armstrong, Eunice	1863	L.	....	1864, æ. 75	*wid.* of —— Tracy.
Ayres, Esther M.	1864	P.	dism.	....	*m.* Levi Toucey.
Ayres, Clorinda B.	1864	L.	....	....	*w.* of Lewis B.
Atwater, Dr. David F.	1864	L.	1883	....	....
Atwater, Sarah	1864	L.	1883	....	*w.* of Dr. D. F.
Atwater, Mary M.	1864	P.	1888	....	*dau.* of Dr. D. F.
Ayres, Lewis B.	1864	L.	....	....	....
Ayres, Charles L.	1864	P.	....	....	*s.* of Lewis B.
Aldrich, Mahala W.	1866	L.	1882	....	*w.* of Wade H.
Aldrich, Wade H.	....	....	....	....	....
Abernethy, Elisha S.	....	....	....	....	....
Abernethy, Charlotte M.	1868	L.	....	1869, æ. 60	*w.* of Elisha S.
Atwater, Charles	1874	P.	1882	....	*s.* of Dr. D. F.
Alvord, Adelaide	1872	L.	1888	....	*w.* of Nelson
Ayres, Mary Cornelia	1876	P.	....	....	*dau.* of Cornelius H.
Adams, Hannah Maria (Hunt)	1878	L.	....	1891	*wid.* of John.
Andrews, Caroline (Mygatt)	1884	L.	....	....	*w.* of Frank S.
Abernethy, Willard P.	1889	L.	....	....	*s.* of John.
Anderson, Percy Paul	1890	P.	....	....	*s.* of John J.
Anderson, Clarence D.	1892	P.	....	....	*s.* of John J.
Burroughs, Edward	bef. July 1813	R.C.	....	....	....
Burroughs, Elizabeth	bef. July 1813	R.C.	....	....	*w.* of Edward.

Name.	Admission.	Dismission.	Death.	Remarks.
Backus, Simon	1809 R.C.	....	....	....
Backus, Alice	1809 R.C.	....	....	w. of Simon.
Burroughs, Polly	1811 R.C.	....	....	....
Beach, Barnum	1813 R.C.	....	....	....
Beach, Betsey	1813 R.C.	....	....	w. of Barnum.
Bartlett, John	1814 R.C. / 1815 P.	....	1872, æ. 87	....
Bartlett, Sally	1814 R.C. / 1815 P.	....	1881, æ. 92	w. of John.
Beach, Caleb	1815 R.C.	....	....	....
Beach, Agur	1819 R.C.	....	....	....
Beach, Mary	1819 P.	1854	1886	w. of Agur.
Booth, Roswell	1824 R.C.	....	....	....
Booth, Minerva	1824 R.C.	....	....	w. of Roswell.
Backus, Huldah	1807	1830	....	w. of Joseph.
Baldwin, Elizabeth	1811	....	....	....
Baldwin, Josiah Brinsmade	1813	1830	....	....
Backus, Eunice Alice	1814	....	....	w. of Simon, Jr.
Burroughs, Pamela	1814	....	1825, æ. 42	w. of Stephen, Jr.
Burroughs, Stephen, 2d	1815	....	1845, æ. 82	....
Backus, Oswald	1815 P. / 1838 L.	1830	1863	....
Bussy, Enos	1815	....	af. 1818	....
Benedict, Epenetus	1815	1826	....	entered the ministry.
Houghton, Nathaniel	1815	....	....	entered the ministry.
Benedict, Ann	1815	rem.	....	....
Beardsley, Sally	1815	....	1849	....
Benedict, Hulda	1815	....	....	w. of Jesse.
Blake, Polly	1815	....	....	w. of Seeley.
Beard, Spencer Field	1816	....	....	....
Burroughs, Thankful	1816	....	....	w. of Stiles.
Beach, Elizabeth	1816	....	....	w. of Barnum.
Brisco, Nathan	1816	rem.	....	....
Benedict, Sarah	1817	....	....	w. of Comfort.
Brown, Elizabeth D.	1817	....	....	....
Beardsley, Syrena	1818	1847	....	....
Benton, Priscilla	1818	rem.	....	w. of John M.
Benjamin, Mary	1819	rem.	....	w. of Barzillai.
Baldwin, Nathan	1821	1830	....	....
Bulkley, John William	1821	1828	....	....
Baldwin, Eliza	1821	1827	....	w. of Eli. [bury.
Baldwin, Charlotte	1821	1859	....	m. —— Hubbell ; rem. to Sims-
Bouton, John Mills	1821	rem.	....	....
Burr, William	....	....	1825, æ. 41	....
Burr, Lewis	1821	exc.	....	....
Brooks, John, Jr.	1821	1830	....	....
Baldwin, Jennett Augusta	1821	....	1828	w. of Josiah B.
Bussey, Mary	1821	....	1832	w. of Enos.
Brooks, Maria	1821	1830	....	w. of John, Jr.
Burr, Alisia	1821	....	....	....
Brooks, Jannett	1821	....	....	....
Burrows, Maria	1821	....	....	m. —— French.
Baldwin, Lyman	1821	1830	....	....
Baldwin, Esther	1822	1830	....	from Trumbull.
Benedict, Manson	1824	....	....	entered the ministry.
Burr Ann	1824	1830	....	w. of William ; from Wilton.
Bradley, Elizabeth	1824	1830	....	w. of Enos.

Name.	Admission.		Dismission.	Death.	Remarks.
Brown, Sally	1827	P.	1830	....	*wid.* of —— Brown.
Basset, Ann Eliza	1827	P.	....	....	*m.* —— Sherman.
Basset, Louisa	1827	P.	....	....	....
Baker, Caroline	1827	P.	rem.	....	....
Bartram, Urana	1828	L.	dism.	....	w. of John.
Bateman, Helen	1828	L.	1830	....	....
Blank, Susan Palmer	1828	P.	....	1889, æ. 89	w. of Albin P.
Bliss, Betsey	1828	P.	1831	....	....
Backus, Jennett	bef. 1826	....	1830	....	....
Beach, Eliza	1821	....	1829	....	w. of Isaac.
Bolen, Mary	bef. 1826	....	rem.	....	....
Benedict, Alanson	bef. 1826	....	rem.	1833	entered the ministry.
Brown, Mary E.	bef. 1830	....	1832	....	....
Betts, James	1828	....	....	1858	....
Betts, Esther	1828	....	....	1859	w. of James.
Blatchford, Rev. John	1830	....	1837	....	to Chicago.
Blatchford, Frances	1830	....	....	....	w. of Rev. John.
Beach, Elizabeth	1821	P.	1885	....	....
Bartlett, Julia	1831	....	....	....	....
Beardsley, Hiram	1831	....	....	....	....
Baker, Jesse	1831	....	....	1832	....
Blakeman, Abijah	1831	....	1837	....	....
Betts, James B.	1831	....	1833	....	to Charleston, S. C.
Black, Mary Ann	1831	....	....	....	to Baptist Church.
Bray, William	1832	....	exc. for withdraw		ing to Baptist Church.
Bray, Sarah E.	1833	....	....	....	w. of Judson.
Beers, Samantha	1833	....	....	....	....
Bartram, Maria	bef. 1830	....	....	....	w. of Ira.
Beach, Isaac E.	1832	....	....	1877, æ. 75	....
Baldwin, Charity	1831	....	....	1852, æ. 80	*wid.* of Timothy.
Beers, Hannah	1833	....	....	....	*wid.* of ——.
Bradley, Harriet	1831	....	....	....	[Norwalk.
Beach, Dr. and Dea. Samuel, bef.	1834	L. fr. Stamf'd	May 6, '53	drowned in railroad disaster at
Beach, Mary	1834	L.	dism.	....	w. of Samuel.
Bunnell, William R.	1835	L.	....	1872	clerk of church 1856 to 1870.
Bunnell, Sarah H.	1835	....	....	April 1835	w. of Wm. R., *dau.* of S. S. Haight.
Brewster, Jane	1836	....	....	....	....
Bunnell, Diantha	1836	....	....	1858, æ. 80	*wid.* of Rufus.
Bolin, Eliza A.	1836	....	dism.	....	....
Beach, Julia Ann	1837	....	dism.	....	....
Bliss, Henry H.	1837	....	dism.	....	....
Bliss, ——	1837	....	dism.	....	w. of Henry H.
Bunnell, Mrs. Thomas	1838	....	dism.	....	....
Burr, Margaret M.	1838	P.	1868, 1894	....	*wid.* of Rufus.
Bixby, Harriet	1839	L.	....	....	from Valatie, N. Y.
Boughton, Hannah	1840	....	....	1860, æ. 84	*wid.* of ——.
Beecher, Frances Julia A. (Jones)	1840	P.	....	....	w. of Rev. Thomas K.
Beecher, Rev. Thomas K.	....	....	1857	....	to Elmira, N. Y.
Booth, Sarah C.	bef. 1841	....	....	....	....
Bassett, Freeman C. (soc. 1834).	1841	P.	....	1858, æ. 72	....
Bassett, Maria	1841	P.	....	1864, æ. 68	w. of Freeman C.
Birch, Eliza	1842	P.	....	1867, æ. 69	*dau.* of Stephen Burroughs.
Beardsley, Rev. Bronson B. (soc. 1840	{ 1843 1864	P. L.	1870	....	....
Backus, Susan W. (Seymour)	1845	L.	....	....	w. of Oswald.
Baldwin, Rachael	1845	....	1848	....	....
Beardsley, Nichols (soc. 1835)	1848	P.	1870	....	....

Name.	Admission.	Dismission.	Death.	Remarks.
Beardsley, Anna W.	{ 1848 .... { 1861 L.	1852 1868	....	w. of Wilson.
Birch, David M.	1849 P.	....	1853	....
Blank, Miss Sarah	1849	....	1850	[Henry S. Parrott.
Bradley, Lucinda	1849 L.	....	....	w. of Morehouse, W., 2d w. of
Baldwin, George	1850 ..	1870	....	....
Baldwin, Abigail	1850 L.	1870	....	w. of George.
Benham, Mary S.	1850	1863	....	w. of Julius.
Beardsley, Dea. Agur (soc. 1863)	1852 L	....	....	....
Beardsley, Lucinda (Nichols)	1852 L.	....	1865, æ. 70	w. of Agur.
Blake, Henry T.	1852 L.	1864	....	....
Blank, Abram P.	1859 L.	....	....	....
Burr, Rufus	....	....	....	....
Brooks, Joseph W.	....	1867	....	....
Brooks, Elizabeth	....	1867	....	....
Beardsley, Wilson (soc. 1849)	....	1852	....	....
Bradley, Morehouse W. (soc. '44)	1858 P.	....	1860, æ. 42	....
Benham, Julius (soc. 1841)	....	1863	....	....
Balcom, Sumner	1854 L.	....	1864, æ. 61	....
Blackman, Treat	1855 L.	....	....	....
Bishop, Mary Jane	....	dism.	....	....
Brooks, Samuel H.	1857 L.	1860	....	....
Brooks, Frances E.	1857 L.	1858	....	....
Brown, Rebecca W.	1858 P.	....	....	wid. Dr. Henry C.
Bunnell, James S.	1858 P.	1872	....	to San Francisco.
Beach, J. Wickliff	1858 L.	1860	....	to Yale College.
Brown, Dr. Henry C. (soc. 1856)	....	....	....	....
Beach, George E.	1858 P.	....	1877, æ. 44	....
Bray, George A.	1858	....	1864	....
Balcom, Jennie S.	1858 P.	1865	....	m. —— Holcomb.
Balcom, Mary Elizabeth	1858 P.	....	....	m. Samuel E. Blinn.
Birk, Charles H.	1858 P.	1859	....	....
Blinn, Samuel E.	1864 P.	1873	....	....
Barlow, Daniel S.	1858 P.	....	1876	....
Beardsley, Sarah A.	1858 L.	....	....	w. of Henry N.
Beach, Mary E.	1858 P.	....	....	w. of John H.
Beach, John H. (soc. 1856)	....	....	....	....
Baker, Margaret L.	1859 L.	1865	....	w. of Elisha.
Beardsley, Marcia	1859 P.	1870	....	....
Bennet Mary	1859 L.	....	....	....
Bradley, Theodore F. (soc. 1870)	1860	1876	....	....
Baker, Elisha	....	1865	....	....
Baldwin, Jennie	1860 P.	1865	....	....
Buss, Persis H.	1860 L.	1874	....	w. of R. T.
Bishop, James P.	1860 L.	1868	....	....
Bishop, Charles K.	1860 L.	1868	....	....
Bishop, Celestia O.	1860 L.	1868	....	w. of James P.
Buss, R. T. (soc. 1861)	....	....	....	....
Bissell, Mary	1861 L.	....	....	....
Bunnell, Katharine S.	1863 P.	1892	....	m. Dr. George F. Lewis.
Beardsley, Mary W.	1861 L.	1870	....	w. of Rev. B. B.
Baldwin, Eliza V.	1863 L.	1869	....	m. Dr. Joseph H. Grier.
Barlow, Daniel S. (soc. 1857–'68)	....	....	....	....
Barnum, Emeline L.	1864 P.	1872	....	....
Bishop, Edward W.	1864 P.	....	....	....
Basset, Charles H.	....	....	....	....
Barnum, Lydia	1864 L.	....	....	....

—205—

Name.	Admission.		Dismission.	Death.	Remarks.
Backus, Joseph S.	1865	P.	....	Oct. 27, '65 æ. 16½.	
Burrill, ———	1865	P.	....	....	w. of Villeroy.
Bradbury, Frank B. (soc. 1868)	....		....	....	....
Beebe, James I.	....		....	....	....
Bradley, Eliza N.	1867	L.	1876	....	w. of Theodore F.
Brinsmade, Hobart	1867 / 1889	L. / L.	1890	....	
Barnum, Eunice G. (McD.)	1867	P.	....	....	w. of W. H.
Barnum, W. H. (soc. 1865)	....		....	....	[Dale.
Brown, Maggie	1868	L.	....	....	dau. of James D., w. of T. N.
Brown, Margaret	1868	L.	....	....	w. of James D., M.D.
Brown, James D.	....		....	....	
Brown, Catharine S.	1868	P.	....	....	m. 1868, Jos. P. French, M.D.
Brown, Miss Matilda	1869	L.	....	....	
Bronson, Orlando H. (soc. 1872)	1878	....	....	....	s. of Peleg.
Balcom, Laura	1854	L.	....	1888	wid. of Sumner.
Backus, Mary P.	1858	L.	....	1880	wid. of Oswald.
Banks, Cornelia C.	1861	P.	....	1885	w. of Edwin.
Barlow, Charity	1863	P.	....	....	w. of Daniel S.
Bradley, Edward H.	1864	P.	....	....	
Bradbury, Susan E.	1866	L.	1883	....	w. of Frank B. [Thomas.
Bracken, Alice H. (Hanford)	1874	P.	....	....	dau. of James Hanford, w. of
Bunnell, Cornelia S.	1831	P.	....	1883	wid. of Wm. R., dau. of David
Birch, Juliette	1842	P.	....	....	[and Deborah Sterling.
Birdsey, Ezekiel (soc. 1837)	1844	P.	....	....	
Brooks, Eleanor H.	1844	P.	....	....	wid. of Joseph W.
Birch, Mary A.	1858	P.	....	....	wid. of George E.
Birdsey, Martha W.	1858	P.	....	....	w. of Geo. K., dau. of Horace
Birdsey, George K.	1858	P.	....	....	[F. Hatch.
Blinn, Mary E.	1858	P.	....	....	wid. of Samuel.
Bronson, Ann E.	1857	P.	....	....	w. of Peleg.
Brown, Rebecca W.	1858	P.	....	....	wid of Dr. H. C.
Beach, Mary E.	1858	P.	....	....	w. of John H.
Bronson, Peleg	1858	P.	....	....	
Burton, Oriana (Sprague)	1859	P.	....	....	w. of Silas.
Bunnell, Julia H.	1863	P.	....	....	dau. of William R.
Beebe, Bessie Howard	1866	P.	....	....	w. of Jabez L.
Bronson, Maria Frances	1870	P.	....	1878	w. of Orland H.
Beecher, Charles M.	1872	L.	1894	....	
Benedict, George	1873	P.	1883	....	entered the ministry. [Hawes.
Beardsley, Ella Cornelia	1873	P.	....	....	w. of George B., dau. of E. N.
Brigham, Edwin G. (soc. 1868)	1871	L.	....	....	
Brigham, Marietta P.	1871	L.	....	1882	w. of Edwin G.
Brigham, Arthur L.	1871	L.	1880	....	
Beecher, Anna Johnson	1874	L.	1894	....	w. of Charles M.
Beeman, Mary Eliza A.	1876	P.	1880	....	w. of Geo. S Waller. [Beach.
Briggs, Lizzie H.	1874	P.	....	....	w. of Warren R., dau. of Geo. E.
Baldwin, Emily P.	1876	L.	....	....	w. of Sherlon I. [Sterling.
Baillie, Gertrude Maria	1877	P.	1892	....	w. of Wm. E., dau. of Dan. H.
Baillie, Matilda McCoy	1877	P.	....	....	dau. of Daniel H. Sterling.
Beach, James Eaton	1876	P.	....	....	
Beers, Mary J. (Hanford)	1876	P.	....	....	w. of Seth J.
Beach, David Sherman	1876	P.	....	....	s. of John H.
Barrow, Adelaide	1877	P.	1879	....	dau. of George.
Beach, Isaac Eaton	1877	P.	....	....	s. of George E.
Bennetto, Elizabeth Ann	1877	P.	1891	....	wid. of John.

Name.	Admission.	Dismission.	Death.	Remarks.
Botsford, Henry C.	1877 P.	1888	....	s. of H. H.
Burr, Anna J.	1878 L.	....	1892	
Bullock, Anna C.	1878 L.	1890	....	w. of Israel M.
Beach, Herman ....May,	1878 P.	....	May, 1878	
Barnum, Marcus	1879 L.	1882	....	
Barnum, Mary J.	1879 L.	1882	....	w. of Marcus.
Beach, Matilda B.	1879 L.	....	....	w. of James E.
Birdsey, Herbert	1879 P.	....	....	s. of George K.
Brown, Samuel	1879 L.	....	....	
Bodwell, Minnie Alice (Fuller)	1879 P.	....	....	
Beecher, Maria	1880 L.	....	....	
Beecher, Fanny Maria	1880 P.	....	....	
Beardsley, George Blakeman ..	1880 P.	....	....	
Bartley, Joseph Dana	1883 L.	1892	....	
Hartley, Mary Atwood	1883 L.	1892	....	w. of Joseph D.
Bartley, Helen Preston	1883 L.	1892	....	dau. of Joseph D.
Bartley, William Tenney	1883 P.	1894	....	s. of Joseph D.
Bennetto, John	1883 P.	1883	....	
Brundage Elizabeth T.	1883 L.	....	....	
Busse, Annie M. (McKinnon)..	1882	1891	....	w. of Franz Theo.
Banks, Sarah C.	1831 P.	....	1885	wid. of Charles B.
Baldwin, Sherlon L.	1884 P.	....	....	
Bronson, Fanny Louisa	1884 L.	....	....	w. of Orland H.
Birdsey, Mary Gertrude	1885 P.	....	....	dau. of George K.
Botsford, Emeline Eliza	1885 L.	1888	....	
Burr, Mary Hammond	1884 L.	....	....	w. of Ebenezer.
Blachly, Mary L.	1886 L.	....	....	dau. of Jos. W.
Bartram, Mattie L.	1887 L.	....	....	w. of Edgar B.
Beach, Mary Jane	1886 L.	....	....	
Bishop, William F.	1889 L.	....	....	
Boardman, Ellen L.	1887 L.	....	....	
Baldwin, Alice May	1889 P.	....	....	dau. of Sherlon L.
Bishop, Mary Linda	1889 P.	....	....	dau. of William F.
Blodgett, Dr. Henry	1887 L.	....	....	
Brinsmade, Ella M.	1889 L.	1890	....	w. of Hobart B.
Brinsmade, Robert Bruce	1889 P.	1890	....	s. of Hobart B.
Barrett, Lucy A.	1890 L.	1892	....	
Beardsley, Morris B.	1890 P.	....	....	
Beardsley, Lucy J.	1890 L.	....	....	w. of Morris B.
Beardsley, Samuel F.	1891 P.	....	....	s. of Morris B.
Burlison, James	1890 P.	....	....	
Benson, Abel T.	1892 L.	1893	....	
Benson, Martina	1892 L.	1893	....	w. of Abel T.
Beers, Cora May	1893 P.	....	....	dau. of Mary J.
Beers, Mary J.	1893 L.	....	....	
Baldwin, Lewis Palmer	1894 P.	....	....	s. of Sherlon L.
Beardsley, Lucy May	1894 P.	....	....	dau. of Morris B.
Curtis, Matthew	1809 R.C.	....	....	
Curtis, Polly	1809 R.C.	....	....	w. of Matthew.
Cable, Polly ....May 6,	1810	....	1810, æ. 40	w. of Samuel.
Croford, Hannah	1815	....	....	
Clark, Dorothy	1816	....	....	
Crawford, George	1816	1826	susp.	
Cable, Thomas	1820	1828	exc.	
Cannon, Mary	1821	....	....	
Chichester, Alfred	1821	1827	....	

—207—

Name.	Admission.	Dismission.	Death.	Remarks.
Crosby, Nathaniel P.	1821	exc.		
Carrier, Alpha	1821	1835		
Cannon, Elizabeth	1823 L.			from Stratford.
Chandler, Moses	1823 L.	1826		
Curtis, Andrew	1823 L.	rem.		
Cable, Eliza	1824			w. of Thomas; fr. Meth. Ch.
Canfield, Lucretia	1827 P.	1830		
Curtis, Victory		1830		
Curtis, Susan		1830		
Coty, Cornelia M.		1830		
Chichester, Susan	bef. 1826	1827		w. of Alfred.
Curtis, Hepsa	1831		1866, æ. 82	
Caswell, Joana	1831		1851	wid. of ——.
Crane, Horace F.	1831		rem.	
Curtis, George A.	1831		rem.	
Cooke, Elizabeth	1832		1836	
Crawford, Harriet	1832		dism.	wid. of Bronson.
Croninberger, Hannah	1832		1855	w. of Joseph.
Conklin, Isaac M.	1833		1861, æ. 60	
Cannon, Lavinia	1835			
Cameron, Roxanna	1835 P.		1875, æ. 67	w. of Robert.
Clark, Susan A.	1838	exc.		
Clark, Andrew	1840 L.			from Milford.
Curtis, Janetta (Peck)	bef. 1841			w. of George.
Chatfield, Susan (Kippen)	1841		1851	
Clark, Eliza B.	1841	dism.		
Clark, Dr. James H.	1841 L.	1844?		
Clark, Mary Elizabeth	1841	dism.		
Clark, Sereno B.	1844 P.	dism.		
Clark, Lydia	{ 1850 L. / 1870 L.	1863 / 1888?		wid. of Elijah.
Clark, Mary Jane	{ 1850 L. / 1870 L.	1863	1863	dau. of Elijah.
Conklin, Sarah E.	1851 L.	1853		
Chappel, Caroline	{ 1851 P. / 1854 L.	1852 / 1858		
Caswell, Alanson	{ 1831 / 1851 L.	1860		
Caswell, Mary	1851 L.	1860		w. of Alanson.
Clark, William A.	1851	1855		
Chatfield, Elizabeth (Brooks)	1852 L.	1867		w. of Henry W.
Cummings, Cornelia A.	1852 L.	1854		wid. of ——.
Curtis, Rodney		1868		
Curtis, ——	1831	1868		w. of Rodney.
Cronenberger, Joseph	1837		1855	
Chatfield, Henry W. (soc. 1841)	1844 P.	1867		
Clark, Mr.		1863		
Cummings, Cornelia			1854	
Curtis, Israel I.	1857 L.	1858		
Chambers, Mary A. (Bulkley)	1858 L.			w. of Francis.
Chambers, Francis	1858 P.	1859		
Cronenberger, Augusta E.	1858 P.		1855	
Cole, Julia M.	1858 L.			w. of ——.
Curtis, Alfred H.	1859 P.	1862		
Carter, Gilman	1859 L.		1866	
Carter, Ida Augusta	1859 L.	1867		w. of Gilman.
Curtis, Miss Cornelia M.	1861 P.			

Name.	Admission.		Dismission.	Death.	Remarks.
Curtis, Daniel	....	....	....	....	....
Capen, Christopher	1863	L.	....	1877, æ. 67	....
Coffin, Edward W.	1861 ?	...	....	....	....
Capen, George C.	1864	P.	....	1873	....
Chapman, T. P.	1866	L.	....	1869, æ. 49	....
Chapman, Anna H.	1866	L.	1870	....	w. of T. P.
Cate, Adelia E.	1867	L.	1874	....	w. of Stephen M. [W. Coe.
Cate, Adelia E.	1867	L.	1868	....	dau. of Stephen M., m. Irving
Curtis, Homer S.	1867	L.	....	1874	....
Carr, Dabney	1868	P.	1870	....	....
Conklin, Betsey	1833	...	....	1893	wid. of Isaac M.
Campbell, Mary (Bissell)	1861	L.	....	....	....
Cameron, Robert (soc. 1834)	1858	P.	....	1886	....
Curtis, Julia	1861	P.	....	....	wid. of Daniel.
Curtis, Alice (Bradley)	1864	P.	1886	1886	wid. of Homer S.
Capen, Lydia	1863	L.	1869	....	wid. of Christopher.
Coffin, Mary W.	1863	L.	....	1888	w. of Edwin.
Cate, Stephen M.	1867	L.	1881	....	....
Collier, Margaret E. A.	1868	P.	....	....	w. of James.
Clark, Elizabeth A. (Birdsey)	1870	P.	....	....	dau. of Ezekiel Birdsey.
Cowles, George B.	1871	L.	1881	....	....
Cowles, Cordelia W.	1871	L.	1881	....	w. of George B.
Cole, John H. (soc. 1868)	1874	L.	....	....	....
Cole, Margaret A.	1874	P.	....	....	w. of John H. [Beach.
Curtis, Amelia M. (Beach)	1876	P.	1887	....	w. of G. S., dau. of John H.
Canfield, William Edwin	1877	L.	....	....	....
Canfield, Mary Elvira	1877	L.	....	....	w. of William Edwin.
Cowles, George Burr	1877	P.	1881	....	....
Carter, John Robert	1880	P.	....	....	....
Conklin, Alexander Bowen	1879	P.	....	....	....
Cogswell, Richard Baldwin	1881	P.	....	....	....
Cogswell, Lucy Maria	1881	L.	....	....	w. of Richard B.
Cogswell, Mary Kate	1882	P.	....	....	dau. of Henry C.
Cogswell, Sarah Jane	1883	P.	....	....	w. of Henry C.
Canfield, Alice W.	1882	P.	....	....	w. of Charles S.
Campbell, Andrew Chambre	1883	P.	1892	....	....
Carter, Maria C.	1883	P.	....	....	....
Crump, Frances Bell (Hastings)	1883	P.	....	....	w. of Henry S.
Crane, Carrie J. (Nichols)	1884	L.	1895	....	w. of L. B.
Campbell, Hattie Barrett	1885	L.	1892	....	w. of Andrew C.
Conklin, Ann	1885	L.	....	....	....
Cowles, Martin	1885	L.	....	....	....
Cowles, Cynthia B. K.	1885	L.	....	1887	....
Cameron, Ann Elizabeth	1886	L.	....	....	....
Cogswell, Richard William	1888	P.	....	....	s. of Richard B.
Cogswell, Grace Maria	1891	P.	....	....	dau. of Richard B.
DeForest, Philo	1808	R.C.	....	....	....
Darling, Samuel	1807	...	....	....	....
Darling, Nancy	1807	...	....	....	w. of Samuel.
Dudley, Hannah	1808	...	....	....	....
DeForest, Betsey	1808	...	....	....	....
DeForest, Nancy	1808	...	....	....	w. of Philo.
DeForest, Eleanor	1824	...	....	1825, æ. 71	wid. of ———.
Doane, Susan	1827	P.	1830	....	....
DeForest, Mary L.	1827	P.	1830	....	....
DeForest, Louisa	....	...	1830	....	....

Name.	Admission.	Dismission.	Death.	Remarks.
Davy, Emily	1831	dism.		
Davy, Harriet	1832	dism.		
Davis, Robert C.	1834			
Dunning, William M.	1836 P.		after 1861	
Dunning, Amelia Louisa	1836 P.			w. of William M.
Davies, David	1838	dism.		
Dyer, Emeline	1832 / 1851 L.	dism.	1890	w. of William B.
Day, Emily Jones	1842 L.		1869	w. of Daniel, Jr.
Day, Daniel, Jr.			1869	
Dyer, William B.	1851	exc.	1866, æ. 67	
Donaldson, Sarah M.	1855 L.	1873		
Donaldson, Thomas				
Davis, Phebe	1861 P.		1864	
Dayton, Phebe M.	1861 P.		1870	m. Seth Hill.
Day, John B.	1863 P.	1870		
Day, Mary Elizabeth	1863 P.	1870		m. —— Willmer.
Davis, Victoria V. (Trulock)	1864 P.		1869	w. of Guernsey W.
Davis, Guernsey W.				
Dana, Mary S.	1868 L.	1870		w. of ——.
DeForest, Isaac	1869 L.			
DeForest, Sarah Ann				
Dickerman, Mary Lacey	1869 L.	1887		m. S. S. Hunter.
Day, Rev. Dea. Guy B.	1855 L.		1891	
Day, Mary (Barnes)	1855 L.			wid. of Guy B.
Durand, Lizzie	1864 P.			dau. of Mrs. H. T. Wheeler.
Durfee, Amelia	1867 P.			sister of Mrs. Jas. B. Prescott.
DeForest, Eliza L.	1871 L.		1885	w. of Marcus.
Day, Julius Barnes	1876 P.	1884		s. of Guy B.
Day, Emily Bradford	1876 P.			dau. of Guy B.
Dana, Ellen R.	1877 P.	1890		dau. of George E. Wheaton.
Diller, Laura J. (Paul)	1878 L.	dism.		w. of J. S. Diller.
Dyer, Minnie Lawson	1882 P.			dau. of William B.
Dyer, Ann Eliza	1882 P.			wid. of William B.
Davenport, Mary Eliza	1884 L.			w. of Daniel.
Day, Arthur Whittlesey	1884 P.			s. of Guy B.
Dickerman, Ezra Day	1884 P.	1891		
Edgerton, Lucretia	1816	1830		
Eells, Waterman	1817	1830		
Eells, Luthenia	1817			w. of Waterman.
Edwards, Charity	1818		1821, æ. 34	w. of Daniel.
Edwards, Thomas	1822			
Edwards, Chloe	1822	susp.		
Edwards, Cloe	1823	rem.		wid. of Thomas.
Ellis, Nancy	1827 P.	1830		
Ellis, William	1828 P.	1830		
Evertson, Eliza	1836			
Edwards, Charles (soc. 1857-'75)				
Easland, John B.	1855 L.	1858		
Elliott, Henry	1859 L.	1867		
Elliott, Anna G.	1859 L. / 1872	1867	1886	w. of Henry.
Ely, Seymour W. (soc. 1868)				
Englehart, Charles				
Ennisley, William (soc. 1868)		1870		
Ennisley, Eliza				w. of William.

—210—

Name.	Admission.		Dismission.	Death.	Remarks.
Ellis, Fannie J.	1868	P.	....	....	w. of Ellis.
Ely, Mary E. (Wheeler)	1859	P.	....	....	w. of Seymour W.
Edwards, Sophia	1844	P.	....	1895	w. of Charles.
Englehart, Elizabeth A.	1857	L.	....	....	w. of Charles. [Hawley.
Eaton, Mary W. (Hawley)	1863	P.	....	....	w. of Levi W., dau. of Thos.
Edwards, Eleanor	1873	P.	....	....	dau. of Charles.
Earle, John Baptist	1877	P.	....	....	....
Earle, Barbara Innes	1877	P.	....	....	w. of John B.
Eames, Carlos Sidney	1881	P.	1894	....	....
Eames, Carrie Belle	1881	P.	1894	....	....
Edmonds, Mary Hopper	1882	L.	1892	....	w. of George B.
Englehart, Elizabeth S.	1894	P.	....	....	....
French, William	1809 R.C.		....	....	....
French, Betsey	{ 1809 R.C. 1810 .... 1815		....	1866, æ. 80	w. of William.
French, Susannah	1810		....	1835, æ. 74	w. of Gamaliel, Jr.
Fitch, Charles	1815		dism.	....	....
French, Joseph B.	1815		....	1862, æ. 75	....
French, Drusilla	1815		....	1830	w. of Joseph.
French, Ebenezer	1816		....	1843	....
French, Susan	1821		....	....	....
Fish, Catharine G.	1827	P.	1830	....	....
Fowler, Hannah	bef. 1826		....	....	....
French, Marie	bef. 1830		....	1832	m. —— Glasco.
French, Maria	1821		....	1853	w. of Wheeler.
French, Mary E.	1821		....	1869	w. of Ebenezer.
Freeman, Rose Ann	1831		dism.	....	....
French, Ann Eliza	1832		....	....	....
Foot, Hepsa Ann	1837		....	....	....
Foster, Junius	1847	L.	1855	....	....
Fancher, Caroline	1852	L.	....	1872	wid. of ——.
Fairweather, Mrs. Daniel	....		....	1858	....
French, Wheeler (soc. 1835)	....		....	1853	....
Fairchild, Eliad	....		....	....	....
Foster, Irwin	....		....	....	....
Fairchild, Amanda	....		1862	....	....
Farron, Charlotte	1853	L.	1858	....	wid. of John.
Foote, Charles, Jr.	....		1862	....	....
French, Hattie N.	1858	P.	1868	....	....
French, Caroline Louisa	1861	P.	....	....	....
Fisherdick, George H.	1867	P.	1874	....	....
Fisherdick, Eunice M. (Webster)	1867	L.	1874	....	w. of George H.
Fowler, Arabella S.	....		1859	....	....
Fox, William S. (soc. 1868)	....		....	....	....
Fox, Mary I.	1868	P.	....	1871	w. of William S.
French, Harriet B.	1831	P.	....	1884	w. of Henry N.
French, Susan M.	1831	P.	....	....	....
French, Henry N.	1832	P.	....	1884	....
French, Polly B.	1834	P.	....	1879	wid. of Capt. Joseph B.
Fairchild, Thedosia	1844	L.	....	1882	wid. of Eliud W. [Tomlinson.
Forsyth, Mary L. (Tomlinson)	1864	P.	1888	....	w. of John, dau. of Stephen
French, Catharine B.	1868	L.	....	....	w. of Dr. Joseph L.
Follansbee, John L.	1868	L.	1887	....	....
Follansbee, Eunice R.	1868	L.	1887	....	w. of John L.
Foster, Evelyn Matilda (Smith)	1883	P.	1890	....	w. of C. L.

—211—

Name.	Admission.		Dismission.	Death.	Remarks.
Fairchild, Lilian Maud (Wilson)	1884	P.	1886	....	w. of R. N.
Fuller, Mary Augusta	1885	P.	....	1893	w. of John E.
Fancher, Ann Augusta	1885	L.	....	....	wid. of Sherman.
Fitzgerald, Mary Isabella	1885	L.	1886	....	dau. of Charles M. Gaylord.
French, Burr H.	1894	P.	....	....	
Gouge, Thomas ....bef.	1813 R.C. 1827		....	1848	
Gouge, Ruth ....bef.	1813 R.C.		....	....	w. of Thomas.
Gregory, Hulda (F.M. 1777)	1813	....	....	1861	wid. of Thaddeus? d. in N. Y.
Grounderson, Salome	1815	....	....	....	wid. of Peter.
Grant, John	1816	....	....	....	
Gray, Joseph	1821	....	....	1827, æ. 23	
Gregory, Ezra, Jr.....F.M. 1810,	1827	P.	....	1871	
Gray, Ann M.	....	....	1830	....	
Gordon, Elizabeth	1823	....	1856	....	w. of Alexander.
Gregory, Bethia	1815	....	....	after 1851	w. of Ezra.
Gregory, Mary E.	1831	....	1837	....	
Griffith, Harriet	1831	....	dism.	....	
Graves, Hannah	1836	P.	....	....	m. George F. Tracy.
Goulden, Joseph	....	....	....	....	
Griffith, Maria A.	1839	L.	dism.	....	
Griswold, Matilda	1839	L.	....	....	w. of George W.
Gridley, Charlotte	1844	....	....	1862	w. of George E.
Griffith, Ann Elizabeth	1845	....	dism.	....	
Gates, Robert W.	1851	L.	....	1868, æ. 48	For many years S. S. Librarian.
Gates, Mary Elizabeth	1851	P.	....	....	w. of Robert W.
Gridley, George E. (soc. 1841)	....	....	....	1862	
Gregory, Elizabeth L.	1856	L.	1856	....	
Goodale, Joseph H.	1856	L.	dism.	....	
Goodale, Melinda	1856	L.	dism.	....	w. of Joseph H.
Goodale, Mary	1856	L.	dism.	....	
Golden, Josiah R.	1858	P.	....	1859, æ. 22	
Graham, Alva C.	1858	P.	....	after 1860	
Gardner, Albinus M.	1860	P.	....	....	
Gould, N. (soc. 1856)	....	....	1859	....	
Grounderson, Mary L.	1867	P.	....	1867, æ. 42	w. of Peter.
Grogan, Andrew	....	....	1871	....	
Grogan, Harriet Preston	....	....	1871	....	
Goulden, Lydia	1837	L.	....	1878	wid. of Joseph H.
Grounderson, Peter	1858	P.	....	1884	
Gray, Rhoda M.	1864	L.	....	....	wid. of Joseph H.
Goulden, Lydia	1837	L.	....	1878	
Gould, Lucinda (Nichols)	1864	L.	....	....	wid. of Jonathan. [E. C. Goff.
Goff, Louise W. (Lyon)	1868	P.	1878	....	wid. of Asahel L. Lyon, w. of
Gawley, Mary Elizabeth	1873	P.	....	1881	w. of Dr. Samuel S. [Sterling.
Gamsby, Carrie M. (Sterling)	1874	P.	....	....	w. of Alfred H., dau. of Walter
Gawley, Lizzie	1874	P.	1885	....	dau. of Samuel S.
Griswold, George W. (soc. '42)	1869	P.	....	1885	
Gordon, Alexander S.	{ 1832	....	1858	1882	
(soc. 1826) Rest.	{ 1875	P.			
Griffith, Fanny	1876	P.	....	....	dau. of Thomas.
Gilbert, Kathleen Estelle	1885	P.	....	....	
Gamsby, Alfred Henderson	1884	P.	....	....	
Gaylord, Carlotta M.	1885	L.	....	....	w. of Rev. S. D.
Gaylord, Bessie Theoda	1885	L.	dism.	....	dau. of Carlotta M.
Gaylord, Carlotta Jennie	1885	L.	1886	....	dau. of Carlotta M.

—212—

Name.	Admission.	Dismission.	Death.	Remarks.
Gaylord, Harry Clayton	1885 L.	....	1889	s. Carlotta M.
Garlick, Dr. Samuel Middleton	1887 L.	....	....	....
Garlick, Harriet Trubee (Knapp)	1887 L.	....	....	w. of Samuel M.
Garlick, Almira Elizab'th Trubee	1894 P.	....	1895	dau. of Samuel M.
Gedney, Josephine	1885 L.	....	....	....
Hawley, Samuel	bef. 1813 R.C.	....	....	....
Hawley, Gurdon	bef. 1813 R.C.	....	....	....
Hawley, Ebenezer	bef. 1813 R.C.	....	....	....
Hawley, Zalmon	bef. 1813 R.C.	....	....	....
Hubbell, Ezekiel	bef. 1813 R.C.	....	....	....
Hubbell, Catharine	bef. 1813 R.C.	....	....	w. of Ezekiel.
Hubbell, Aaron	bef. 1813 R.C.	....	....	....
Hubbell, Sally	bef. 1813 R.C.	....	....	w. of Aaron.
Hubbell, David	bef. 1813 R.C.	....	....	....
Hubbell, Anne	bef. 1813 R.C.	....	....	w. of David.
Hubbell, Anson	1813 R.C.	....	....	....
Hubbell, Betsey	{ 1813 R.C. / 1821 .... }	....	1870, æ. 81	w. of David, 3d
Hubbell, Charles Benjamin	1814 R.C.	....	....	....
Hubbell, Eliza	1814 R.C.	....	....	w. of Charles Benjamin.
Hawley, Monson	1824 R.C.	....	....	....
Hawley, Matilda	1824 R.C.	....	....	w. of Monson.
Hawley, Abijah	1824 R.C.	....	....	....
Hawley, Talcot	1807	....	....	....
Hall, Narcissa	1808 P.	....	....	....
Holburton, Sally	1810	....	....	....
Hawley, Lucy, 2d	1811	1830	....	w. of Samuel.
Hubbell, Abiah	1814	....	1830	w. of David.
Hubbell, Bethiah	1815	....	....	w. of Samuel.
Hubbell, Elisha	1815	1843	....	....
Hawley, Stephen	1815	1830	....	....
Hawley, Betsey	1815	1830	....	w. of Samuel.
Hildrop, Mary	1815	dism.	....	....
Holburton, Eunice	1815	1830	....	....
Hawley, Temperance	1815	1830	....	w. of Stephen.
Hull, Errata	1815	....	1846	w. of Wakeman.
Hatch, Nancy	1815	1846	1853, æ. 76	w. of Daniel.
Hyer William	1815	exc. 1823	....	....
Hawley, George	1816	1830	....	....
Hawley, Caroline	1816	1830	....	....
Hawley, Sally	1816	....	....	....
Hull, Sarah	1817	1828	....	m. William Mallett.
Hubbell, Asa	1821	dism.	....	....
Hawley, Ransom	1821	....	....	entered ministry.
Hawley, Samuel, 3d	1821	....	....	....
Hawley, Lucy, 3d	1821	1830	....	....
Hall, Sarah Marietta	1821	1828	....	....
Hubbell, David, 3d	1821	....	after 1837	....
Hubbell, Josiah	1821	....	after 1824	....
Hull, Ellen	1821	dism.	....	....
Hull, Fanny	1821	....	....	....
Hawley, Emeline	1821	....	....	....
Hawley, Elizabeth	1821	....	....	....
Hawley, Eliza	1821	....	....	....
Hawley, Mary	1821	1830	....	....
Hawley, Ann Maria	1821	....	....	m. —— Gray.

—213—

Name.	Admission.		Dismission.	Death.	Remarks.
Hawley, Marietta	1821				m. —— Knapp.
Hawley, Anson T.	1821			1892	
Hall, Josiah B. (soc. 1820)	1827	P.	1830		
Hall, Elizabeth	1827	L.	1830		w. of Josiah B.
Hawley, Frederick	1827	P.		Dec. 1827	
Hubbard, Harriet	1827	P.	1830 1831		
Hawley, Elizabeth	1827	P.			
Hilliard, Hannah	1827	L.	1830		
Higby, Hervey	1828	P.	1830		
Higby, Charlotte	1828	P.	1830		
Hawley, Bronson	1828	P.	1830		
Hall, Marietta S.			1830		
Hawley, Mary B.	bef. 1826		1830		
Hubbell, Marlott	bef. 1830		1833		w. of Josiah.
Hubbell, Laura (Wordin)	1828			1883	wid. of Alfred.
Hatch, Daniel	1831		1859		to Christ Church.
Hawley, Julius W.	1831				
Holly, William H.	1831			1835	
Husted, Stephen St. John	1831		1833		
Hall, Samuel	1831		rem.		
Hart, Hannah	1831				
Hamlin, Mary	1833				w. of Alanson.
Hunter, Rev. John H.	1838		1845		
Hull, Amos G.	1839				
Hull, Emily	1839				w. of Amos.
Hubbell, Julia	1831			bef. 1868	
Hatch, Daniel B., Jr.	1831		1866		to New York.
Hatch, Anna	1831			1848	
Haight, Joseph	1836		dism.		
Howick, Ann	1836			1852	
Howick, Henry H.	1838			1849	
Hunter, Sarah	1839	L.	dism.		
Hunter, Julia M.	1839	L.	dism.		w. of Rev. J. H.
Hatch, Sheldon	1840	L.		1843	
Hartwell, Sherman	1840	L.		1876, æ. 85	
Hartwell, Rachel	1840	P.	dism.		
Hatch, Mary A.	1842	P.			w. of Horace F.
Hull, Abigail	1844	P.			
Hatch, Sarah (Gregory)	1844	P.		bef. 1851	
Hopkins, John (soc. 1840)	1844	P.		1873	
Hall, Eleanor	1844	P.			m. Joseph W. Brooks.
Hull, Eliza	1845	P.			
Hubbell, Charles B.	1848	P.		1873, æ. 84	
Hubbell, Eliza (Thompson)	1848	P.		1862, æ. 70	w. of Charles B.
Hubbard, Calista S.	1849	L.		1868	w. of T. B. [Hubbard.
Hartwell, Cornelia	1850	P.		1871	dau. Sherman, m. Dr. Robert
Hall, Delia	1852	P.			w. of Charles H.
Hall, Charles H. (soc. 1850)					
Hincks, Dea. John W.	1852	L.		1875, æ. 57	
Hincks, Sarah A.	1852	L.		1864, æ. 43	
Hull, Wakeman (soc. 1854–1868)					
Hall, Sarah E.	1853	L.		1871	w. of Turney.
Hubbell, David M.					
Hawley, Charles (soc. 1855–'49)					
Hall, Samuel B. (soc. 1856–1868)					
Hanford, Stephen (soc. 1856)	1838	P.			

Name.	Admission.	Dismission.	Death.	Remarks.
Hanford, Louisa.	1838	P.	....	1853	w. of Stephen.
Hawley, Lucy C. (Wordin)	1841	....	dism.	....	w. of Edmund S.
Holcomb, William W. (soc. 1842)	1844	P.	exc. 1856	....	....
Holcomb, Julia	1844	P.	dism.	....	w. of William W.
Hall, Polly I.	1844	P.	1875	....	dau. of Dea. David Sherwood.
Hawley, Edmund S.	....	....	dism.	....	....
Hopkins, Abigail	1845	L.	....	1862, æ. 60	....
Hubbard, T. B. (soc. 1849)	....	....	1868	....	....
Hall, Charles H. (soc. 1850)	....	....	....	....	....
Hubbell, Caroline.	1854	L.	....	1869	w. of Elbert E.
Hoyle, George	....	....	....	1893, æ. 83	....
Hatch, Daniel B.	1855	P.	1858	....	to DuQuoin, Ill.
Hall, Esther A.	1855	P.	....	....	w. of F. L.
Hand, Elizabeth W.	1855	P.	1856	....	....
Hall, F. L.	....	....	....	....	....
Hotchkiss, Josiah	1858	L.	....	1860, æ. 72	....
Hotchkiss, Betsey	1858	L.	1866	....	....
Hotchkiss, Jarvis	1858	L.	....	1862, æ. 61	....
Hotchkiss, Sarah E.	1858	L.	1865	....	w. of Jarvis.
Hall, Fannie	1858	P.	....	....	m. William Van Gasbeck.
Holcomb, ———	....	....	1865	....	to Granby.
Haux, Mary C.	1858	P.	....	....	m. James Turner.
Hincks, Edward Y., D.D.	1858	P.	1862	....	to Church at Yale College.
Higgins, Jane C.	1859	L.	....	1866, æ. 57	....
Hanford, Juliette W.	1859	P.	....	....	wid. of Stephen S.
Huth, Lucy	1860	P.	....	....	w. of Charles Lewis.
Havens, George O.	1860	L.	1868	....	....
Havens, Clara M.	1860	L.	1868	....	w. of George O.
Hall, Louisa S.	1861	P.	....	1888	dau. of Samuel B.
Huth, Charles L.	....	....	....	....	....
Hawley, Thomas.	1862	L.	....	1875	....
Hubbell, Charles E.	1863	P.	1871	....	to Stratford.
Hincks, John Howard	1863	P.	....	1877	entered the ministry.
Hatch, Sarah S. G.	1864	P.	1870	....	....
Hubbard, Josephine C.	1864	P.	1868	....	to Stratford.
Hubbard, Sarah E.	1864	P.	1868	....	to Stratford.
Hanford, Harriet A.	1864	P.	....	....	....
Hanford, James.	....	....	....	....	....
Hull, Dr. Calvin E., F.M. 1868	....	....	....	....	....
Hotchkiss, Lucinda	1868	P.	1869	....	....
Hatch, Horace F.	1831	P.	....	....	....
Hawley, Eliza J.	1831	P.	....	1894	wid. of Charles.
Hawley, Frances S.	1832	P.	....	1887	w. of Anson T.
Hall, Sarah (Walker)	1832	P.	....	....	wid. of Samuel B.
Hincks, Ann B. (Wordin)	1832	P.	....	....	wid. of John W.
Hubbell, Elbert E.	1831	P.	....	1889	....
Hartwell, Sophia	1840	L.	....	1882	wid. of Sherman.
Hoile, Elizabeth L.	1854	L.	....	1890	w. of George.
Hubbard, Dr. Robert	1852	L.	....	....	....
Hartshorn, Catharine A.	1857	P.	....	....	wid. of Tyler.
Hawley, Maria	1862	L.	....	1887	wid. of Thomas.
Hincks, William B., Dea.	1858	P.	....	....	s. of John W.
Hubbell, Isabella (Stillman)	{ 1845 / 1862 }	P. / L.	1894	1894	wid. of Elbert E.
Hubbell, Howard G.	1864	P.	....	....	s. of Elbert E.
Hall, Henry	1864	P.	....	....	....

Name.	Admission.	Dismission.	Death.	Remarks.
Hill, Dr. Seth	1863	P.	1870	
Hincks, Enoch Pond	1863	P.	....	s. of John W.
Hincks, Mary L. (Hart)	1867	P.	1890	w. of William B.
Hincks, Cornelia E. (Hart)	1867	P.	....	w. of Enoch P.
Hanford, Susan A.	1864	P.	1892	w. of James.
Hawley, Jane M.	1867	L.	1890	w. of Charles E.
Hull, Almira J.	1865	L.	1892	w. of Dr. Calvin E.
Hunter, Mary L.	1869	L.	1887	w. of Samuel S.
House, Frances M.	1868	L.	....	w. of James A.
Hoag, Mary	1869	L.	....	
Hall, George B.	1869	L.	....	
Hall, Lucy	1869	L.	....	w. of George B.
Hall, Turney (soc. 1856)	1868	P. rem.	....	
Hart, Charlotte Irene	1873	P.	....	[V. Hawes.
Hewitt, Cora Almira	1873	P.	....	w. of Hewitt, dau. of Edmund
Hincks, Jane Isabel	1873	P.	....	dau. John W. [R. Wilmot.
Hobbs, Florence E. (Wilmot)	1874	P.	....	w. of Willis F., dau. of Samuel
Hubbell, Isabel	1870	P.	1878	dau. of George H.
Hine, Annie Louise (Dyer)	1874	P. 1889	....	dau. of William B. Dyer.
Hawes, Edmund V.	1874	P.	1882	
Hartshorn, Tyler W.	1877	P.	....	s. of Tyler.
Hartshorn, Kittie Salter	1877	P.	1882	dau. of Tyler and Catharine.
Huth, Charles Sackett	1877	P.	....	s. of Charles Louis.
Hatch, Mary Jane	1878	P.	....	dau. of Leavitt.
Harrington, Henry Martyn	1878	L.	....	
Hatch, Elvira	1878	P. 1888	....	dau. of Leavitt.
Holley, Rev. Platt T.	1878	L.	1889	
Hopkins, Mary Elizabeth	1881	P.	....	dau. of L. M.
Hobbs, Willis Farrar	1881	L.	....	
Hurd, George B.	1880	L. 1886	....	
Hull, Frederick Wellington	1881	P. 1890	....	
Hull, Margaret Jane (Nichols)	1881	P. 1890	....	w. of Frederick W.
Hubbell, Rebecca A. (Gould)	1881	L.	....	w. of Howard G.
Hubbard, Sophia Todd	1883	L. 1887	....	dau. of Dr. Robert.
Hubbard, Cornelia Elizabeth	1883	P. 1892	....	m. C. M. Everest.
Harrington, Jessie	1882	P.	1891	dau. of Henry M.
Hughes, Anne J.	1884	L.	....	w. of Frank J.
Harris, Eva M.	1884	L. 1889	....	
Horr, Weston Henderson	1884	P.	....	s. of William L.
Harvey, Alice Anna	1884	L.	....	wid. of Frank.
Harlem, J. L.	1885	L. 1887	....	
Harlem, M. A.	1885	L. 1887	....	w. of J. L.
Hayes, Chester N.	1885	P.	....	
Hincks, Annie Hart	1886	P.	....	dau. of Enoch P.
Hubbell, Emily Stillman	1886	P.	....	dau. Elbert E., m. Ralph Tilton.
Hincks, Edward Baldwin	1888	P.	1890	s. of William B.
Hilgerson, Matilda	1888	L.	....	
Hunter, Mabel Harlakenden	1889	P. 1892	....	dau. of Samuel S.
Hawley, Sarah B.	1887	L.	1893	
Hall, Frank S. S.	1888	P.	1889	
Hawley, George Waller	1889	P.	....	s. of Alexander.
Hincks, Robert Stanley	1889	P.	....	s. of William B.
Hawley, Alexander William	1891	P.	....	s. of Alexander.
Hincks, Henry Pond	1890	P.	....	s. of Enoch P.
Hincks, William Thurston	1891	P.	....	s. of William B.
Hoile, Frances E.	1890	P.	....	m. Fred. Somers. [Gold. M.D.
House, Gertrude	1861	P.	....	dau. of James A., m. James D.

Name.	Admission.	Dismission.	Death.	Remarks.
Hugo, Josephine Eva	1893 P.	....	....	....
Hubbell, Gertrude G.	1894 P.	....	....	*dau.* of Howard G.
Irish, Eliza M.	1831	dism.	....	....
Ingersoll, Emily E.	1864 P.	1866	....	....
Ingham, Julia A.	1869 P.	1868	....	*w.* of Samuel W.
Ingham, Samuel W. (soc. 1857)	....	1868	....	....
Ingersoll, Marietta	1866 L.	....	....	....
Jennings, Robert Ross	1810 R.C.	....	....	....
Jones, Widow Mary	1810	....	1819, æ. 78	from Episcopal Church.
Jennings, Rhoda	1810	1830	....	*w.* of Ross.
Jennings, Sarah	1810	1830	....	*w.* of Eliphalet.
Jackson, Ezekiel	1813 L.	....	....	....
Jackson, Polly	1813	....	....	*w.* of Ezekiel.
Jennings, James	1815	1830	1838	*s.* of Eliphalet.
Jackson, Henry	1815	rem.	....	....
Jones, Seth B.	1821	1830	....	....
Jones, Susan	1821	1830	....	*w.* of Seth B.
Judson, David	1822	1830	....	....
Judson, Aurelia	1822 L.	....	....	....
Jones, Emily E.	1841	1851	....	*m.* Daniel J. Day.
Judson, Kath. A. T. (Chappel)	1851 L.	1863	....	....
Judd, Elizabeth A.	....	....	....	....
Judson, Dr. Fred. J. (soc. 1856)	1862	....	Feb. 1862, æ. 58.	
Judson, Maria	1851 L.	abs. 1868	....	*w.* of William H.
Johnson, William H.	....	....	....	....
Judson, Henry	1856 L.	....	....	....
Jennings, Josephine Maria	1857 P.	1858	....	....
Joy, Jesse	1858 L.	1860	....	....
Jordan, Augusta	1858 P.	1861	....	*m.* —— Smith.
Judson, Janette	1859 L.	1861	....	....
Judson, Harriet E.	1861 P.	1863	....	....
Jackson, Daniel B.	1861 L.	....	1868, æ. 50	....
Jackson, Adelia S.	1861	1873	....	*w.* of Daniel B.
Jones, Morris	1862 L.	1866	....	....
Jones, Henry W.	1858 P.	1858	....	....
Jordan, Mary Ann (Platt)	1869	....	....	*w.* of Stephen.
Jordan, Stephen (soc. 1850-1874)	....	....	....	....
Johnson, Mary Walker	1869 P.	....	....	*w.* of J. R.
Johnson, J. R. (soc. 1870)	....	....	....	....
Jones, Eliza S. (Webster)	1839 L.	....	1888	*w.* of Rev. Henry.
Jones, Rev. Henry (soc. 1838)	1858 L.	....	1878	....
Judson, Charlotte	1857 P.	1894	....	*wid.* of Henry.
Jackson, Henry S. (soc. 1870)	1861 L.	....	....	....
Joy, Andrew Eliott	1878 L.	....	1882	....
Jones, Clara J. (Stillman)	1879 L.	1888	....	*dau.* of John J. Stillman.
Jarvis, Emma Augusta	1880 P.	....	....	....
Johnson, Lizzie Cecile	1883 P.	1888	....	....
Jones, Florence	1884 P.	....	....	....
Jacoby, Addie Florine	1886 P.	....	....	*w.* of John.
Jones, Annie M.	1887 L.	....	....	....
Johnson, Anna Tina	1894 P.	....	....	....
Knapp, Ephraim	1814 R.C.	....	....	....
Knapp, Sarah	1814 R.C.	....	....	*w.* of Ephraim.
Kipping, George	1818 R.C.	....	....	....

Name.	Admission.		Dismission.	Death.	Remarks.
Kippen, Betsey	1816		....	1864, æ. 72	w. of George.
Kippen, George	1816		1853	....	
Knapp, Joseph	1821	vote	....	Dec. 1857	
Knapp, Abigail	1821	vote	....	Jan. 1857	w. of Joseph.
Knapp, Burr	1821		1830	....	
Knapp, George	1821		....	1822, æ. 18	
Knapp, Maria	1821		1830	....	m. —— Lacey.
Keeler, Sally	bef. 1826		1830	1851, æ. 80?	
Kippen, Mary E.	1831		....	....	
Knapp, Eliza	1831		....	....	
Kelsey, Charles	1832		1853	....	
Kenworthy, Martha	1841	P.	abs.	....	
Knapp, Mrs. Ephraim	1844	P.	....	bef. 1851	Ephraim d. 1831.
Kippen, Jane	1845	L.	1853	....	
King, Mary H.	1853		1856	....	w. of L. A.
Kelsey, Mary (Newton)	1835		1853	....	w. of Charles.
Keeler, Edward	....		....	....	
Kimball, ——	....		....	....	w. of Henry.
Knowlton, Wm. S. (soc. 1870-'76)	....		....	....	
King, L. A.	....		1856	....	
Kimball, Jane E.	1855	P.	....	....	w. of Henry.
Kimball, Henry	....		....	....	
Kippen, Anne	1858	P.	1869	abt. 1871	m. —— Mead, 1867.
Knapp, Anna E.	1864	P.	....	....	
Keeler, Theodore (soc. 1875)	....		....	1884	
Keeler, Caroline	1844	P.	1891	1894	wid. of Edward.
Knowlton, Stella	1852	L.	....	1884	w. of Wm. S.
Kelsey, Courtland (soc. 1856)	1858	P.	....	....	
Keeler, Mary E.	1864	P.	....	....	dau. of Edward.
Keeler, Villeroy E. (B)	1865	P.	....	....	w. of Justin S.
Keeler, Catharine M.	1867	L.	1886	....	w. of Theo. A.
Kohlns, J. C. H. L.	1868	L.	....	....	
Kelsey, Clarence H.	1874	P.	1888	....	s. of Courtland. [Tomlinson.
Kelsey, Elizabeth B.	1874	P.	1888	....	w. of Clarence H., dau. of Ste.
Kelsey, Sarah Hoyt	1875	L.	....	....	w. of Courtland.
Kelsey, Stephen Clifford	1879	P.	....	....	s. of Courtland.
Kelsey, Louise Hoyt	1879	P.	....	....	dau. of Courtland.
Kimberly, William Gilead	1881	L.	....	....	
Kimberly, Laura A.	1881	L.	....	....	w. of William G.
Kirchoff, Charles Francis	1883	P.	....	....	
Kirchoff, Margaret F.	1883	P.	....	....	w. of Charles F.
Keeler, Sylvester R.	1884	L.	1894	....	
Keeler, Mary B.	1884	L.	1894	....	w. of Sylvester R.
Keeler, Jennie	1884	P.	1886	....	
Keyes, Mary Virginia	1885	P.	....	....	
Kelsey, Annie Hoyt	1885	P.	....	....	dau. of Courtland.
Knapp, George S.	1885	L.	....	....	
Knapp, Jennie A.	1885	L.	....	....	w. of George S.
Keeler, Birdie Raymond	1888	P.	1894	....	dau. of Sylvester R.
Kellogg, Emily Peck	1894	P.	....	....	
Lewis, Daniel	1815	R.C.	....	....	
Lord, Daniel	1808		....	1825, æ. 64	
Lord, Annie	1808		1830	....	w. of Daniel.
Lacey, Daniel, Jr.	1808		....	....	
Lewis, Mary	1808		....	....	m. Daniel Lacey, Jr.
Lacey, Catharine	1808		....	....	wid. of ——.

Name.	Admission.	Dismission.	Death.	Remarks.
Lewis, Hulda	1815	1830	....	w. of Daniel.
Lockwood, Frederick	1815	1824	....	
Lockwood, Rebecca	1815	rem.	....	
Lewis, Alanson	1815	1863	....	
Lacey, Ellen	1815	1830	....	
Lockwood, Elizabeth	1816	1826	....	
Lewis, Eunice	1816	....	....	
Lacey, David, F.M. 1810	1816	1822	....	
Lacey, Laura	1816	1822	....	w. of David.
Lacey, Ruth	1816	1830	1838	
Lewis, Mary Ann	1816	rem.	....	
Lacey, Sally	1817	rem.	....	m. —— Sherwood.
Lockwood, Roe	1819	....	....	
Lord, Joshua	1821	1830	....	
Lewis, Fanny	1821	1830	....	w. of Roswell.
Lockwood, Julia	1821	....	....	
Linsley, Philip	1823	....	....	
Lord, Willis	1827 P.	1830	....	
Lord, Sally	....	1830	....	
Lacey, Maria	....	1830	....	
Lewis, Julia	1821	1863	....	w. of Alanson.
Lindsley, Phebe	bef. 1826	1830	....	w. of Jeremiah.
Love, Alexander	1834	....	....	
Love, Margaret	1834	....	....	w. of Alexander.
Love, Sophia	1834	....	....	
Love, Janette	1834	....	....	
Lockhart, Margaret	1834	....	....	
Lockwood, Lucretia	1836	....	....	
Lum, Edward	1836	dism.	....	
Lacey, Jane E	1831	....	1857	w. of Rowland B.
Lord, Matthew	1835	1868	....	
Lord, Jane	1835	1868	....	w. of Matthew.
Loyd, Hannah	1836	....	....	m. —— Coster.
Langridge, Levi	1839 L.	....	....	
Lamoux, ——	1841 P.	....	....	lost at sea.
Lord, Anna	1845	....	1859, æ. 94	
Leach, Caroline	1845 P.	....	....	
Logan, Eliza S.	1847 L.	1855	....	
Lamont, Helen	1850 L.	1868	....	wid. of ——.
Lamont, Anna Maria	1850 L.	1868	....	
Lyon, Marietta	1851 L.	....	1859	w. of Asahel.
Lyon, Jarvis (soc. 1842-1849)	....	....	....	
Lyon, Asahel (soc. 1859)	....	....	1859	
Lockwood, Minerva	1855 L.	1870	....	w. of Hezekiah.
Loomis, James C. (soc. 1845-75)	....	....	1877	
Lyon, Frederick H.	1850	dism.	....	
Lockwood, Hezekiah	....	1870	....	
Lathrop, Margaret	1856 L.	1864	....	w. of John W.
Lathrop, John W. (soc. 1857)	....	1864	....	
Lacey, Mary Louisa	1858 P.	1865	....	
Lewis, Margaret J.	1858 P.	1863	....	
Livingston, Julia A.	1861 L.	....	1864	w. of ——.
Lindley, Miss Mary A.	1861 P.	1868	....	
Lathrop, George L. (soc. 1863-'68)	....	....	....	
Lord, Fanny I.	1863 P.	1868	....	
Lafarge, Fanny E.	1864 P.	....	....	
Lane, Esther M.	1864 P.	1868	....	

Name.	Admission.	Dismission.	Death.	Remarks.
Littell, Margaret	1865	....	—, æ. 83	wid. of ——.
Lyon, Louisa W.	1868	P.	....	w. of Asahel L.
Lacey, Dea. Rowland B.	1837	L.	....	....
Lyon, Emeline (soc. 1868)	1838	....	....	wid. of Jarvis.
Loomis, Mary B.	1855	P.	....	wid. of James C.
Lemmon, Jane Cameron	1857	P.	....	w. of Lionel.
Lyon, Bessie	1855	P.	dism.	....
Lyon, Hanford (soc. 1834)	1858	P.	1879	....
Lyon, Annie M.	1858	P.	....	wid. of Hanford.
Lacey, Elizabeth R.	1859	L.	1894	w. of Rowland B.
Lathrop, Esther	1863	P.	1894	w. of George L.
Lyon, Adelaide	1864	P.	....	dau. of Hanford.
Lewis, Catharine S.	1865	P.	1892	w. of Dr. George F.
LaMonte, Abram H.	1867	L.	1881	....
LaMonte, Helen Dean	1867	L.	1881	w. of Abram H.
Lewis, Dr. George F.	1868	L.	1892	....
Lacey, David Sherman	1874	P.	1878	s. of Rowland B.
Lacey, Henrietta Boardman	1874	P.	....	dau. of Rowland B.
LaMonte, May	1874	P.	1881	dau. of Abram H.
LaMonte, Isabel Dean	1874	P.	1881	dau. of Abram H.
Lockwood, Lizzie Chappelle	1876	P.	....	w. of Frederick J. Lockwood,
Lineburg, William Golden	1878	L.	....	[dau. Thos. C. Wordin.
Lineburgh, William Golden, Jr.	1878	P.	....	
Lineburgh, Ann Eliza	1878	L.	....	w. of W. G., Sr.
Lewis, Julia Waterman	1878	L.	1884	wid. of Alanson F.
Lewis, Margaret Isham	1878	L.	....	dau. of Alanson F.
Lewis, Minnie Prescott	1879	P.	....	w. of Walter.
Lewis, William Henry	1880	P.	....	....
Langley, Lillie L.	{ 1883 / 1891	L. / L.	1885 / 1892	w. of Wm. A.
Levake, Eliz. Statira (Robinson)	1883	P.	1894	w. of Burnside.
Lyon, Katharine	1883	P.	1888	....
Lewis, Willis Grant	1884	P.	....	....
Lewis, Hattie Allen	1884	L.	....	w. of Willis G.
Lamson, Warren H.	1887	L.	....	....
Lamson, Mary McC.	1887	L.	....	w. of Warren H.
Lamson, Harrison G.	1889	P.	....	s. of Warren H.
Lund, Peter Lauritz Petersen	1890	P.	....	....
Lemmon, Jennie C.	1890	P.	....	dau. of Lionel.
Lynn, Catharine C.	1892	L.	....	....
Levy, Louis Lazar	1894	P.	....	....
Levy, May	1894	P.	....	w. of Louis L.
Morehouse, Abijah	bef. 1813	R.C.	....	....
Meeker, Esther	bef. 1813	R.C.	....	w. of David.
May, Henry	1808	R.C.	....	....
May, Almira	1808	R.C.	....	w. of Henry.
Mallett, William	1811	R.C.	....	....
Mallett, ——	1811	R.C.	....	w. of William.
May, Joseph	1811	R.C.	....	....
May, Sophia	1811	R.C.	....	w. of Joseph.
May, Sylvester	1811	R.C.	....	....
May, Grace	1811 R.C. / 1815	....	rem.	w. of Sylvester.
Munn, Hannah	1808	....	....	w. of James ?
Mallett, Harriet	1815	....	1830	....
Mallett, Avis	1815	....	1829	....

Name.	Admission.		Dismission.	Death.	Remarks.
Meeker, Nancy	1815		....	1853	
Meeker, Susan	1815		....	....	
Montross, David Ira	1817		....	1823	
Merwin, Sally	1817		....	....	w. of Charles of Stratford.
Maloney, Emily	1821		1828	....	
Munn, Henry	1821		dism.	....	
Milton, St. John	1821		rem.	....	
Mallett, Lauretta	1821		1830	....	
Miles, Susan	1821		....	....	m. Curtis.
Morehouse, Mary	1823		rem.	....	
Morse, Sally	1823		1830	....	w. of Samuel.
Mallory, Daniel	1825		....	....	fr. New Milford.
Munson, Eliza	1826	L.	....	....	
Moore, Luther	1827	L.	1830	....	
Mead, Rufus, F. M. 1827	1828	L.	1830	aft. 1856	
Mead, Elizabeth	1828	L.	1830	....	w. of Rufus.
Middlebrook, Ephr'm, F.M. 1826	1828	L.	1830	....	
Middlebrook, Betsey	1828		1830	....	w. of Ephraim.
Morris, Eliza E.	....		1830	....	
Mills, Polly	1828		....	....	
Moore, Ann S. bef.	1827		1841 ?	....	w. of Mark.
Moore, Catharine	1834		rem.	....	
Merserole, Mary L.	1835		rem.	....	
Milne, Huldah	1832		dism.	....	
Morehouse, Roxana	1836		....	....	
Merril, Charlotte	1839	L.	....	....	
McCauley, Irene M.	1838	L.	....	....	w. of ———.
Mott, Joseph	1844	P.	dism.	1879	
Miner, Isaac	1851	L.	abs.	....	
Miner, Esther I.	1851	L.	....	....	w. of Isaac.
Miner, Charles M.	1851	L.	1868	....	
Miner, Harriet H.	1851	L.	1868	....	
Marsh, Helen C.	1852	L.	1858	....	w. of Egbert.
	1884	L.	1886		
Mallard, Caroline	1845	P.	....	1871	w. of William.
Middlebrook, E. B. (soc. 1868)	....		....	....	
Marsh, Egbert (soc. 1856)	1857	P.	1858	....	
Meeker, Mary E.	1855	L.	1862	....	w. of Geo. H.
Meeker, George H	....		1862	....	
Mallory, Benajah	1856	L.	....	1862, æ. 74	
Mallory, Catharine	1856	L.	....	1869, æ, 77	w. of Benajah.
Murdock, Isabella	1857	L.	....	1867, æ. 71	
Murphy, Mary Ann	1857	P.	1862	....	
Mallory, George	....		....	....	
Murdock, Hugh	....		....	1867	
Mills, Thomas	1858	L.	....	....	
Mills, Emma	1858	P.	....	1868, æ. 58	w. of Thomas.
Mills, Susan W.	1858	P.	1870	....	w. of Benj. K.
Mallory, Eliza B.	1858	P.	1858	....	w. of Thomas D.
Mallory, Thomas D.	1857	L.	1858	....	
Marsh, William E. (soc. 1861)	....		....	....	
Morris, Lydia E.	1859	L.	1861	....	w. of Joseph L.
Morris, Joseph L.	....		1861	....	
Marsh, Dr. William E.	....		....	....	
Marsh, Anna	....		....	....	
Marsh, David H.	....		....	....	
Marsh, Susan	....		....	....	

—221—

Name.	Admission.		Dismission.	Death.	Remarks.
Moore, Elizabeth	1864	P.	....	1867	w. of Jas. H.
Moore, James H., (soc. 1857-68)	....	....	....	....	....
Mills, Abbie M	1867	L.	1870	....	w. of Walter K.
Mills, Walter K	....	....	1870	....	....
Mead, Annie K	....	....	....	abt. 1871	....
Mead, George W	....	....	....	....	....
Middlebrook, Mary B.	1850	L.	1878	....	w. of Dr. E. B.
Marsh, Nancy W	1858	P.	....	....	w. of Wm. E.
Mott, Grisel A	1844 / 1873	L. / L.	1865	1883	wid. of Joseph.
Moore, Elizabeth W	1874	L.	....	....	w. of Jas. S.
Middlebrook, Mary Ida	1874	P.	....	....	w. of Clarence M., dau. of
Mills, Benjamin K. (soc. 1857).	1876 Rest.		....	....	[Peleg Bronson.
Morris, Jeannette	1877	P.	1886	....	dau. of John H.
Middlebrook, Stiles M	1878	L.	....	1883	....
Middlebrook, William N	1878	L.	....	....	s. of Stiles M.
Middlebrook, Jessie Elizabeth	1878	P.	....	....	w. of Wm. N:
Middlebrook, Clarence M	1878	P.	....	....	s. of Charles.
Mathern, Elizabeth (Aucher)	1877	P.	....	1885	w. of John.
Mott, Anna E	1879	L.	....	....	wid. of John J.
Mott, Josephine Augusta	1880	P.	....	1894	dau. of John J.
Moody, Ella Aurora	1880	P.	....	....	....
Mahony, Emily Belle (Fuller)	1880	P.	....	....	w. of Jas. P.
Miner, Mary J.	1879	L.	....	....	....
Marsh, Egbert	1884	L.	1886	....	....
Mathern, Bertha	1885	P.	....	....	....
Miller, Rachel Buckley	1884	L.	....	1887	....
Miller, Frederick Buckley	1884	L.	....	....	s. of Rachel.
Moore, Margaret Amanda	1884	L.	1886	....	....
Miller, Elizabeth	1885	P.	....	....	....
Mahr, Mrs. Frances	1885	L.	1886	....	....
Martensdale, Carolina	1888	L.	....	....	....
Mathern, Charlotte	1889	P.	....	....	....
Middlebrook, Lillian Louise	1888	P.	....	....	....
Mott, Ann Helen (Orr)	1890	L.	....	....	w. of Willard H.
Mott, Willard Henry	1890	P.	....	....	....
Mott, Edward Henry	1890	P.	....	....	s. of John J.
Morris, Lulu Evelyn	1891	L.	....	....	....
Mott, Nellie Louise	1894	P.	....	....	....
McGrath, Helen Fannie	1886	L.	....	....	....
Meeker, Lucy Jones	1892	L.	....	....	w. of Edward F.
Nichols, Polly	1811	....	1830	....	....
Nichols, David	1815	....	1830	....	to South Carolina.
Nichols, ——	1815	....	....	....	w. of David.
Nichols, Phebe	1815 / 1828	....	1830	....	w. of Stiles.
Nash, William Burr	1815	....	....	....	from Fairfield.
Nichols, Mary	1815	....	....	....	....
Nails, Esther	1815	....	....	....	....
Nash, Esther	1815	....	....	....	....
Nichols, Lavinia	1821	....	1830	....	to South Carolina.
Northrup, Liba	1822	....	1830	....	....
Northrup, Phebe	1822	L.	....	....	w. of Liba.
Northrup, Eliza	1822	L.	rem.	....	w. of Norman.
Nichols, David B	1826?	....	....	1838	....

—222—

Name.	Admission.	Dismission.	Death.	Remarks.
Northrup, Nicholas, F.M. 1823.	1827 P.	1830	....	....
Nichols, Wheeler	1827 P.	1830	....	....
Nichols, Jane M.	1827 P.	1830	....	....
Nash, William B.	1827 L.	1830	....	....
Nash, Ruth Martha	1827 L.	1830	....	....
Nichols, Eliza	1828 L.	1830	....	....
Northrup, Caroline	bef. 1826	1830	....	w. of Nicholas.
Naramore, Mary	1831	dism.	....	wid. ———.
Nichols, Nancy	1834	....	1863, æ. 72	....
Niles, Samuel (soc. 1834)	1841	....	1850	....
Nichols, Lucinda	1844 P.	1859	....	m. ——— Gould.
Nichols, Charles A.	1851	....	....	to New Haven.
Nichols, Lucy (Betts)	1844 P.	....	....	w. of Nelson C.
Nichols, Nelson C.	1847 L.	....	1868, æ. 64	....
Naramore, Susan W.	1858 P.	....	....	m. Dr. Abelardo DeLuna.
Nicholson, Samuel G.	....	....	....	....
Nichols, Eli T. (soc. 1856)	1864	....	1867, æ. 49	....
Nash, William B., M.D.	1862 L.	....	1872	....
Nash, Anna	1862 L.	....	....	w. of William B.
Nichols, Eliza L.	1871 L. / 1884 L.	....	....	w. of Walter.
Norton, Sarah E. (Averill)	1868 L.	1887	....	w. of Wilfrid E.
Naramore, Caroline (Worden)	1839 P.	....	....	w. of William W.
Naramore, William W.	1844 P.	....	....	....
Nichols, Stephen	1831 P.	....	1893	....
Nichols, Emeline	1838 P.	....	1890	w. of Stephen. [C. Niles.
Nichols, Eliza N. (Faulkner)	1841 P.	....	1893	wid. of David B., wid. of Sam'l.
Nicholson, Harriet E.	1858 P.	....	....	w. of Samuel.
Nash, Dr. David H.	1862 L.	....	1882	....
Nash, Susan	1862 L.	....	1888	w. of Dr. David H.
Norton, Wilfrid E.	1868 L.	1887	....	....
Nash, Isabel Bullock	1876 P.	....	....	w. of Andrew E.
Nichols, Frances S.	1884 L.	....	....	....
Northrop, Joseph Walter	1885 L.	1887	....	....
Northrop, Mary Elvira	1885 L.	1887	....	w. of Joseph Walter.
Naramore, Annie B.	1889 L.	....	....	....
Nash, Susan Sterling	1889 L.	....	....	dau. of Andrew E.
Nothnagle, Lucy Johnson	1891 L.	....	....	....
Nichols, Martha	1864 P.	....	....	wid. of Eli.
Oviatt, Mary	1815	1830	....	w. of Daniel.
Oviatt, Nancy	1816	....	....	....
Oviatt, Daniel B.	1818	1830	....	....
Ogden, Lucinda A.	1821	1827	....	m. ——— Ayres.
Olmstead, Eliza	1827 P.	....	....	wid. of ———.
Oviatt, George A.	1827 P.	1832	....	to Yale College.
O'Neil, Esther	bef. 1826	....	....	....
Oakley, William B.	1844 P.	1859	....	....
Oakley, Ann Eliza (Fancher)	1844 P.	1859	....	w. of William B.
Olmstead, Hiram	1844 P.	....	....	....
Olmsted, Julia W.	1847	dism.	....	w. of ———.
Overton, Samuel	1855 L.	....	1860, æ. 52	....
Oakley, Mary M.	1867 P.	....	1869, æ. 40	wid. of Hezekiah.
Oakley, Hezekiah	....	....	....	....
Overton, George S.	....	....	....	....
Overton, Deborah	1855 L.	....	1893	wid. of Samuel.
Overton, Mary Isabel (Stratton)	1869 L.	....	....	w. of George S.

—223—

Name.	Admission.	Dismission.	Death.	Remarks.
Odell, William Sair	1880 L.	1884	....	....
Odell, Kate Mortimer	1881 P.	1884	....	w. of William S.
Ockington, Mary E.	1881 L.	1885	....	w. of B. F.
Ott, Minnie L.	1883 P.	....	....	w. of George C.
Orford, Margaret Frances	1886 L.	....	....	....
Olaidatter, Hilda C.	1888 L.	....	....	....
Parrott, Abraham	bef. 1813 R.C. 1815	....	....	....
Parrott, ——	bef. 1813 R.C. 1815	....	....	w. of Abraham.
Parrott, Abraham, Jr.	bef. 1813 R.C.	....	....	....
Parrott, Lucy W.	bef. 1813 R.C.	....	....	w. of Abraham, Jr.
Platt, Moses	bef. 1813 R.C.	....	....	....
Platt, ——	bef. 1813 R.C.	....	....	w. of Moses.
Porter, Ellen	1809	....	1867, æ. 86	w. of Samuel.
Penfield, Hannah	1812	....	....	wid. of ——, from Fairfield.
Pierce, Clarissa	1815	1830	....	w. of Nathaniel.
Parsons, Mercy	1816	....	....	w. of Titus.
Peabody, Cornelia Maria	1821	....	....	m. —— Coty.
Price, Zalmon	1821	dism.	....	....
Peck, Eliza	1821	1842	....	w. of Starr.
Porter, Polly Ann	1822	rem.	....	....
Perry, Sally	1827 L.	1830	....	w. of Tolman.
Post, Edward	1827 P.	dism.	....	....
Porter, Otis	1827 P.	1830	....	....
Pool, Abigail	1827 P.	....	....	....
Porter, Sarah M.	1827 P.	1830	....	....
Porter, Edward	bef. 1826	1830	....	....
Peet, Lucy	bef. 1826	....	1861	....
Porter, Samuel	bef. 1830	....	1842	....
Parrott, Esther	bef. 1830	....	1852	wid. of ——.
Platt, Lavinia	1831	1859	....	....
Peck, Harriet	1831	dism.	1856	....
Parrott, Legrand	1831	1868	....	....
Parrott, Charlotte	1831	1868	....	w. of Legrand.
Porter, Elizabeth	1839 P.	....	....	....
Page, Emily B.	1847 L.	1854	....	w. of Rev. Benjamin St. J.
Porter, Edward E.	1847 L.	dism.	....	....
Piersall, Mary J.	1851	1853	....	....
Peet, Seeley	....	....	....	....
Preston, John (soc. 1850-1880)	....	....	....	....
Page, Rev. Benjamin St. John	1846	1854	....	....
Peck, Benedict	1853 P.	1856	....	....
Pye, Grace M.	1853 L.	1853	....	wid. of ——.
Parsons, Lavinia Platt	1857 L.	1872	....	w. of ——.
Parsons, Frederick A. (soc. 1850)	....	1872	....	....
Preston, Catharine Ann	1857 P.	1862	....	....
Parrott, Julia B.	1858 P.	....	1859	....
Peters, Mary G.	1858 P.	1860	....	....
Perry, John L.	....	1868	....	....
Peet, Gordon L.	1859 P.	1872	....	....
Pease, Lucinda E.	1861 L.	1862	....	....
Patterson, Stephen J. (soc. 1850)	....	....	....	....
Patterson, Harriet S.	1862 P.	....	....	w. of Stephen J.
Platt, Mary C.	1863 P.	....	....	....
Parrott, Henry R. (soc. 1856)	....	....	....	....

—224—

Name.	Admission.		Dismission.	Death.	Remarks.
Pond, John E. (soc. 1868)	....	....	....	1889	....
Pond, Maria N. (Niles)	1863 / 1868	P. L.	1865	....	w. of John E.
Preston, Nettie E.	1864	P.	1871	....	m. Isaac B. Lefergy.
Parsons, J. Morton.	1865	L.	1868	....	....
Porter, Clarence D.	....		....	....	....
Price, Betsey	1867	L.	1870	....	w. of ——.
Parsons, Harriet Alice	1867	P.	....	....	w. of J. Morton.
Pitcher, Miss Mary Louise	1867	P.	....	1869, æ. 31	....
Parrott, Fred. W (soc. 1837-'82)	....		....	....	....
Prescott, James B.	....		....	....	....
Platt, Benjamin W.	1831		....	....	....
Peck, Jennetta	1831		....	....	....
Parrott, Mary Ann	1832		....	....	....
Pease, Hannah	1833		....	....	....
Preston, Phebe Ann	1839	L.	....	1883	w. of John.
Prout, Asenath	1842	P.	....	1883	w. of Hiram.
Porter, Henry H.	1856	P.	....	....	....
Porter, Eliza F. H.	1848?	P.	....	....	....
Parrott, Henry S.	1858	P.	....	1890	[Middlebrook.
Perkins, Mary J. M.	1858	P.	1878	....	w. of Robert, dau. of Dr. E. B.
Preston, Alice A.	1858	P.	....	....	dau. of John.
Parrott, Annie J. (Garland)	1863	P.	....	1895	w. of Henry R.
Parrott, Lucretia A.	1867?	P.	....	....	w. of Frederick W.
Prescott, Juliette D.	1868	L.	1890	....	wid. of James B.
Pond, Edwin Walter	1866	L.	....	....	....
Porter, Isabella (Mills)	1866	P.	....	....	w. of Clarence D., dau. of Thomas
Palmer, Rev. Charles Ray, D.D.	1872	L.	....	....	Pastor Emeritus, Sept. 1, 1895.
Palmer, Mary Barnes	1872	L.	....	1888	w. of Rev. C. Ray.
Porter, Fanny Sherwood	1874	P.	....	....	dau. of Henry H.
Paddock, Susie Roberta	1877	P.	....	....	w. of Miner H.
Petersen, John	1876	L.	1879	....	....
Petersen, Mina	1876	L.	1879	....	w. of John.
Peck, Rev. Charles Huntington	1877	L.	1882	....	....
Peck, Anna Crossman	1877	L.	1882	....	w. of Charles H.
Prescott, Lucy H.	1879	P.	....	....	....
Preston, Mary Emily (Stillman)	1880	P.	1894	....	w. of Dr. James C.
Peck, Maria E.	1882	L.	....	....	....
Parrott, Hattie G.	1882	P.	....	1893	dau. of Henry R.
Palmer, Alfred Barnes	1883	P.	....	1892	s. of Rev. C. Ray.
Palmer, Edith Burr	1885	P.	....	....	dau. of Rev. C. Ray.
Petersen, Thekla Josephine	1884	P.	....	....	dau. of John.
Petersen, John M. Trombold	1885	P.	....	....	....
Petersen, Minnie Elizabeth	1885	P.	....	....	w. of John M.
Plumb, Luzerne D.	1880	P.	....	....	....
Poirier, Elizabeth P. (Warner)	1884	P.	....	....	w. of George C.
Patterson, Harriet S.	1862	P.	....	....	w. of Samuel J.
Pond, Elise Falconer	1889	P.	....	....	dau. of John H.
Pagels, E. H. Victor	1891	L.	1892	....	....
Peck, Vincent C.	1892	L.	....	....	....
Porter, Emily	1893	P.	....	....	....
Palmer, Maria Waud	1887	L.	....	....	....
Palmer, Harriet Shepard	1887	L.	....	....	....
Pierce, George E.	1894	L.	....	....	....
Pierce, Florence H.	1894	L.	....	....	....
Pierce, Florence C.	1894	P.	....	....	....

Name.	Admission.	Dismission.	Death.	Remarks.
Quintard, John H...............	1860 L.	1862	....	....
Risley, Hezekiah...............	1809 R.C.	....	....	....
Risley, Laura...................	1809 R.C.	....	....	w. of Hezekiah.
Rockwell, David S.............	1821	1833	....	....
Ryan, Marsh	1831	rem.	....	....
Robinson, James W...........	1831	1868	....	....
Riggs, Harriet	1839	1850	....	....
Robinson, Julia.................	1844 P.	1868	....	w. of James.
Rood, Edwin	1845 P.	1845	....	....
Robinson, Maria C.	1856 L.	1861	....	w. of ——.
Rogers, Lucy A.	1856 P.	1860	....	....
Rogers, Abner...................	1856 L.	abs.	....	....
Rogers, Lucy M.................	1856 L.	1860	....	w. of Abner.
Reid, Martha.....................	1859 P.	....	....	....
Ross, Betsey	1864 L.	....	1866, æ. 73	wid. of —— Spooner.
Rogers, Isaac R.	....	....	....	....
Richards, Rev. George (Pastor).	1866 L.	1871	....	....
Richards, Ann Maria..........	1867 L.	1871	....	w. of Rev. George.
Richards, Josephine E........	1867 L.	1871	....	dau. of Rev. George.
Richards, Anna W.	1867 L.	1871	....	dau. of Rev. George.
Richards, George J............	1868 P.	1871	....	....
Robie, John A. (soc. 1868–1874)	....	....	....	....
Rolf, Margaret E. A............	1868 P.	....	....	m. James Collin.
Richards, William Rogers	1870 P.	1871	....	....
Robinson, Sarah E.	1859 L.	....	....	w. of George L. (soc. 1856?)
Rowland, Catharine...........	1861 L.	....	bef. 1886	w. of George M.
Rogers, Abby L.	1865 L.	....	....	w. of Isaac.
Russell, Rev. Charles H.	1864 L.	1892	1895	....
Russell, Anna A.	1868 L.	....	1888	w. of Charles H.
Robie, Sibyl B...................	1867 L.	1880	....	wid. of John A.
Rogers, Samuel T.	1870 L.	....	....	....
Russell, Mary Tallman	1882 L.	1885	....	....
Robinson, John H..............	1886 L.	1887	....	....
Robinson, M. J..................	1886 L.	1887	....	w. of John H.
Strong, Joseph ....bef.	1813 R.C.	....	....	....
Summers, Stephen.......bef.	1813 R.C.	....	....	....
Sterling, David...........bef.	1813 R.C.	....	....	....
Sterling, Sarah...........bef.	1813 R.C.	....	....	wid. of ——.
Sterling, Philip...........bef.	1813 R.C.	....	....	....
Sterling, Ruth............bef.	1813 R.C.	....	....	w. of Philip.
Sterling, Jesse, F.M. 1809 ..bef.	1813 R.C. 1816	1830	....	....
Sterling, Sally ....bef.	1813 R.C. 1816	1830	....	w. of Jesse.
Standish, John..................	1809 R.C.	....	....	....
Standish, Naomi	1809 R.C.	....	....	w. of John.
Seeley, Joseph...................	1809 R.C. 1810	....	1873	....
Seeley, Ruth.....................	1809 R.C.	....	....	w. of Joseph.
Snow, John.......................	1819 R.C.	....	....	....
Snow, Hannah...................	1819 R.C.	....	....	w. of John.
Sherman, Ira	1819 R.C. 1856 P.	....	1869, æ. 76	....
Summers, Alice..................	1808	....	1823, æ. 62	w. of ——.
Sherman, Mary, 2d............	1808	....	1832	....

— 226 —

Name.	Admission.	Dismission.	Death.	Remarks.
Smith, Phebe	1808	1830	....	m. —— Gouge.
Summers, Urania	1808	....	....	dau. of Elnathan.
Summers, Betty	1808	....	....	w. of Matthew.
Sturges, Isaac	1809	....	....	
Sturges, Joseph Porter (soc.1834)	1809	dism.	aft. 1856	to Greenfield Hill.
Sturges, Sarah	1809	....	....	w. of Isaac.
Seeley, Betsey	1809	....	1823, æ. 39	w. of James I.
Sherman, Dea. Isaac (soc. 1809)	1812	....	1863, æ. 75	m. Maria Burroughs; s. of David
Sterling, Dea. Silvanus	1812	....	1848	[and Rebecca (French).
Sherman, Maria	1812	....	1868, æ. 77	w. of Isaac.
Sterling, Polly	1812	....	1866, æ. 74	gave the parsonage to church.
Seeley, Ruth	1815	....	....	w. of Joseph.
Slater, Joel	1815	dism.	....	
Seeley, Mary	1815	....	1875	
Skinner, Abigail	1815	....	....	w. of Nathaniel L.
Standish, Naomi	1815	....	....	w. of John.
Smith, Mehitable	1815	1834	....	
Seeley, Nancy	1816	....	....	
Spinning, Elijah Crane	1818	....	1853	
Shipman, Harriet	1819	....	1858	wid. of ——.
Sherman, Laura	1819	....	1881	w. of Ira.
Selby, Maria Antoinette	1821	rem.	....	
Sherman, Anson	1821	rem.	1835	
Sherman, Caroline	1821	....	....	
Sterling, Ann Strong	1821	....	....	m. —— Moore.
Summers, Susan	1821	rem.	....	
Sterling, Legrand	1821	....	1860	
Summers, Lucinda Maria	1822	1827	....	
Sterling, George	1827 P.	1830	1871	
Shepherd, Minerva	1827 L.	1827	....	w. of Dr. William.
Shepherd, Mehitable	1827 P.	1830	....	
Sherman, Mary	1827 P.	....	1857	
Sterling, Jane E	bef. 1826	1830	....	w. of Sherwood.
Southworth, Mary	bef. 1826	1833	....	
Spinning, Salome	bef. 1826	....	1877	w. of Elijah Crane.
Summers, Hulda (Wakeley)	bef. 1826	....	1837, æ. 83	w. of Anson or Aaron.
Sterling, Emma	bef. 1826	....	....	w. of David, Jr.
St. John, Milton	bef. 1826	rem.	....	
Seeley, Polly	1815	1823	....	w. of David V.
Sherman, ——	bef. 1830	....	....	w. of Anson.
Sherman, Ann Eliza	bef. 1830	....	....	wid. of Isaac, Jr.
Sterling, Capt. Danl., F.M. 1808	1828	....	1853, æ. 76	s. of Abijah and Eunice.
Sherwood, Mary	1828	....	1877	
Sherwood, Sally	1817	....	....	w. of Seeley.
Sterling, Deborah	bef. 1830	....	1848	
Stillman, Emily	1831	....	1869, æ. 55	dau. of Wyllys.
Stillman, Clarissa	....	....	1875, æ. 88	w. of Wyllys.
Sherwood, Albert E.	1831	....	1868, æ. 74	
Sherwood, Dea. David	1831	....	1873	s. of Stephen.
Sherwood, Anna	1831	....	1852	w. of David.
Stillman, Henry W.	1831	1868	1889	
Stillman, Asenath	1831	....	1874	w. of Henry W. [man.
Sherman, Jane E.	1831	....	1857	m. R. B. Lacey, dau. Isaac Sher-
Sterling, Eloisa	1831	....	1852	w. of Legrand.
Sterling, Margaret A	1831	....	1866, æ. 54	m. —— Hussey.
Sherman, Eliza	1831	1837	....	m. J. G. Adams.
Smith, Harriet	1831	....	....	

—227—

Name.	Admission.		Dismission.	Death.	Remarks.
Street, Debby Ann	1831		....	....	
Smith, William	1831		exc. 1834	....	
Smith, Howard (soc. 1835)	1831		....	....	
Smith, Lucina D.	1831		....	....	
Southmayd, Thomas	1832		....	....	
Smith, Isaac	1832		....	....	
Selleck, Deborah	1833		....	1834	w. of Warren W.
Shadbolt, Robert	1834		....	....	
Samis, Abigail	....		....	1859	
Stevens, Margaret	1834		....	....	
Sherwood, Eliza	1835	P.	....	1868, æ. 59	w. of Albert E.
Suydam, William	1835		....	....	
Suydam, Sarah	1835		dism.	....	
Smith, Mary Ann	1837		dism.	....	
Selleck, Phebe	1838		1867	....	
Suydam, Julia A.	1838	L.	....	1845	
Stillman, John J.	{1838 / 1880	/ L.	1867 / 1881	....	
Stillman, Margaret J.	1838		....	....	wid. of Rufus Burr.
Suydam, Martha	1839	P.	....	....	
Sterling, Hannah (Judson)	1840	P.	....	1852	w. of Capt. Daniel.
Smith, Mary	bef. 1841		....	1849	wid. of ——.
Spinning, Caroline	1844	P.	....	....	
Spinning, Anna M.	1845		....	....	m. John F. Wheaton.
Spinning, Elizabeth	1845	P.	rem.	....	
Selleck, ——	1841	L.	....	....	w. of Warren W.
Seeley, Maria	1845	P.	....	....	
Stillman, Grace L.	1845	L.	dism.	....	
Stillman, Arabella	1845	P.	1859	....	m. Hickson Fowler.
Stillman, Caroline S.	1847	L.	....	1867, æ. 40	w. of John J.
Stillman, John J.	1847	L.	1870	....	
Seeley, Morgan	1852	L.	1870	....	
Seeley, Sally	1852	L.	1870	....	
Seeley, David V.	....		....	....	
Sherwood, Seeley	....		....	....	
Stillman, Wyllys	....		....	1852, æ. 71	
Smith, Edwin	bef. 1870		....	aft. 1891	
Stillman, Emily	....		1868	....	
Sterling, Nathaniel	....		....	....	
Strong, Henry P.	1853	L.	1856	....	
Strong, Sarah Adelia	1853	L.	1856	....	w. of Henry P.
Sherman, Starr	1854	L.	1860	....	
Sherman, Harriet	1854	L.	1860	....	w. of Starr.
Sprague, Nathan G.	1854	L.	....	1858, æ. 36	
Slosson, Henry V.	1855	P.	1855	....	
Sterling, Emily	1855	P.	....	1860	in Illinois.
Smith, Evelina	1857	L.	1859	....	
Seeley, Elizabeth A.	1855	L.	1870	....	dau. of Morgan.
Smith, A.	....		1861	....	w. of ——.
Sterling, Walter	1858	P.	....	1870, æ. 55	engineer, Housatonic R. R.
Sherman, Henry B.	1858	P.	....	1859	
Staples, Georgiana A.	1858	P.	1862	....	
Sterling, Mary M. H.	1857	L.	....	1860	w. of Legrand.
Smith, Rev. Matson M.	1859	L.	1865	....	
Smith, Mary S.	1859	L.	1865	....	
Sammis, Franklin	1859	L.	1871	....	

Name.	Admission.		Dismission.	Death.	Remarks.
Sammis, Sabra V.	1859	L.	1871	....	....
Scott, Elizabeth	1859	L.	....	....	....
Sterling, Nancy	1859	L.	....	1863, æ. 78	....
Sanderson, Harriet J.	1859	L.	....	....	w. of John H.
Smith, William E.	1859	P.	1867	....	....
Smith, Julia	1860	L.	1867	....	w. of William E.
Sturdevant, Mary S.	1861	....	1864	....	w. of ——.
Shaw, Mary Jane	1862	L.	....	....	....
Storrs, Fanny A.	1863	P.	1865	....	....
Sanderson, Mary R.	1863	P.	....	1867, æ. 21	dau. of John H.
Seeley, Ezra N.	1863	P.	1867	....	....
Smith, Norman W.	1863	P.	1865	....	....
Smith, Emily Stewart	1863	P.	1865	....	....
Stewart, Adelia A.	1864	P.	....	....	....
Stewart, Imogene	1864	P.	....	....	....
Staniford, Henry E.	1864	L.	1870	....	to South Church.
Stewart, John L. (soc. 1856-1868)	....	....	....	....	....
Smith, Lydia A.	1865	P.	1866	....	m. S. B. Terry.
Smith, Edward W.	1865	P.	....	....	....
Sanderson, George W.	1866	P.	....	April 7,	1866, æ. 24. Soldier.
Stevenson, John C.	1866	L.	....	....	....
Stevenson, Eleanor A.(McGrath)	1866	L.	....	....	w. of John C.
St. John, Joseph	1867	P.	1870	....	s. of George A.
St. John, Anna E.	1867	P.	1870	....	dau. of George A.
St. John, George A.	1867	L.	1870	....	....
St. John, Adaline	1867	L.	1870	....	w. of George A.
Slosson, J. P.	1867	L.	1870	....	....
Scoville, Seward	....	....	....	....	....
Scoville, Lemuel	1867	L.	1868	....	....
Scoville, Augusta C.	1867	....	1868	....	w. of Lemuel.
Sanborne, Anson	1861	P.	1862	....	....
Sanborne, Hannah	1861	P.	1862	....	....
Sanderson, Emma J.	1868	P.	....	....	....
Stratton, Henrietta	1869	P.	1870	....	....
Sterling, Lorenzo B.	1831	P.	....	1881	....
Selleck, Warren W.	1853	L.	....	1884	....
Smith, Sally	1837	L.	....	....	wid. of Edwin.
Sprague, Lucretia E.	1854	L.	....	1858	w. of Nathan G.
Sterling, Sabra S.	1852	L.	....	....	wid. of Walter.
Sage, Dr. Henry L.	1857	L.	....	1880	....
Selleck, Eliza D.	1858	P.	....	....	wid. of Warren W.
Spinning, Harriet A.	1856	P.	....	....	w. of Edgar.
Spinning, Anna B. (Lendeveg)	1858	L.	....	1883	w. of Theodore A.
Smith, Elizabeth	1857	L.	....	....	w. of Horace.
Smith, Horace	1858	P.	....	....	....
Spinning, Theodore A.	1858	P.	....	....	....
Spinning, Edgar G.	1862	L.	....	1885	....
Sterling, Henrietta E.	1862	L.	....	1891	wid. of Legrand.
Sanderson, John H.	1859	L.	....	....	....
Sanderson, Jane	1859	L.	....	....	dau. of John H.
Seeley, Carrie A.	1863	P.	....	....	dau. of Morgan.
Sherwood, Charles	1864	P.	....	....	....
Stewart, Mary L.	1864	P.	....	....	wid. of John L.
Smith, Eli C.	1864	P.	....	....	s. of Horace.
Stillman, Horace C.	1864	P.	....	....	s. of John.
Scott, Samuel T.	1863	P.	....	....	....

—229—

Name.	Admission.	Dismission.	Death.	Remarks.
Sage, Lavinia Todd	1865	L.	....	w. of Dr. Henry L.
Stillman, Grace M.	1868	L.	1882	dau. of William M.
Stillman, Sarah M.	1869	P.	1895	w. of William M.
Stillman, Caroline A. G.	1873	L.	1893	w. of F. M.
Selbie, Patrick	1874	P.	1881	
Stanley, H. Dwight	1874	P.	....	
Stanley, Emma A. (B)	1874	L.	....	w. of H. D.
Sammis, Francis B.	1875	L.	....	
Sterling, Ada C.	1874	P.	....	dau. of Walter.
Stewart, Ruth	1874	L.	....	w. of Hector L.
Sherwood, Emma C.	1874	P.	....	w. of Charles, dau. of S. J. Pat-[terson.
Sherwood, Clara Ann	1874	P.	1887	dau. of Dea. David.
Smith, Mary E. (Wright)	1875	L.	....	w. of Eli C.
Smith, Horace Winfield	1876	P.	....	s. of Horace.
Stillman, Albert W.	1876	P.	....	s. of William M.
Spencer, J. Parker	1876	P.	....	
Sanderson, Hattie Alice	1876	P.	....	dau. of John H.
Sanborn, Isabella Maria	1877	P.	1888	w. of Joseph F.
Sterling, Maria McCoy	1876	P.	....	wid. of Daniel H.
Stark, Dana (Hatch)	1878	L.	1885	w. of Leonard H., dau.of Leavitt.
Stewart, John Wesley	1877	P.	....	
Sammis, Frances Allen	1878	P.	....	w. of Francis B.
Stillman, Caroline M.	1880	L.	1881	
Smith, Julia Elizabeth	1880	L.	1893	w. of H. M.
Sterling, John Tolman	1881	L.	....	s. of Charles.
Sterling, Harriet Elizabeth	1881	L.	....	w. of John T.
Sterling, Matilda L. (Werner)	1882	L.	1884	
Stillman, Helen Blakeman	1882	P.	....	dau. of William M.
Sirrett, Sarah M.	1883	L.	1895	wid. of William.
Stevenson, Lucinda	1883	P.	1894	wid. of William G.
Sanderson, Lucien	1884	L.	....	
Swan, Fanny Bixby	1884	L.	....	w. of Clarence.
Swan, Clarence	1884	P.	....	
Sanborn, Joseph Franklin	1884	L.	....	
Sprague, Lucy D.	1884	L.	....	w. of Arthur J.
Spencer, Samuel C.	1884	P.	....	
Spencer, Annie Elizabeth	1884	P.	....	w. of Samuel C.
Smith, Ann, Mrs.	1884	L.	1894	
Stillman, Emma Maria	1884	L.	....	w. of Frank P.
Squires, Ida May	1884	L.	1891	
Squires, Emily Loretta	1884	L.	1889	
Salisbury, Newton Hough	1884	P.	....	
Salisbury, Catharine Taylor	1884	P.	....	w. of Newton H.
Stevens, Mary E.	1884	L.	....	
Seirup, Hans	1884	L.	1890	
Sterling, Charles Sherwood	1885	P.	....	
Sharp, Robert Walter	1885	L.	1887	
Smith, Chary Couch	1885	P.	....	dau. of Horace.
Spinning, Hattie Louisa	1885	P.	....	
Spinning, Verna Balcom	1885	P.	....	
Simonds, Henry D.	1887	P.	....	
Simonds, Fanny Abigail	1887	L.	....	w. of Henry D.
Sterling, Mary Louisa (Osborn)	1887	L.	....	w. of Charles S.
Sage, Bertha Wheeler	1886	P.	....	
Spaulding, Kate M.	1886	L.	1892	
Sirrett, Susan Jane	1888	P.	1892	

Name.	Admission.		Dismission.	Death.	Remarks.
Smith, Mary Esther Wright	1889	P.	....	....	dau. of Eli C.
Sirrett, Robert Harry	1890	P.	1893	....	....
Sibley, Sarah Augusta	1892	L.	....	....	....
Seward, Daniel B. (soc. 1886)	1891	P.	....	....	....
Sawyer, Andrew	1890	L.	1894	....	....
Sawyer, Mary F.	1890	L.	1894	....	w. of Andrew.
Sawyer, Alice M.	1890	L.	....	....	w. of Walter.
Sherman, Florence A. De	1892	P.	1893	....	....
Smith, Daniel Sanford	1894	P.	....	....	s. of Eli C.
Smith, Ada Dearborne	1894	P.	....	....	w. of Horace W.
Treadwell, Sophia	1807		....	....	w. of Robert.
Tomlinson, Caleb	1815		1830	....	....
Thorp, Capt. Joel	1819		....	aft. 1834	
Thorp, Polly	1819		....	1838	w. of Joel.
Thompson, Betsey	1821		1830	....	w. of Lewis.
Thompson, John M.?	1821		....	1848	....
Thatcher, Daniel	1828	L.	....	1867, æ. 79	....
Tomlinson, Susan	....		1830	....	....
Tuttle, Thankful	1816		....	1860, æ. 82	....
Thompson, Marietta	1821		....	1868, æ. 72	w. of Gideon.
Treadwell, Mercy	bef. 1826		....	1831, æ. 77	....
Thompson, Fanny	bef. 1826		....	1835	w. of John M.
Treadwell, Mary	1830		....	....	....
Tobie, Mrs. Thomas	bef. 1830		....	....	....
Tweedy, Samuel L.	1831		exc.	....	....
Thatcher, Julia	1831		....	1852	w. of Daniel.
Thompson, William	1832		1857	....	....
Tracey, Hannah Graves	1836	P.	....	....	wid. of George F.
Thompson, Nobles	1841	L.	dism.	....	....
Thompson, Maria, Mrs.	1841	L.	1864	....	m. Raymond French.
Taylor, Elizabeth	1845	P.	....	1850	....
Tomlinson, Mary H. (Faulkner)	1847	L.	....	....	w. of Stephen.
Thurston, Samuel D.	1852	L.	1858	....	....
Thurston, Jane Maria	1852	L.	1858	....	w. of Samuel D.
Tracy, George F. (soc. 1847)	1858	P.	....	1872	....
Tomlinson, Stephen (soc. 1863)	....		....	....	....
Tracy, Ebenezer	1853	L.	1868	....	....
Tracy, Phebe	1853	L.	1868	....	w. of Ebenezer.
Towne, Rev. Joseph H.	1855	L.	1858	....	Pastor.
Towne, Eliza I. C.	1855	L.	1858	....	w. of Rev. J. H.
Taylor, Rev. ———	....		....	....	....
Thorpe, Catharine	1855	P.	....	1859	....
Terry, Juliette	1855	L.	1857	....	w. of Theodore.
Terry, Theodore	....		1857	....	....
Trulock, Marshall S.	1863	P.	....	....	....
Toucy, Levi	....		1869	....	w. of Levi.
Toucy, Esther M. (Ayres)	....		1868	....	dau. of Stephen.
Tomlinson, Mary (Linsley)	1864	P.	....	....	dau. Geo. F.; m. H. E. Staniford
Tracy, Mary Fanny	1864	P.	1870	....	m. 1866, Gurnsey W. Davis.
Trulock, Victoria B.	1864	P.	....	....	w. of James.
Turner, Mary C.	1858	P.	....	....	....
Treat, Miss Mary B.	1869	L.	....	1870, æ. 55	....
Thatcher, Eunice S.	1863	L.	....	1889	wid. of Daniel.
Todd, Mary C. (Platt)	1863	P.	....	....	w. of Eliphalet.
Tracey, Helen L.	1864	P.	....	....	w. of John D.
Thompson, Gideon (soc. 1824)	1869		....	1888	....

Name.	Admission.	Dismission.	Death.	Remarks.
Thompson, Emma L.	1874 P.	1878	....	dau. of S. S. Hanford ; w. C. S.
Thomas, Emma J. (Kellogg)	1874 L.	1889	....	w. of Dr. J. P.
Treat, Mary Angeline (Clark)	1882 L.	....	1892	w. of Amos S.
Treat, Mary Clark	1891 P.	....	....	dau. of Amos S.
Thompson, Myrtle A.	1891 P.	1893	....	dau. of William S.
Thompson, Phoebe A.	1892 P.	1893	....	w. of William S.
Ufford, Widow Betsey	1821	....	....	....
Underwood, Mary L. (Seward)	1890 P.	1890	....	....
Vail, Franklin Y.	1826	....	....	Pastor.
Vail, Catharine M.	1826 L.	....	....	w. of Rev. F. Y.
Vose, Polly Ann	1827 P.	....	....	....
Vandervoort, Peter	1821	rem.	....	....
Van Sickles, Mathias M.	....	....	....	....
Van Gasbeck, Fannie (Hall)	1858 P.	....	....	w. of William.
Van Gasbeck, William H.	1864 P.	....	....	....
Van Syckel, Amelia	1864 P.	....	....	w. of Matthias M.
Van Dalsan, Rev. Henry A.	1882 L.	1882	....	....
Van Dalsan, Sarah A.	1882 L.	1882	....	w. of Rev. H. A.
Vervait, Stephanie M.	1893 P.	....	....	....
Wade, Nathaniel bef.	1813 R.C. 1828 P.	....	1857	....
Wheeler, Ezra	1809 R.C. 1815	....	Nov.15 '56	....
Wheeler, Polly	1809 R.C. 1815	....	Nov.16 '56	w. of Ezra.
West, William	1813 R.C.	....	....	....
West, Eunice	1813 R.C.	....	....	w. of William.
Wordin, Thomas C.	1815 R.C.	....	....	....
Wordin, Nancy	1815 R.C. 1821	1830	1866, æ. 74	w. of Thomas C.
Wallace, Perlina	1821 R.C.	....	....	w. of Abijah.
Wetmore, Sally	1808	....	1822, æ. 74	....
Wilcox, Alvan	1809	dism.	....	....
Wilcox, Patience	1809	....	....	w. of Alvan.
Wheeler, Sally	1809	....	1821, æ. 58	w. of Benjamin.
Wordin, Susanna	1812	....	1812	dau. of William.
Wordin, Anna	1814	....	1818, æ. 35	....
Whiting, Seymour	1815	1830	....	to New York.
Wheeler, Maria	1815	....	....	....
Wordin, Lucy	1815	....	....	....
Wordin, Mary Ann	1815	....	1820, æ. 24	....
Warner, Hiram	1815	....	....	....
Wakeman, Matilda	1816	....	....	....
Wells, Charity	1817	....	1842, æ. 61	dau. of Jedidiah.
Wheeler, Rosanna	1819	....	....	....
Wade, George	1821	dism.	1879	....
Wanzer, Thomas	1821	rem.	....	....
Waterman, Susan Johan	1821	....	....	....
Wordin, Clara	1821	....	1827, æ. 35	....
Wheeler, Eliza	1821	rem.	....	m. —— Gabandon.
Wheeler, Julianna	1821	rem.	....	....
Wright, William	1821	1830	....	....
Whittemore, Robert J.	1821	1827	....	....
Wheeler, Marietta	1821	....	....	m. Thompson.

Name.	Admission.	Dismission.	Death.	Remarks.
Waterman, Julia A.	1821	....	....	m. Alanson F. Lewis.
Wordin, Laura	1821	....	....	....
Waterman, Emma	1821	....	....	....
Wakeman, Catharine	1821	....	....	....
Wade, Ann	1822	....	1868	wid. of Franklin?
Ward, Thomas	1822	....	....	....
Ward, Anna	1822 L.	....	....	....
Wheeler, Benjamin Samuel	1821	....	....	....
Waterman, Lucy	1824	1830	....	w. of Rev. Elijah.
Wade, Sarah	1825	....	....	w. of James.
Wade, Nathaniel, Jr.	1825	1830	....	died at Yale.
Wheeler, Widow Susan	1825	1830	....	....
Washburn, Betsey H.	1826 L.	....	....	....
Wood, Frances	1827 L.	1830	....	dau. of Joseph and Frances.
Wells, Widow Julietta	1827 P.	1830	....	....
Woodhull, Mary	1827 P.	1830	....	....
Woodhull, Samuel	1827 P.	1830	....	....
Wilson, Jarvis	1827 P.	1830	....	....
Whittemore, Sally	1827 P.	1836	....	....
Williams, Rhoda Ann	1827 P.	1830	....	....
Ward, Caroline	1828 P.	1830	....	....
Wolley, Fanny	1828 P.	1830	....	....
Wordin, Laura	1828 P.	....	....	....
Wolcott, Elizabeth	....	1830	....	....
Waterman, Betsey I.	bef. 1830	1830	....	m. Day.
Wordin, Mrs.	bef. 1830	1830	....	m. Tomlinson.
Weeks, Abigail	1831	....	....	....
Weeks, Charlotte	1831	dism.	....	....
Wordin, Nathaniel S.	1831 P.	....	1889	....
Weeks, Ebenezer	1831	....	....	....
Whiting, Maria	1831	dism.	....	....
Whiting, Sarah C.	1831	....	1855	w. of Ephraim.
Woodworth, W. W.	1831	1837	....	....
Wade, Catharine	1831	....	....	....
Wade, Henry	1831	1834	....	....
Wordin, Susan M.	1831	....	aft. 1857	....
Whitehead, Priscilla N.	1831	....	....	....
Wheeler, Philo C.	1831	....	aft. 1835	....
Wordin, Levi	1833 P.	....	1870, æ. 69	....
Wilson, John	1834	....	1858	....
Wilson, Elizabeth	1834	....	1853	w. of John.
Wilson, Janette	1834	dism.	....	....
Wheeler, Emily	1835	....	....	w. of Philo C.
Woodridge, Mary Ann	1837	1838	....	....
Woodbridge, Mary	1837	1838	....	....
Woodbridge, Emeline	1838	1838	....	....
Woodbridge, Rev. John	1837	1838	....	....
Woodruff, John L.	1839 L.	....	....	....
Woodruff ———	1839 L.	....	....	w. of John L.
Waterbury, Charles	1839	dism.	....	....
Wyatt, Thomas	1839	dism.	....	....
Wyatt, Almira	1839	dism.	....	....
Wordin, Fanny A. (Leavenworth)	1840 L.	....	1892	....
Whiting, Mary	1841	....	1841	....
Wheeler, Rhoda T.	1841 L.	....	1860, æ. 79	wid. of ———.
Waterman, Cordelia (Sterling)	1844 P.	....	1885	w. of Robert H.
Wilson, James	1844 P.	rem.	1852, æ. 82?	....

—233—

Name.	Admission.		Dismission.	Death.	Remarks.
Wheaton, Ann Maria	1845	P.	....	....	w. of John F.
Worden, Elizabeth	1845	P.	....	1852	
Weed, Susan	1840	....	1858	....	w. of Joseph.
Wood, Sarah Ann	1847	P.	....	1888	w. of Sherman S.
Wheeler, Mrs. Ira B.	1848	....	....	....	
Weed, Joseph B.	1848	P.	1858	1864	
Wheeler, Jane	1852	L.	....	1859	w. of Henry T.
Wheeler, Henry T.	1852	L.	....	1887	
Wordin, Mrs. Thomas C.	....	....	....	1864, æ. 74	Dorcas?
Whiting, Ephraim (soc. 1800?)	1837	....	....	1855	
Waterman, Robert H.	....	....	....	....	
Watkins, Maria Seeley	1845	P.	....	1867	w. of Thomas.
Wheaton, John F.	....	....	....	....	
Watkins, Thomas (soc. 1857)	....	....	....	....	
Wheeler, Hannah	....	....	....	1860, æ. 76	
Wheeler, Ira B.	....	....	....	....	
Wells, David F.	1855	P.	1859	....	
Winslow, Elizabeth	1855	L.	1869	....	w. of Andrew.
Winslow, Andrew (soc. 1856, '65)	....	....	1869	....	
Wheaton, Sarah E.	1855	L.	1862	....	
Wilcox, Elias	1855	L.	1858	....	
Wilcox, Eliza	1855	L.	1858	....	w. of Elias.
Wade, Munson (soc. 1868)	1858	P.	....	....	
Wales, Sarah I.	1857	L.	1860	....	w. of ——.
Wales, ——	....	....	1860	....	
Wakeman, Mary	1858	L.	1868	....	w. of David.
Wakeman, David	....	....	1868	....	
Weeks, Emily S.	1858	L.	1866	....	w. of ——.
Weeks, ——	....	....	1866	....	
Winslow, Henry T.	1858	P.	....	1863, æ. 22	returning from war.
Wordin, Helen C.	1858	P.	....	....	dau. of Nathaniel S.
Whiting, John	....	....	....	....	
Waller, Urania	1859	L.	....	1873	w. of George B.
Wales, Caroline M.	1859	L.	1861	....	w. of Henry.
Waller, George B. (soc. 1856)	....	....	....	....	
Whitney, Fanny M. (Parrott)	1858	P.	....	....	w. of John D.
Watrous, Annie	....	....	1870	....	
Watrous, Richard	....	....	1870	....	
Warner, George W.	1861	L.	....	....	
Whiting, Henrietta E.	1862	L.	....	....	m. Legrand Sterling.
Wright, William Burr	1861	L.	....	....	
Wright, Polly (Burr)	1861	L.	....	1890	w. of William Burr.
Winslow, Charles	1863	P.	1869	....	
Waller, Susan H.	1863	P.	....	....	m. Alex Hawley.
Wheeler, Clarissa L.	1863	L.	....	....	w. of Charles B.
Wheeler, Charles B.	....	....	....	....	
Warner, James P.	1864	L.	....	....	
Wordin, Alice	1864	P.	....	....	dau. of Levi.
Wakeman, Julia	1867		1871	....	w. of ——.
Warren, Sheldon (soc. 1868)	....	....	....	....	
Warner, Mary E.	1867	L.	....	....	w. of George W.
Williams, William H.	....	....	....	....	
Williams, A. W. C. (soc. 1868)	....	....	....	....	
Williams, Elizabeth H.	1868	L.	....	....	w. of A. W. C.
Warren, Stanley P.	1870	L.	....	....	
Warren, Sarah North	1870	L.	....	....	w. of Stanley P.
Waldron, Fanny H.	1867	L.	....	....	

Name.	Admission.		Dismission.	Death.	Remarks.
Wheeler, Horace	1864	P.	----	----	----------------
Wordin, Fanny L.	1864	P.	----	----	----------------
Williams, Helen K.	1868	P.	----	1879	*w.* of William H.
Wilmot, Sarah M.	1869	L.	1887	----	*w.* of Samuel R.
Warren, Jane M.	1867	P.	----	----	----------------
Wade, George (soc. 1835)	1868	L.	----	1878	----------------
Waterbury, M. Louise	1871	L.	1879	----	*m.* W. Henshaw.
Wilmot, Samuel R. (soc. 1868)	1874	P.	1877	----	----------------
Wordin, Dr. Nathaniel Eugene	1873	P.	----	----	*s.* of Nathaniel S.
Wilmot, Frank A.	1876	P.	----	----	*s.* of Samuel R.
Wheaton, Ann Elizabeth	1874	P.	----	----	*w.* of George E.
Wheaton, Martha Maria	1874	P.	----	----	*dau.* of George E.
Witmeyer, Israel Long	1877	L.	1879	----	----------------
Wordin, Thomas Cook	1876	P.	----	----	*s.* of Nathaniel S.
Wilson, Rev. John Saul	1878	L.	1891	----	----------------
Wilson, Susie Virginie (Stevens)	1878	P.	----	----	*dau.* of Charles H.
Wheeler, Jennie Griffing	1879	P.	----	----	*dau.* of Henry T.
Weeks, William Warren	1877	P.	----	----	----------------
Wohlers, Norinda J.	1880	P.	----	----	*wid.* of D. H.
Woodhull, Elizabeth Rogers	1880	L.	1893	----	----------------
Woodhull, Emma Augusta	1880	L.	1893	----	----------------
Wilson, Catharine A.	1881	L.	1889	----	*w.* of D. W.
Werner, Mary A.	1882	L.	----	1884	*wid.* of Theo. N.
Werner, Thomas W.	1882	L.	1885	----	*s.* of Mary A.
Wolffe, Clara Sherwood (Porter)	1883	P.	----	----	----------------
White, Robert J.	1884	L.	----	1885	----------------
White, Ellen W.	1884	L.	1886	----	*wid.* of Robert J.
Wordin, Eliza W. (Barnes)	1884	L.	----	----	*w.* of Dr. N. E.
Wilson, William H. E.	1884	P.	----	----	----------------
Whiting, Mary Fanny (Kensett)	1884	P.	1893	----	*w.* of Frank H.
Wilson, Bertha Storrs (Wheaton)	1885	P.	----	----	----------------
Wheeler, Robert Edgar	1886	P.	----	----	[Bryning.
Wilmot, Ethelyn Mildred	1885	P.	----	----	*dau.* of Samuel R., *m.* P. L.
Wilson, Isabella Gertrude	1885	P.	1892	----	*m.* C. M. Baer.
Wells, Joseph S.	1886	L.	1890	----	----------------
Wells, Agnes T.	1886	L.	1890	----	----------------
Wilson, Carrie Somers	1887	L.	----	----	*w.* of F. M.
Wordin, Frances C.	1886	L.	----	----	*w.* of T. Cook.
Warriner, Dr. M. A.	1890	L.	----	----	----------------
Warriner, Flora C.	1889	L.	----	----	*w.* of Dr. M. A.
Williams, Samuel D. P.	1890	L.	----	----	----------------
Williams, Etta Mae	1890	L.	----	----	*w.* of S. D. P.
Withington, Augustus S.	1893	P.	----	----	----------------
Withington, Lucy E.	1893	P.	----	----	*w.* of Augustus S.
Walter, Margaret Bell	1894	P.	----	----	*dau.* of Edward P.
Walter, Sarah Frances	1894	P.	----	----	*w.* of Edward P.
Young, Catharine	----		----	----	----------------
Young, Betsey	bef. 1826		----	----	----------------
Youngs, James	1864	P.	----	----	----------------
Zeller, Samuel Snively	1889	L.	1892	----	----------------
Zeller, Nellie Frances	1889	L.	1892	----	*w.* of Samuel S.
Zeller, Annie Russell	1889	L.	1892	----	*dau.* of Samuel S.

www.ingramcontent.com/pod-product-compliance
Lightning Source LLC
Chambersburg PA
CBHW022007220426
43663CB00007B/992